CONCRETE CENTUR.

Concrete Century

Julius Kahn and the Construction Revolution

Michael G. Smith

UNIVERSITY OF MICHIGAN PRESS
Ann Arbor

For questions or permissions, please contact um.press.perms@umich.edu

Published in the United States of America by the
University of Michigan Press
Manufactured in the United States of America
Printed on acid-free paper
First published September 2024

A CIP catalog record for this book is available from the British Library.

Library of Congress Cataloging-in-Publication Data

Names: Smith, Michael G. (Architecture historian), author. |
    Michigan Publishing (University of Michigan), publisher.
Title: Concrete century : Julius Kahn and the construction revolution /
    Michael G. Smith.
Other titles: Julius Kahn and the construction revolution
Description: Ann Arbor : University of Michigan Press, 2024. | Includes
    bibliographical references and index.
Identifiers: LCCN 2024016800 (print) | LCCN 2024016801 (ebook) |
    ISBN 9780472039746 (paperback) | ISBN 9780472221844 (ebook)
Subjects: LCSH: Kahn, Julius, 1874–1942. | Kahn, Albert, 1869–
    1942. | Reinforced concrete construction—History—20th
    century. | Architecture, Modern—20th century. | Engineers—United
    States—Biography.
Classification: LCC NA737.K28 S65   2024 (print) | LCC NA737.K28
    (ebook) | DDC 338.7/62418341092 [B]—dc23/eng/20240523
LC record available at https://lccn.loc.gov/2024016800
LC ebook record available at https://lccn.loc.gov/2024016801

Cover image: Shift change at the Ford Motor Company plant, Highland Park,
Michigan, 1916. Looking east along Manchester Street. Colorized by the
author. (Library of Congress, Detroit Publishing Company photograph
collection, control number 2016816050)

To Sherry, David, Jennifer, Reid, Christine,
Spencer, Ally, Jake, Noah, and Emma

Contents

Figures

CONCRETE CENTURY

1

Industry on Fire

Detroit's Jefferson Avenue streetcar was making its way east from downtown on March 9, 1901. As it passed the large Olds Motor Works factory, the conductor noticed a small column of smoke issuing from the plant's three-story main building, located between Jefferson Avenue and the Detroit River. On his return trip just 16 minutes later, he was shocked to see that the entire structure had become a flaming ruin; only a few jagged sections of wall remained standing.

The flames had roared through the main structure and into the attached two-story building that housed the machine shop and forging department, incinerating the 230-foot-long structure along with the machinery and tools contained within. The adjacent foundry would have been consumed as well, but for streams of water poured on it by the city's fireboat. It was a Saturday afternoon, so only 20 people were at work in the buildings; had it been a weekday, nearly 300 employees would have been on hand. All 20 escaped the inferno, though the fire spread so rapidly that 10 of them had to leap from second- or third-story windows. Three suffered broken bones as a result.

The large plant was less than a year old, having been constructed the previous spring to manufacture automobiles by the thousands. Reacting to news of the fire, company president Ransom E. Olds stated,

"While the material loss is great, we do not care half so much about that as we do for the setback it has given our business. We had contracted orders to keep us working full time for over a year, and a more inopportune time for such a calamity could not be."[1] Olds had been just days from introducing its automobile to the market when the fire destroyed dozens of completed vehicles and many others in process of construction, as well as parts, raw materials, and machine tools. Fortunately, the detailed plans for the Olds motor car and the company's account books had been secured in a vault the previous day and survived the blaze. The Olds Motor Works suffered a total loss of around $120,000 as a result of the fire, not all of which was covered by insurance.

The fire was caused by a loose fitting on a natural gas pipe. Fed by a three-inch gas main, the fire spread rapidly through the building, igniting along the way the highly flammable materials employed in automobile manufacturing: gasoline, solvents, carbolic acid, paint and thinner, glue, wood finishes, and lubricants for machines. The building was, like nearly every American factory of the era, constructed with wooden beams, columns, and floors—once started, the fire was also fed by the building itself.

The destruction of the Olds Motor factory exemplified an ominous trend at the end of the 19th century: increasing numbers of American manufacturing firms were suffering devastating fires. By 1901, the destruction by fire of major manufacturing firms was reaching epidemic proportions. The same month that the Olds Motor plant went up in flames, the Virginia-Carolina Chemical Works of Savannah, Georgia, burned, causing a loss of more than $115,000; in Kankakee, Illinois, the Archer Starch Company's factory—the largest starch factory in the world—was leveled by fire (loss: $375,000); the third-largest glue factory in the world, Gaenssler & Fisher, in Gowanda, New York, was demolished by a fire that started in the engine room and traveled through a wall ($150,000); the planters' cotton warehouse in Eutaw, Alabama, went up in flames on March 14 ($100,000); that evening in Chicago, the Spring Butt Company hardware factory burned ($100,000); in St. Louis, the Anheuser-Busch ice storage plant caught fire, taking several other factories with it ($200,000); and the Rohlfing and Sons piano factory in Milwaukee was wiped out by fire ($300,000). Finally, on March 27, the Richardson, Roberts & Byrnes overall and shirt factory of St. Joseph, Missouri, was destroyed by a fire that killed one young woman ($100,000). Two other women were badly burned and a fireman was severely injured. The blaze began in the building's engine room where gasoline caught fire.

But March 1901 was a light month for fires in the United States; February was far more impressive with 31 fires, each of which caused a loss greater than $100,000. The worst was the Armstrong Brothers' cork factory fire in Pittsburgh. It also consumed the adjoining factory of the Totten & Hogg Iron and Steel Company and racked up a loss of $750,000. Two days later, the eight buildings of the National Glass Company's Rochester, Pennsylvania, works—the largest drinking-glass factory in the world—were incinerated. Aside from the $1 million loss and elimination of nearly 150,000 tumblers a day in production capacity, the company's molds and patterns were ruined when the vault in which they were stored was crushed by a falling wall.[2]

From 1899 through 1901, fire losses on commercial and industrial buildings nationwide spiked 20 percent above the average of the prior 10 years.[3] By January 1902, the dramatic increase in fire losses drove fire insurance companies out of business; some liquidated, while others simply declined to offer fire insurance. In St. Louis, the number of firms writing fire insurance slumped from 160 to 112 during the prior two years. In February, a meeting of fire insurance companies to address the "fire epidemic" resulted in an immediate increase in fire insurance rates by 25 percent on manufacturing and business properties. The increase did not affect New York, "because rates there have already been raised considerably."[4] In Pittsburgh, though, the 25 percent hike was imposed on top of a 30 percent increase the previous year in the wake of the Armstrong Brothers' fire.[5] Consumers ultimately paid the increased cost of fire insurance in the form of higher prices for the goods they purchased.

Tall office buildings in the late 1800s were built using so-called fireproof construction. Such buildings were supported by an iron or steel frame that, while incombustible, would soften and deform when exposed to the heat of a fire, leading to a collapse of the structure. To prevent this, frame members were fireproofed by enclosing them within an insulating layer of brick, hollow terra cotta tile blocks, or concrete. Though costly, it could be sustained partly due to the high rental rates earned by office buildings in a city's business center, and partly because the building would remain in service for many decades. The high cost of this method of construction, however, could not be justified for a factory, particularly as industrial structures rarely remained in service as long as buildings in a business district. The preferred method

(*Above*): The Michigan Stove Company in 1900 was the world's largest manufacturer of stoves. Located on Detroit's East Jefferson Avenue near the entrance to Belle Isle, the factory is seen here around 1905. (Library of Congress, Detroit Publishing Company photograph collection, control number 2016816940)

(*Facing page*): The stove factory's mill construction buildings after the disastrous fire of January 8, 1907. All that remained of the six-story main building is a small corner of brick (the dashed line shows the space formerly occupied by the structure). Another of the firm's buildings, visible on the right, was completely gutted by the fire. (Walter P. Reuther Library, Wayne State University, Detroit, VMC20053)

for building factories in the last decades of the 19th century was "mill construction" or, more accurately, "slow-burning construction."

Mill construction was a type of brick-and-timber factory design developed during the 19th century by the cotton and woolen mills of New England to reduce the risk of fire. Though not fireproof, these buildings adhered to specific construction standards that reduced fire hazards and, in the event of fire, slowed its spread through a building, giving firefighters more time to extinguish it. At the very least, occupants would have added time to escape, hopefully taking with them valuable tools, plans, and jigs essential for restarting production. Mutual insurance companies—those owned by policyholders—were instrumental in developing and promoting mill construction as an economical factory type that could be insured at lower rates, due to meeting standards for fire resistance.

The brick-and-timber type of building, from which mill construction evolved, was a wall-supported structure—the exterior walls held themselves up as well as the interior structure. Floors were supported by closely spaced wooden joists (essentially small beams) covered by wood planks on top and a finished ceiling below. The joists rested on beams or girders anchored to the exterior walls and on vertical columns of wood or iron. Mill construction differed from other buildings in that the beams and columns were of heavy timber, thick enough that they could maintain their strength for some time even as they burned. Floors were made of thick, interlocking wooden planks covered by fire retardant material. Heavy timber beams supported the floor in place of joists. Concealed spaces where fire could spread unseen were eliminated by leaving the underside of the floor exposed. Brick firewalls extending from basement to roof were used to break up large buildings into smaller sections, and openings in these walls were protected by automatic (heat activated) fire doors. Firewalls enclosed stairways and elevators to prevent fire from spreading from one floor to another. The entire building was protected by automatic sprinklers. Employees were trained in the use of firefighting supplies, which were accessible throughout the building.[6]

Edward Atkinson, president of the Boston Manufacturers' Mutual

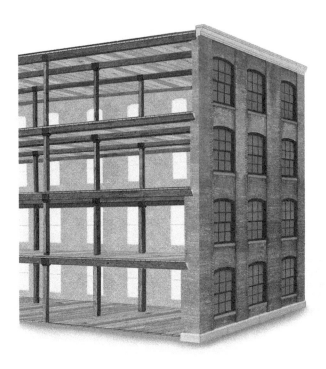

The typical mill construction factory in 1900 had brick supporting walls, timber columns, and wood beams and floors. Because the exterior walls supported the building, windows had to be narrow and limited in size to avoid excessively weakening the structure.

Fire Insurance Company and an important proponent of fire safety, stated the case for mill construction in 1880: "We cannot prevent a building from burning or being destroyed by any method of construction. . . . All we can do is to cause a building to burn as slowly as possible, and thus give time to fight the fire."[7] An article the following year in *Century Magazine* reflected his recommendations: "So long as wood must be used for floors and roofs there can be no such thing as fire-proof building. It is therefore proposed by one of the leading fire insurance companies that all new structures, and particularly factories and shops where wood is to be used, shall be made fire resisting or slow burning." The article described the fire-resisting construction of floors, concluding, "Such a floor will burn, but so slowly that fire would be a long time in eating its way through. The aim is to gain time, for time is the one element of safety at all fires."[8]

The mill construction factory was a successful compromise between cost and safety in the 19th century, but in the two decades prior to 1900, the technology of manufacturing advanced greatly. This period, often described as "the second industrial revolution," saw a dramatic increase in the use of machinery for mass production. These new manufacturing processes commonly employed highly flammable liquids and gases in close proximity to flame and heat. Under these conditions, the slow-burning factory buildings that had been adequate in earlier years had become dangerous by 1900. In spite of the precautions intended to impede the spread of fire, the great volume of highly flammable fuel, solvents, varnish, gases, lubricants, and cleaning solutions used in the modern factory caused fires to roar out of control so rapidly that they frequently consumed the entire factory.

Beyond the heightened threat of fire, mill construction buildings were increasingly obsolete and incompatible with large volume manufacturing. Columns supporting floor beams spaced as little as eight feet apart interrupted the efficient flow of work and interfered with the optimal placement of machines. The forest of columns made it a challenge to assemble large products such as automobiles. The operation of machine tools caused wooden structures to vibrate, making it difficult to consistently manufacture parts to precise tolerances. Vibration affected the machines as well, causing them to wear out more quickly. Artificial lighting was in its infancy, and nearly all work areas were illuminated by natural light entering through windows. Given that the building was supported by its exterior, brick walls, the maximum size of windows was limited: wider windows decreased the amount of wall available to support the weight of the structure above. To make matters worse, as old-growth forests were cleared by loggers, the hefty timbers required for these buildings were becoming increasingly scarce and expensive.

By 1900, the shortcomings of mill construction buildings hampered manufacturing and increased the cost of products. The sensational growth of the automobile industry would shortly place even greater demands on the outmoded building technology.

As Edward Atkinson was advocating adoption of mill construction, Joseph Kahn (1845–1935) was saving money to move his family from Germany to the United States. By 1880, Joseph was in his late thirties and he and his wife Rosalie had six children: Albert (born in 1869), Gustave (1871), Julius (1874), Mollie (1877), Paula (1878), and Moritz (1879).[9] Joseph earned enough as a rabbi to provide a decent living for his family while also setting some money aside. He supplemented his income giving private lessons in French, which he spoke fluently, in addition to his native German and Yiddish.

While the family's prospects appeared promising, Joseph and Rosalie were deeply concerned by recent political and social developments in Germany. In 1871 the loose confederation of German states had unified under the predominant influence of Prussia to form the modern German nation. While the new nation granted full legal rights to Jews (emancipation), the rise of nationalist sentiment resulted in increasing animosity against Jews and Catholics, viewed by some as more loyal to supranational religious organizations than to the new state.

In parallel with the growth of nationalist sentiment in Germany, antisemitism was on the rise as well. The composer Richard Wagner wrote an anonymous essay in 1850 in which he claimed that Jews could never be true Germans; they "could not express true German art; they could not be more than parasites on authentic German creativity."[10] Beyond art, Wagner attacked Jews for their role in banking, by which they "corrupted morals and culture by money," and ridiculed Yiddish, a German dialect spoken by some Jews, as "intolerably jumbled blabber."[11] By 1869, antisemitic attitudes had become sufficiently widespread that Wagner republished the essay under his own name.

The world economy entered a depression following the Panic of 1873, and in Germany the economic calamity was frequently blamed on the supposed machinations of Jewish bankers. In 1879 the popular German historian Heinrich von Treitschke, editor of a widely read journal, published an article claiming that Jews degraded German morals, overly influenced public opinion through their disproportionate numbers working in the press, and were an alien element in German society.[12] The following year, students in Berlin collected thousands of names on a petition demanding a reversal of Jewish emancipation. This led to a debate in the Prussian parliament on the "Jewish Question," in which the majority largely supported antisemitic attitudes. Unsurprisingly, this led to an increase in antisemitic unrest. In the early morning hours of New Year's Day 1881, a crowd of mostly students rioted in front of a number of Berlin cafés often frequented by Jews, smashing windows, yelling "Jews out!", and roughing up those thought to be Jewish.[13]

Soon after, Joseph did get out, sailing from Antwerp to Baltimore and then on to Detroit, where he arrived in June 1881.[14] Detroit had a sizable Jewish community composed largely of German immigrants who had established the city's first Jewish congregation, Temple Beth

El, in 1850. By the time Joseph arrived in Detroit, the congregation had adopted the tenents of Reform Judaism with its abandonment of many traditional practices and greater emphasis on cultural assimilation. The Reform movement had begun in Germany, led by those who sought to modernize their religious worship and bring it more in line with the social and cultural trends of the day. Joseph's own religious practice was formed by this movement, so he would have sought to settle in a city with a Reform congregation such as Beth El.[15] Once established in Detroit, Joseph wrote to Rosalie that it was time for her and the six children to join him. They sailed from Le Havre, France, and arrived in Baltimore the first week of August 1881, completing the trip to their new home in Detroit by train.[16]

Joseph's first effort to support his family in the New World was a restaurant on Woodbridge Street near the Detroit River; the family lived on the second floor. This venture came to an abrupt end one evening in May 1882 when a fire demolished both the eatery and the family home. In the family's rush to escape the burning building, they briefly forgot three-month-old Felix—the family's newest addition. He was rescued from his crib by a policeman.[17]

Joseph began giving private lessons in French and German and achieved a degree of success sufficient to meet his expenses. Finally in 1885, Joseph was hired as the rabbi of a synagogue in Honesdale, Pennsylvania, and moved there with Rosalie and the four youngest children.[18] Albert, now 16, was working for an architecture firm, while Gustave and Julius attended Detroit public schools and worked part-time.[19] While Joseph and Rosalie lived in Honesdale, the eighth and last of the Kahn brood, Louis, was born in 1886.

Joseph spent much time away from the family as an interim rabbi. After two years in Honesdale, he took a similar position in Pennington, New Jersey, until 1888, followed by one year with a congregation in Jacksonville, Florida, before returning to Detroit in 1890. He was once again hired as rabbi for a congregation in New Orleans in 1892, though all of his children now remained in Detroit. A sermon given by Joseph for the Jewish holiday of Yom Kippur, printed in a New Orleans newspaper that year, shows that he was a deeply insightful thinker who could convey moral concepts in a captivating and lyrical manner.[20] The following year found Joseph in Davenport, Iowa, and then in Pensacola, Florida, from 1894 until the synagogue burned down in 1895. He returned to Detroit until 1900, when he left once again, this time to a

The Kahn family around 1888. Joseph and Rosalie Kahn are surrounded by their eight children. Albert is on the far right, Gustave on the far left, and Julius in the center framed by the open door. (Albert Kahn Associates, Inc.)

congregation in Marshall, Texas. His final stint as a traveling rabbi was also his longest, from 1901 until 1904 in Leavenworth, Kansas.[21]

For Albert and Gustave, their formal education ended during middle school, when they went to work to help support the family. Albert found employment in his chosen profession with one of Detroit's better architecture firms. Gustave, in his teens, worked as a peddler, an occupation quite common for European Jews newly arrived in America. Seeing no future in it, he found work with a plumbing and steam-fitting firm and learned the trade.[22] Julius fared better, in part because his two brothers were already working; he was able to graduate high school in 1892.[23] From an early age, Julius worked at several paper routes in the morning before school and at various jobs after. Savings from these jobs, likely supplemented by his older brothers, paid for Julius to attend the University of Michigan's civil engineering program, from which he graduated in 1896 with a Bachelor of Science degree.[24]

Julius immediately found work as a draftsman with the Union

Bridge Company in Athens, Pennsylvania, but he stayed only a short time before moving to New York to become an assistant engineer with the Hecla Iron Works of Brooklyn, a position that he enjoyed, though the pay was not generous. He spent his evenings studying engineering books and journals in the library of the American Society of Civil Engineers. In November 1897 he joined the engineering staff of the Brooklyn Navy Yard. Though the pay was better, Julius complained to his brother Albert, "During working hours I had absolutely nothing to do except to inform myself on the daily news." "Thanks to a little life I have in me," he reported, "I allowed myself to become a lazy government official for only a very short period of time."[25]

After leaving the Navy Yard, Julius joined the C. W. Hunt Company, an engineering firm that specialized in coal and ore handling facilities. This was an advantageous opportunity for Julius as he designed a particularly large coal handling plant for the Calumet and Hecla Mining Company on the shore of Torch Lake, just south of Lake Linden, Michigan. The steel structure consisted of five movable towers, about 60 feet tall, each having a boom from which hung a large shovel used to empty the coal from ships. Each shovelful of coal weighed two tons, and the shovel itself weighed three. The engineering involved in the structure was quite complex due to the stresses placed on the steel components, as the coal-filled shovel was rapidly accelerated and stopped during operation. Safety measures had to anticipate accidental overloading of the components: for example, if the shovel caught on a part of the ship while being lifted. An unusual aspect of the structure was the 44-foot-long boom, which Julius described as "a heavily trussed structure, of a peculiar shape . . . approximately a parabolic segment." Although complex to engineer, the towers were "reduced to great simplicity in their general design," shrinking the cost and time required to construct them, and resulting in reliable, high-capacity operation. Each tower could hoist one shovel of coal and dump it into a hopper every 50 seconds. If all five towers were in operation on a five-hatch ship, the facility could unload 10 tons of coal per minute.[26]

Noting that a detailed treatment of the unusual engineering challenges posed by coal processing facilities had yet to be discussed in the journal of the American Society of Civil Engineers, Julius decided to write an article. His detailed and engaging discussion of the design considerations and solutions devised for the Calumet and Hecla facility appeared in the December 1898 issue of the society's journal. The society awarded Julius the Collingwood Prize for his piece, "The Coal Hoists of the Calumet and Hecla Mining Company."[27]

Julius was an astute observer of business practices, and as he acquired engineering experience, he also refined his understanding of effective management. During a period when the Hunt Company's president, Charles Hunt, was in Europe, Julius noticed that "everything seems to be at a standstill. No one seems to have any authority to say anything. No one dare do anything of his own accord, but everything must pass through Mr. Hunt's hands before leaving the office."[28]

Having acquired the necessary work experience, Julius received the degree of civil engineer from the University of Michigan in March 1899. Not long after, and perhaps as a result of his article on coal handling, Everett Welles Frazar (1867–1951) of Frazar and Company, the largest American company trading with China, Japan, and Korea, contacted Julius. (Frazar & Co. was founded by E. W. Frazar's father, Everett Frazar.) Frazar offered Julius a job as chief engineer of a sulfur mining startup in Japan, the Kubo Moyoro Sulphur and Iron Mining Company (also known in Japan as Futayama Shokai) of Yokohama. Julius had what was described by a coworker as a "keen interest" in Japan; he accepted the offer and sailed for Japan from Vancouver on April 16, 1900.[29]

While the position with Kubo gave Julius experience managing others, the decision to join the firm turned out not to have been to his advantage, as the company was woefully undercapitalized and unable to pay many of its creditors. Julius wrote to Albert that, while he enjoyed the work, he was in "continual fear of being paid for it." Concerned that if he simply quit, he would lose the pay he was owed, Julius hatched a clever plan that might allow him to leave and be paid in full. "Keeping myself well informed in regard to the times when the concern was apt to be a little unusually flush," wrote Julius, "I approached Mr. Kubo one day when he was in an exceptionally good humor, and after an hour's talk convinced him what a great saving it would be if he would allow me to close my contract with him, thereby saving my exceedingly large salary, and the work, I convinced him, would proceed just as well." Kubo, under the impression that Julius wished to return to the United States, agreed to pay his salary in full and release him from his contract. After three weeks of fretting over whether Mr. Kubo would actually follow through, Julius received his back pay and left the firm.[30] It went bankrupt the following year.

Julius, however, did not return home. E. W. Frazar had arranged for him to join Frazar and Company as an engineering advisor and sales agent for various types of industrial equipment and machinery. According to Julius, this included "marine engines, rice cleaning plants, mail making machinery, locomotives, woodworking machinery," and so forth. The work afforded him an opportunity to become familiar with a much broader swath of the industrial economy, giving him "a superficial knowledge of all matters in engineering," a benefit that would prove valuable later. Dealing directly with clients, he also acquired a fair appreciation of the sales process.[31]

Frazar was pleased with Julius's work, and asked him to stay for three more years before returning to the States. Though appreciative, Julius had not planned to remain that long in Japan. He wrote to Albert, "In consideration of the training in business method which I am receiving, I can well afford to give them a year of my time, but that is all."[32]

In early June 1901, Julius received a letter from Albert with the extraordinary suggestion that, upon his return to the States, he become a partner in Albert's architectural firm. Julius assumed the proposal was Albert's way of looking out for his younger brother by assuring that he would have a job in Detroit. Though Julius appreciated Albert's generosity, with no background in architecture, he considered himself a poor candidate for the position. He did allow that the partnership might work if Albert was willing to wait a couple of years while Julius attended architecture school.[33] Albert, however, had a completely different plan in mind that had nothing to do with Julius working as an architect; he would reveal that plan in detail once Julius returned home.

Julius sailed from Yokohama on October 5, 1901 and arrived in Marseilles on November 25, having made stops in Kobe, Hong Kong, Singapore, and Suez. He toured Europe, but with little interest in the work of European engineers as he believed that, in America, "we are considerably ahead of the Europeans."[34]

In late January 1902, Julius arrived home in Detroit. Albert shared the idea he had for a partnership, and once Julius had taken it all in, he quickly committed. This partnership laid the groundwork for one of the most important inventions of the 20th century.

2
Kahn and Kahn

Albert's architectural partnerships prior to this time had lacked stability. He learned his trade working under George D. Mason and Zachariah Rice in the office of Mason and Rice, leaving in 1895 to partner with George W. Nettleton and Alexander B. Trowbridge. That firm, Nettleton, Kahn and Trowbridge, lasted until 1897, when Trowbridge left to accept a position at Cornell University as a professor and dean of the School of Architecture.[1]

Continuing on as Nettleton and Kahn, the firm met with success designing mostly residences, ranging from moderately priced spec houses to mansions for such notables as James E. Scripps, founder of the *Detroit News*. There were a small number of larger projects: Bethany Presbyterian Church (1897), Grace Hospital's Nurses' Home (1898), Sigma Phi fraternity house in Ann Arbor (1900, demolished), and Pierson Apartments (1899, demolished).[2] Then in December 1900, George Nettleton died of tuberculosis in Colorado, leaving Kahn alone in the practice.[3]

Kahn's former employer, George Mason, had been on his own since his parting from Zachariah Rice in 1899. Mason needed the help of a skilled architect for his prosperous practice, and Kahn needed someone to share the rent. The two men established the firm of Mason and

Kahn in early February 1901, and Mason moved his office into the larger space occupied by Kahn in Detroit's Union Trust Building.[4] During 1901, the firm was chiefly occupied with the design of luxurious homes costing between $5,000 and $10,000. Though this was considered desirable work, custom built mansions required the architect to spend a significant amount of time in meetings with the client to meet their expectations. In addition to these smaller commissions, Mason and Kahn secured a number of significant projects: the Palms Apartment Building, with a construction cost of $80,000; Belle Isle Park's aquarium and horticulture buildings, with a total cost of $125,000; the University of Michigan Psychopathic Hospital and a new Engineering Building, costing $50,000 and $140,000, respectively; and the Century Association Club, at $40,000.[5]

Architects were compensated on a percentage basis, typically receiving between 3 and 6 percent of the construction cost for designing and superintending a project.[6] Consequently, larger projects generated significantly more income for the architect than did residences. While major structures such as hospitals and educational buildings were desirable commissions, the most common large projects were factories.

In 1901 Detroit was on the cusp of an industrial boom, but Albert Kahn anticipated that future growth would be different. The *Detroit Free Press* column "Real Estate Field" appeared each Sunday, usually on the same page as "News of the Architects." Kahn may have read a column on November 11, 1900, stating, "The recent election victory in this country is, in more respects than one, a triumph of industrial forces. It means more factories to be built and enlarged in Detroit and vicinity."[7] This was a reference to the victory of President William McKinley—a supporter of the recently enacted gold standard—over William Jennings Bryan, who advocated a return to bimetallism. On March 24, 1901, "Real Estate Field" reported, "Manufacturers are quietly looking for building sites and vacant buildings. The local supply of vacant buildings suitable for manufacturing purposes is very limited."[8] The same page included the additional note "Homer Warren & Co. report a splendid demand for factory sites of late."[9] On April 7, 1901, the same column stated, "Manufacturing enterprises are passing by Detroit simply because she has no factory buildings to rent."[10] It was shortly after this last story appeared that Albert wrote to Julius in Japan suggesting that they form a partnership upon his return to the States.[11]

These news stories indicated that industrial concerns were grow-

Julius (*left*) and Albert Kahn around the time they became partners in Kahn and Kahn, Architects and Engineers. (Albert Kahn Family Collection, Leo M. Franklin Archives, Bloomfield Hills, MI)

ing in Detroit at an unprecedented rate. More significantly, from his own observations and from reading trade journals, Kahn realized that modern manufacturers increasingly required buildings tailored to their needs, and that factories were becoming larger and more complex. Kahn concluded that, for industrial structures, the role of civil engineers specializing in factory buildings would become progressively more important, ultimately relegating architects to a marginal role.

Kahn's plan, then, was to partner with his brother, a civil engineer, so that the firm could provide both services, an unusual arrangement for the time, but perfectly in line with Albert's vision for the future of industrial architecture. Kahn and Kahn would be the only Detroit firm offering both architecture and engineering, and one of the first in the nation to do so. Julius's education and experience would give the firm an advantage over other local architecture firms in securing commissions for large industrial and manufacturing facilities.

Albert's vision was of a different type of architecture firm, one in which the architect retained the chief leadership role and oversight of a project, delegating tasks to specialists in design, architecture, engineering, mechanical systems, and construction supervision. The client would retain the benefits of a trained and experienced architect to conceptualize the structure, while experts worked out the details. This, in fact, was exactly the type of firm Albert built over the coming decade.

Combining architecture and civil engineering in a single firm was not unique; a small number of firms offered both prior to 1902. One of those was Lockwood, Greene and Company of Boston, which designed many mills in New England and the South. The company was established prior to the Civil War as a one-man mill consulting practice and by 1900 had grown into a large operation primarily engaged in designing and outfitting mills throughout the southern states. Another such firm was Wilson Brothers and Company, Architects and Consulting Engineers, established 1876 in Philadelphia. The three founders were civil engineers, two of whom were also architects. The firm's early projects were railroad stations and bridges, taking advantage of the 16 years of experience one of the founders had as a civil engineer for the Pennsylvania Railroad. Though railroad stations figured prominently on the firm's list of jobs, by 1900 their commissions included a variety of consequential buildings.

Both of these firms began as highly specialized engineering practices focused on a particular industry, evolving over time as the demands of their client base became more varied. Unlike these firms' slow evolution, Albert's plan to bring on Julius as a civil engineer was an ambitious and innovative leap that would alter the nature and size of his business. Motivated by his ambition to grow the firm and possessed of great insight into the types of buildings that would be required in the future, Kahn devised a strategy that would place his firm in the most advantageous position.

Albert was aware that his business plan might fail, but civil engineering involved another type of risk. On the afternoon of November 5, 1898, twelve workers were killed by the collapse of the Wonderland Theater, under construction on Monroe Street at Campus Martius in downtown Detroit. The theater was designed by the architecture firm of John Scott and Company. The firm was founded by William Scott of Windsor, Ontario, a former civil engineer for Britain's Great Western Railway, as William Scott & Company of Detroit. Scott had turned the business over to his two sons, John (1850–1928) and Arthur H. (1852–1931), around 1888 and they later renamed the firm John Scott and Company. Both John and Arthur began their careers as engineers, though it is not clear they received any formal training other than from their father. John had a preference for architecture, so gave up engineering in 1875 to practice as an architect. Prior to rejoining his brother in the family business, Arthur had been employed for around 12 years as a civil engineer with a railroad.[12]

The coroner's investigation into the Wonderland collapse began November 11. The coroner impaneled a jury and subpoenaed over 70 witnesses; the various parties involved were represented by a "small army of attorneys."[13] The inquest went on for a month and was extensively covered in the newspapers, usually on the front page, with much of the testimony published verbatim. On December 9, the jury received the case and, within two hours, returned with a unanimous decision "fixing the responsibility for the accident on John Scott & Co., architects of the building."[14]

The cause of the collapse became clear early in the proceedings: the large steel trusses carrying the roof over the expansive theater had failed, allowing the roof and trusses to come crashing down. The falling mass collapsed the upper balcony, smashed onto the lower balcony, and cascaded forward into the orchestra pit, carrying with it many of the more than 30 men working in the building. Later that evening, as over 150 people were attempting to free the dead and injured from the wreckage, the east wall of the building fell, taking out the electric lights that had been rigged up and plunging the entire scene into darkness. As rescuers scrambled for safety, some fell through voids in the floor and landed in the basement, further increasing the number of injured.[15]

The failed trusses had been designed by Arthur Scott. Testifying at the coroner's inquest, Scott admitted he had not calculated the weight the trusses would be required to support, but had essentially copied the design of trusses used to construct the adjacent Detroit Opera House.[16] From his other testimony, it became apparent that Scott was not capable of doing the calculations. The prosecuting attorney asked him to compute for a particular section of one of the building's trusses the weight that it could safely support: "He made an attempt to do so, but finally said that he would be unable to do it in court."[17] Scott's engineering experience, it turned out, was limited. Trusses he previously designed "were all simple ones" and he had "never designed a truss before that was the same as the Wonderland truss."[18] Scott could have hired an outside consultant to assist in the design of the steel work; his reason for not doing so may have been a desire to avoid the expense. When asked why he did not hire an inspector to assure the steel was correctly manufactured by the mill and installed by the contractor, Scott testified "that an engineering company could have skimmed the job in many ways, had it set out to do so."[19]

Albert Kahn would certainly have considered the consequences should a similar calamity befall his firm. To surmount these concerns, Albert must have had a great deal of confidence in Julius, even though he had not seen or spoken with his brother, other than by mail, in two years.

In mid-February 1902, Albert Kahn and George Mason dissolved their year-old partnership. On March 16, the *Detroit Free Press* carried a notice that Julius Kahn "has opened up a practice as consulting engineer at 1117 Union Trust Building."[20] The following week the paper reported that, with the firm of Mason and Kahn having ended, "[Albert] Kahn will continue to practice at No. 1117 Union Trust Building with the collaboration of Julius Kahn, civil engineer." To allay any concerns of Mason and Kahn's clients concerning ongoing projects, the article stated that "buildings designed by Mason & Kahn, now in course of erection, will be continued to completion under their joint supervision. They include the aquarium at Belle Isle, the Temple Beth El, the apartment houses of Dr. J. B. Book and Frank C. Andrews."[21]

The new firm of Kahn and Kahn quickly secured a number of modest industrial projects. Albert's work designing and altering expensive homes for Detroit's business leaders proved a considerable advantage, as nearly all the new industrial commissions came through previous residential clients. The most important of these clients was Joseph Boyer (1848–1930), head of the Boyer Machine Company of Detroit. Prior to 1900, Boyer's company had been located in St. Louis and manufactured pneumatic hammers—a hand-held tool used for driving rivets—for the Chicago Pneumatic Tool Company. Boyer devised a significant improvement in the design of the hammer, which was subsequently manufactured and sold by Chicago Pneumatic; the widespread adoption of the "Boyer Hammer" made him a wealthy man. Prior to this success, Boyer had rented space in his shop to William S. Burroughs (1857–1898), who was working on a mechanical adding machine. The machine proved difficult to develop, and Boyer often assisted Burroughs in working out problems. This gave rise to a relationship between the two men that later resulted in Boyer becoming president of American Arithmometer, the company that Burroughs established to manufacture the highly successful machine. (The firm was later renamed the Burroughs Adding Machine Company.)

In 1900, Boyer relocated himself and the Boyer Machine Company from St. Louis to Detroit, claiming that the move was motivated by climate—having grown up in Canada, Boyer found the summers in St. Louis to be "infernally hot." Perhaps more relevant was the superb quality of Detroit's machine tool industry, which, largely through the influence of Henry M. Leland, was machining parts to closer tolerances than elsewhere, facilitating their interchangeability in manufactured products.[22] Boyer's new Detroit factory was designed by St. Louis architect Louis Mullgardt (1866–1944) and built on the northwest corner of Second Avenue and Amsterdam Street.[23] Mullgardt's design took an innovative approach to the manner in which natural light was provided to the single-story building. At the time, in order to supply adequate illumination for the precise machining work that took place within, it was common to construct such buildings with a glass or sawtooth roof containing north-facing windows. These roofs had disadvantages: they were prone to leaking, and the large, south-facing area of the sawtooth caused heat buildup in the summer. Alfred Doughty, Boyer's general superintendent of the tool factory, suggested to Mullgardt that the sawtooth windows be placed across the width of the building—parallel with the roof trusses—instead of along its length. The result was essentially a gable roof with numerous small saw teeth at right angles to the roof's ridge. This design not only solved the leaking and heat problems but eliminated many of the interior support posts necessary for a traditional sawtooth roof.[24]

Boyer, though new to the city, quickly integrated himself into the top echelons of its businesspeople. In January 1901 he joined with William Maybury, mayor of Detroit, and Homer Warren, head of the city's leading real estate firm, to form the Detroit Industrial Bureau, charged with recruiting industrial businesses to relocate to the city.[25] Later that year Boyer hired Albert Kahn to design alterations to his home.[26] On the last day of 1901, Boyer merged his machine company with Chicago Pneumatic and was appointed a director of the firm and head of the Detroit operation.[27] Shortly after, Chicago Pneumatic allocated funds for two minor additions to its Detroit plant, the former Boyer Machine

Company factory on Second Avenue. For these additions, Boyer chose Albert Kahn as the architect, perhaps because he had worked with Kahn the previous year on his house; it was Albert and Julius Kahn's first industrial job. One of the additions was a 48-foot extension to a section in the rear of the factory, completed in March or April of 1902. The design work entailed little more than copying Mullgardt's plan for the existing section and labeling it "extension." The second addition was for a rudimentary warehouse along the railroad tracks behind the building. The permit for this 50-by-200-foot structure was issued in early May and listed its cost as $5,300.[28] The modest cost of the warehouse reflected the structure's simple construction: wooden posts, steel roof trusses, dirt floor, and steel exterior cladding.

Kahn and Kahn found more challenging work with two jobs that leveraged Julius's previous experience designing coal-handling structures. The first was a project for the Brown and Brown Coal and Ice Company of Detroit. Brown and Brown was founded by David A. Brown (1875–1958), a savvy businessman who belonged to Congregation Beth El—as did Albert and Julius—and who, two years later, married their sister, Paula Kahn. The Brown and Brown job included enlarging the firm's office on the northeast corner of Woodward Avenue and Elizabeth and constructing a coal storage warehouse and coal elevator on the east side of Woodward Avenue between East Baltimore Street and the railroad tracks, completed during spring 1902.[29] (Though one of the largest and most modern facilities in the city, Brown and Brown was forced to abandon the site in 1910 when the railroad constructed an overpass over Woodward Avenue. Raising the tracks to pass over the street made it impossible to maintain the siding by which coal was brought in to the Brown and Brown facility.[30])

The Kahns' second project was for the Detroit City Gas Company, headed locally by Dexter M. Ferry (1833–1907). Ferry had hired Albert for alterations to his home in 1900, so the brothers had an established contact through which they could pursue work with the company. Julius was hired by the gas company in April 1902 to design a coal elevator and conveyor for the Station B coal gas plant located at the end of Wight Street east of Meldrum near the Belle Isle Bridge, while Albert was engaged for a project at the company's Station A on West Jefferson Avenue at 21st Street.[31] Julius's elevator remained on the property through the 1950s.

Late in the year Joseph Boyer brought two more jobs for Chicago

Pneumatic to the brothers. The first was a large addition to the machine shop of nearly 150 feet, but the job was canceled at some point after the plans were drawn up.[32] The second job, however, was quite significant. John Duntley, head of Chicago Pneumatic, found a substantial market for his tools in Europe and decided to build a factory in Scotland to manufacture them for the company's European subsidiary, Consolidated Pneumatic Tool Company. He selected Fraserburgh, a fishing town of 10,000 people, about 400 miles north of London.[33] Duntley sought to have the factory operate in the same manner as did the one in Detroit, using American equipment and management methods. Naturally the factory itself would be designed by an American architect and be similar to the Detroit plant. Though Kahn and Kahn had not designed Boyer's Detroit factory, Duntley and Boyer had acquired sufficient confidence in the brothers to hire them to design the Consolidated Pneumatic plant.

The factory in Scotland had two distinct sections, a two-story office building and a single-story manufacturing area, itself composed of two long bays featuring the same novel sawtooth roof as the Detroit plant. The bays were wider than those in the Detroit building, achieved by redesigning the roof truss and providing a row of support columns. The office building was of stone in an attractive style similar to that of the substantial buildings in the nearby town. Plans for the factory were completed in November, and construction began in January 1903.[34] There is no record of Albert Kahn having designed a factory prior to this; as strange as it may seem, the first factory Kahn designed was in Scotland.[35]

These were the significant industrial projects of Kahn and Kahn through the end of 1902, all of them secured through previous residential clients or personal contacts.[36] It was not a bad start, though the firm lagged behind another Detroit architecture and engineering firm begun in September 1902 by architect Harry Stevens and engineer Gustave Blume—Stevens and Blume, Architects and Engineers. In the first three months of operation, the partners secured two sizable commissions: an office, factory, machine shop, and foundry for Detroit Brass Works, and a large foundry for the Sheffield Car Company in Three Rivers, Michigan.[37]

The office of Kahn and Kahn was busy, though, with important holdovers from Mason and Kahn: the Palms apartment building; two jobs for the University of Michigan—a psychopathic hospital and an engineering building; and a small addition for the American Can Company. The Palms building was of particular interest. It was planned in early 1901 as a seven-story building with 24 luxury residences. Some large suites had ten rooms, including three or four bedrooms and servant's quarters. Construction began on the $80,000 "fireproof" building in the fall of 1901, even as plans for the upper floors were being revised. The drawings for the building were completed between December 1901 and January 1902, prior to Julius partnering with Albert.[38]

The Palms was constructed much like an office building, supported by an internal frame of steel columns and beams. The typical practice for making such a building fireproof was to enclose the columns within hollow three- or four-inch-thick terra cotta tiles and to bridge the area between beams with specially designed terra cotta blocks that supported the floor and enclosed the beams. The terra cotta was often topped with several inches of cinder concrete as a filler material to create a level surface upon which to attach the flooring material.[39] To make the Palms fireproof, though, Mason and Kahn elected to employ a new method of floor construction: concrete reinforced with expanded metal. Concrete was widely used for basement floors, foundations, sidewalks, platforms, docks, and other applications where it was fully supported from beneath at all points. It was typically strengthened by embedding within it some type of wire mesh, either fencing wire or expanded metal lath. In 1901, when the Palms was designed, the idea of building concrete floors above ground level was new and relatively untried. Only a handful of significant buildings in the country had been or were being constructed with such floors, and none had yet been built in Detroit.[40]

Concrete floors of this type were supported—much like a traditional wood floor—by regularly spaced, parallel steel joists beneath the floor's surface; the joists were supported at each end by the beams of the building's steel frame. The concrete that spanned the area between two floor joists, unlike concrete laid directly upon the ground, had no support beneath. To prevent the concrete from giving way when weight was placed on it, expanded metal lath was embedded within it near its lower face.[41]

The performance of commonly used structural materials was well known at the time. The maximum weight that could be supported by a steel or timber beam, brick or stone arch, or other structure, could be computed using standard engineering tables or mathematical equa-

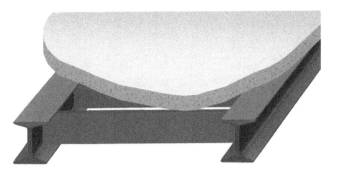

The Palms Apartment building has an internal frame of steel and iron. The floor is supported by beams and joists connected to the frame. Unlike concrete laid directly upon the ground, the concrete in the Palms spans the distance between each joist without any direct support underneath. At the time the Palms was built, there was no engineering data to guide such an arrangement; the floor's design was based on guesswork.

tions. Due to the many foreseeable and unforeseeable defects and errors that inevitably arise in human endeavors, buildings are always constructed with a generous safety factor built in. At the time, the typical factor of safety was four, meaning, for example, that if a particular beam was required to support 25,000 pounds, it would be designed to support at least 100,000 pounds. The ability to make these engineering calculations was absolutely essential to the safe construction of buildings.

While it seemed reasonable that concrete, reinforced with steel lath, could sustain the weight that was likely to be imposed on it across a span of two feet or less between joists, there were no established standards for calculating its strength. Its safety when used as a floor was based entirely on unscientific guesswork. A 1901 article in the journal *Insurance Engineering* claimed that "other things being equal, the reenforcement of concrete construction with expanded metal increases its strength from three to four hundred per cent."[42] This assertion may have inspired confidence in the ability of concrete and expanded steel to support weight, but in reality it was meaningless. Concrete, when unreinforced and unsupported from below, has so little ability to support weight across a span that its load-carrying strength is usually assumed to be zero, so a 300 or 400 percent increase is still zero. Moreover, stating "all things equal" glossed over the most essential variables: type of concrete and its mixture, thickness of concrete floor, thickness of the expanded steel, the location of steel within the floor slab, method used to manufacture the steel, manner in which the sheets of steel were connected at seams, and so forth.

The Palms Apartment building at 1001 East Jefferson Avenue in Detroit. (Photo by the author)

In April 1902, as the Palms neared completion, the Detroit building inspector received a report that the concrete floors in the building appeared to be unsafe. Given the unprecedented nature of concrete floors and the absence of any method by which to calculate the weight the concrete could support, the building inspector decided the floors needed to be tested to assure safety. After locating what appeared to be the weakest area in the building, the inspector had a load of six tons placed on the floor, nearly six times what it was expected to support. There were no untoward consequences to this extreme overloading of the floor, so the inspector approved the construction.[43]

The Palms continues to serve its purpose as an apartment building at the corner of E. Jefferson Avenue and Rivard Street in Detroit. Years after its construction, though, Albert Kahn admitted that his use of concrete floors, "a system then little known," may have been foolish. "We had to depend much upon the advice of the promoters of the system," he said.[44] The Cleveland Silex Stone Company of Detroit, headed by Frank P. Cleveland, installed the concrete floors of the Palms. Prior to 1901, Cleveland Silex advertised itself as a provider of concrete sidewalks, carriage blocks, hitching posts, laundry tubs, and barn and basement floors. It's unclear what qualified Frank Cleveland to provide "advice" on the safety and construction of concrete floors. His extensive hands-on experience likely would have been adequate to specify a floor so overbuilt that it was nearly indestructible (as well as expensive and wasteful of materials). Subsequent to his work on the Palms, Cleveland secured commissions to install floors in local buildings by other architects: the Washington Arcade Building (1520 Woodward Ave.), the Elks' Temple (Monroe St.; demolished), Detroit Boat Club (Belle Isle), Eloise Hospital Building D (Westland, Michigan; demolished), and Murphy Building (151 W. Congress St.).[45]

Concrete floors were specified by Mason and Kahn in their design for the West Engineering Building at the University of Michigan (now West Hall). The regents of the university required that the building be fireproof, achieved in part by constructing the floors in the same fashion as those in the Palms.[46] The plans for the building were approved by the university regents early in 1902, and the construction contract was awarded in late June to Herch and Son of Grand Rapids. In January 1903 as work was proceeding on the building, a dispute arose between the contractor and the university over the cost of the concrete work for the floors. Years later Julius stated that the university was "compelled by state law to let the contract to the lowest bidder, who happened to be utterly unacquainted with the vagaries—in those days they were vagaries—of reinforced concrete floors." The contractor's ignorance of concrete work had resulted in an underestimate of the cost to perform it. Making matters worse, the contractor fell well behind in the work and, rather than completing the building by June 1903 as promised, had made only two floors ready by January 1904; the rest of the building did not open until that fall.[47]

The use of concrete for floors was significantly lower in cost than terra cotta tile fireproofing, which proved a strong incentive for its increased use during this era. The lack of scientific understanding of the principles of concrete construction, combined with workers' unfamiliarity with concrete, however, resulted in numerous dramatic accidents, often fatal. In October 1902, the four-story Otsego Hotel, under construction in Jackson, Michigan, suffered a partial collapse. The luxury hotel was of traditional wall-bearing construction—the exterior walls supported the building—but concrete floors were installed instead of wood to achieve fire resistance. Architect Harrison Albright of Charleston, West Virginia, designed the floors to be supported by cables attached to the 16-inch-thick walls of the building; wire fencing material embedded within the concrete reinforced the floors. The weight of the wet concrete of the newly installed fourth floor was supported by shoring standing upon the third floor, which had been poured just three weeks prior. Suddenly, a section of the third floor and rear wall of the building gave way, though it's not clear whether the floor or wall gave way first. The entire mass collapsed through the second floor onto the ground level of the building, killing one man and seriously injuring three others, including the city building inspector. The contractor for the building, Samuel Pickles, was also mayor of the city, so it was no surprise when the coroner's inquest exonerated both Pickles and architect Albright. The coroner blamed the accident on "wet weather" that weakened the mortar of the wall and added to the weight of the concrete. Soon after, though, a committee of three Detroit architects, hired to review the building plans, found the design to be unsafe. The interior of the building had to be demolished and rebuilt.[48]

In Chicago, the Paddington Apartments (also known as Pattington Condominiums), a four-story building at 660 to 700 West Irving Park Road was under construction in December 1902 when a section of the concrete fourth floor collapsed and crashed down through the lower floors to the basement, killing one worker. The building was originally designed to have wood floors and floor joists, but it was later decided the building should be fireproof and concrete floors were substituted. The concrete was reinforced with expanded metal and half-inch round steel rods anchored to the walls. In constructing a concrete floor, wooden forms held the liquid concrete in place until it became solid and, like a mold, gave it shape. To shore up the concrete floor until it was sufficiently hard to support its own weight, stout wood posts were wedged between the underside of forms and the floor below. The forms could be removed within a few days, and often were as they were needed to construct the next floor, but the shoring had to remain in place for a few weeks until the concrete developed strength. On the day of the

Paddington accident, workers were removing just the wooden forms, while leaving in place the supporting shoring. One of the workers was new to concrete construction and, misunderstanding his instructions, set about removing both the forms and the shoring. The floor, inadequately cured, surrendered to gravity, killing the neophyte worker and injuring another.[49]

During 1902, while the Palms was under construction and plans for the West Engineering Building were finalized, Julius Kahn found himself baffled by his brother's use of concrete floors. He asked Albert, "How do you calculate the strength of the reinforced concrete?" Albert replied, "By guess. There are no scientific data."[50] Beyond his immediate concern over the safety of the floors, the strength of which could not be determined, Julius was curious as to why no one had yet developed a scientifically sound theory for calculating the strength of concrete reinforced with steel.

Seeking to better understand why there was no theory of reinforced concrete, Julius researched the subject in scientific and engineering journals. One of the best treatments of the subject was a paper presented to the Indiana Engineering Society in January 1902 by William Kendrick Hatt (1862–1952), a professor of civil engineering at Purdue University. His paper, "Theory of the Strength of Beams of Reinforced Concrete," was reprinted in the journal *Engineering Record* in May of that year.[51] Hatt succinctly summarized the state of concrete science: "There is no widely-accepted method of computation for the strength of concrete reinforced with steel, and the elements of the strength of the constituent parts are not well ascertained." Hatt set out a series of assumptions and then devised three different and highly complex equations to compute the strength of a reinforced concrete beam. His ultimate conclusion, however, was rather discouraging: "Considering all the elements affecting the strength of reinforced beams, . . . it is evident that the use of refined theories of computations are not justified."

Hatt wasn't done. He carried out a series of tests on concrete, reporting the outcomes in the June 28, 1902, edition of *Engineering Record*.[52] His hope was that tests conducted under laboratory conditions would reveal consistent results upon which a theory of concrete's load-bearing capacity might be based. His first test on both plain concrete cylinders and cylinders reinforced with vertical wrought-iron rods was disappointing: he found the "reinforced cylinders were weaker than the plain cylinders, and the forms of rupture are abnormal." Hatt's tests on reinforcing bars in beams ran into problems as well. "The tension tests were not satisfactory in that the heads of the bars, with some exceptions, pulled off," making it necessary to extrapolate data from a limited number of results.

One of the most important tests conducted by Hatt was of concrete's adhesion to embedded reinforcing bars. If a reinforcing bar can be pulled loose or slip within a concrete beam when weight is imposed, the beam fails. The maximum safe load on a beam, therefore, is either the point at which the reinforcement bar snaps or the bar is pulled loose from the concrete, whichever occurs first. Hatt found there was considerable variation in the strength of adhesion. This was due, at least in part, to inconsistent contact between the concrete and reinforcement bars, a condition he discovered when the concrete was broken apart and inspected after the test. Consequently, any theory of concrete beams reinforced with rods must, for the sake of safety, assume the adhesion between concrete and bar is no better than that of the most poorly adhered bar, the same principle as a chain being only as strong as its weakest link.

Hatt set aside the problem of the bar slipping from the concrete; the theory he proposed for calculating the strength of a reinforced concrete beam was based on the assumption that "there is no slipping between the concrete and the steel reinforcement." He acknowledged that his theory, at best, applied only to beams where no reinforcing rod was pulled loose; if the rod slipped within the concrete beam, his calculations were meaningless. This was a significant limiting factor, as the adhesion of concrete to steel was little understood and, as with Hatt's tests, empirical data varied widely.

3

Experimental Methods

The fact that there was "no widely-accepted method of computation for the strength of concrete reinforced with steel" did not prevent concrete's use in construction. In Europe, a number of systems for reinforcing concrete with steel had been in regular use since around 1890. Of these the most successful was the Hennebique system, patented in 1892 by French engineer Francois Hennebique (1842–1921). By 1900, Hennebique, and the firms to which he had licensed his system, had completed several thousand projects.[1] Hennebique's method of reinforcement, though well thought out, was based on his own informal experimentation, not on any scientific theory. While the trial and error approach taken by Hennebique and others enabled the construction of safe buildings, it was inefficient. In most cases much more steel and concrete was used than would have been necessary if the load-carrying capability of concrete beams, floors, and columns could have been accurately calculated. Albert Kahn once quipped, "Anyone can plan a building to stand up by putting in plenty of materials. The trick is to design adequately in every way but economically and without waste."[2]

Hennebique's system was popular in Europe, but used only occasionally in the United States. The complexity of the system required installation by skilled workers at the construction site and, while these laborers were plentiful in Europe at reasonable cost, in the US their relative scarcity and high wages made the system impractical.

In the United States, the first known use of concrete reinforced with iron was in an unusual house constructed from 1873 to 1876 by William E. Ward (1821–1900) on Magnolia Drive in Rye Brook, New York. Ward, a mechanical engineer, became interested in the idea of reinforcing concrete with iron when in 1867 he observed workers attempting to remove dried cement from their tools. He noticed the cement could only be removed with great difficulty, suggesting to Ward that "the utility of both iron and [concrete] could be greatly increased for building purposes, through a properly adjusted combination of their special physical properties, and very much greater efficiency be reached through their combination than could possibly be realized by the exclusive use of either material separately."[3] The floors of Ward's house were supported by concrete beams, each one reinforced by an embedded iron I-beam; the concrete floor slabs were reinforced by a lattice of iron rods. Ward conducted extensive testing to determine the amount and proportions of concrete and iron required to achieve a strength well in excess of that which would ever be required of the structure. He also tested one completed section of the home's floor by placing a 30-ton load upon it. Though the floor deflected (or sagged) slightly under the weight, once the weight was removed, the deflection disappeared.[4]

What is most impressive about Ward's experimental use of reinforced concrete is that he fully grasped key aspects inherent in the combination of metal and concrete. He understood that concrete reinforced with metal could support a far greater load than an equal quantity of either material by itself. He found that the two materials used together retained an adequate amount of elasticity, such that a beam under a heavy load would deflect, and then return to its original state once the load was removed.

Significantly, Ward appreciated that placing the metal reinforcement near the bottom of the beam was the most efficient location. All beams, regardless of their material composition, resist gravity in the same manner. Along the bottom of the beam are pulling or stretching stresses, much like that on a simple rope bridge. As a pedestrian walks out on to the bridge, the rope stretches slightly and deflects downward under the weight. When the pedestrian steps off, the rope returns to its original state. The top of a beam, however, reacts quite differently: as weight presses down on the beam, attempting to deflect it downward, the top of the beam comes under compressive forces. (These forces can be visualized with a hair comb. Place the comb between two supporting objects and press down on it. If the teeth are facing down, they will move farther apart, and if up, closer together.)

These stresses are greatest at the extreme bottom and top of a beam, and weakest along the center, which is why an I-beam has a broad band of metal along the top and another along the bottom. The bottom band withstands the stretching or tensile stress and the top band withstands the compressive stress. The main purpose of the vertical metal between the top and bottom bands is to connect the two; there is far less stress along the center of the beam. Ward stated that his reason for placing the iron beam so near the bottom of the beam "was to utilize its tensile quality for resisting the strain" along the bottom of the beam where the stress was greatest. Along the top of the beam, concrete "was relied on for resisting compression."[5]

The composite beam Ward built functioned like a steel I-beam. He placed the metal reinforcement along the bottom of the concrete beam to handle the tensile stress in the same manner as the band of steel on the bottom of an I-beam. Instead of using metal to handle the compressive stress in the top of the beam, Ward substituted concrete. By using concrete in place of metal, Ward's composite beam reduced the amount of iron or steel required to construct the building. Iron and steel were (and are) quite costly compared to concrete, which is inexpensive and readily available. There were other important advantages to this arrangement. By embedding the iron within concrete, it was protected from rust and corrosion. The home was essentially fireproof, as the iron, being embedded in concrete, was largely insulated from the heat of a fire which would otherwise cause it to soften and lose strength. Although Ward presented a paper to the American Society of Mechanical Engineers with details of his experiments and home construction in 1883, his efforts failed to spark further interest in reinforced concrete construction.

Ward used Portland cement to make the concrete in his home. Though natural cements have been used in construction for thousands of years, the Portland cement widely used today was invented in England by Joseph Aspdin in 1824. He called it Portland cement due to its resemblance to Portland stone, a popular, high-quality English building stone. Cement is manufactured by crushing limestone, mixing it with clay or shale, heating the mixture in a kiln to 2,642 degrees Fahrenheit, and grinding the result to a fine powder. Concrete is created by mixing cement with sand and stone. The ratio of each ingredient varies depending on the particular application, but a common mixture might have one part cement to two parts sand and three or four parts stone. When water is added to the mixture, a chemical reaction takes place within the cement, causing it to harden. Though most of its strength is developed during the first few weeks, the hardening process continues for years. If cement is allowed to dry too rapidly, or if it becomes frozen, the chemical reaction will be inhibited and the concrete will not reach its full strength.

The benefit of using concrete as an inexpensive and fireproof construction material was recognized by a small number of individuals, among them Franklin W. Smith (1826–1911). Smith was a wealthy Bostonian described as "an amateur architect and amateur builder, with a skill in both arts."[6] Desiring a Moorish style winter home in St. Augustine, Florida, Smith found that building stone was unavailable in the state and transporting it from up north would be prohibitively expensive. While traveling in Europe, Smith was impressed by a house he saw with walls that appeared to be of stone, but were actually concrete cast in molds. Concrete, Smith realized, could serve as an alternative to stone.

In 1882, Smith began construction of Villa Zorayda (83 King St., St. Augustine), his winter home.[7] Though the home was built of concrete, it was not reinforced concrete; there were no composite structural elements as in the Ward house, where greater strength was achieved by a combination of materials. The walls of Villa Zorayda were poured, 10 inches at a time, into molds. Every second day, the height of the mold was built up and another 10 inches of concrete was poured. The molds contained vertical iron rods embedded in the concrete as the wall rose, but the purpose of these was to bond layers of concrete poured on different days, not to sustain structural loads.

After successfully completing his home, Smith assisted in the construction of the Ponce de Leon Hotel (now Flagler College), built by Henry M. Flagler and completed in 1887. The hotel was located across the street from Villa Zorayda and constructed using the same methods as used by Smith on his home. Flagler built a second concrete hotel, the Alcazar (now the Lightner Museum), opposite the Ponce de Leon in 1887. The same year, on the property across King Street from the Alcazar, Smith constructed the concrete Casa Monica Hotel (95 Cordova St.), completed the following year.

As Casa Monica was nearing completion, the era of reinforced concrete in America got underway in earnest through the efforts of Ernest L. Ransome (1852–1917), an English engineer who had relocated to California. Ransome was superintendent of San Francisco's Pacific Stone Company, a firm that manufactured artificial stone using a process invented in England by Ransome's father. In an effort to find a less expensive method of reinforcing concrete sidewalks in places where they were unsupported from below, Ransome sought to use inexpensive square iron bars in place of costly bent rods with washers at each end.[8] The smooth, square bars, however, could be more easily pulled from the concrete than the bent rods. It occurred to Ransome that twisting the square bars to give them a spiral, ridged surface would improve their resistance to being stripped from the concrete. In experiments, Ransome found not only that concrete gripped twisted bars better than untwisted ones, he unexpectedly discovered that the bars actually became stronger as a result of being twisted. He was granted a patent for his bars in 1884 and began using them in small concrete projects.

Ransome's claim that twisting the bars increased their strength was scorned by the scientific community. "I was simply laughed down," reported Ransome of his presentation to the technical society of California, "the consensus of opinion being that I injured the iron." "One gentleman kindly suggested that if I did not twist my iron so much I might not injure it seriously."[9] His findings, however, were subsequently borne out by experiments.

The first significant use of Ransome's bars was in 1884 for two buildings he designed and constructed for the Arctic Oil Works on the San Francisco wharf. Arctic Oil processed raw whale oil into illuminating oil, candles, and other products. Due to the flammability of the oil, the processing and warehouse buildings had to be fireproof. A three-story processing and office building was completed in early 1884. It was 150 by 40 feet in size, with walls and a chimney of concrete reinforced with Ransome's twisted bars. The press lauded the building for its durability, though its appearance was found wanting, "strength rather than beauty having been the apparent purpose of the builders."[10] Later that year Ransome constructed a warehouse on the Arctic Oil site with a concrete floor, walls, and a novel vaulted roof. As a protective measure in case of fire, the warehouse roof contained a reservoir of water that could be released through perforated iron pipes located beneath the eaves.[11] These two buildings are generally recognized as the first reinforced concrete buildings of their kind in the United States.

Four years later Ransome used his patented bars to construct an addition to the Pacific Coast Borax Works in Alameda, California, the first reinforced concrete factory in the United States.[12] This building, begun in 1888 and completed the following year, had reinforced concrete columns, which Ransome claimed were "probably the first ever erected."[13]

Ransome's next major project was engineering the floors of the California Academy of Sciences building in San Francisco, a job that encountered significant criticism from architects and members of the academy. Ransome's opponents made an attempt to have the fire warden condemn the concrete floors, there being no provision for that type of construction in the city's building ordinances. The warden nevertheless demurred, as the concrete floors were not susceptible to damage from fire. Ransome was able to tamp down the controversy by loading a section of the completed floor with gravel to a weight of over 400 pounds per square foot, leaving it in place for four weeks with no resulting damage.[14] The building, begun in 1889, was completed late in 1890, but was destroyed by the 1906 earthquake and fire.[15]

During 1890, Ransome designed and built for the US government a torpedo (floating mine) storage shed on Yerba Buena Island (known at the time as Goat Island) in San Francisco Bay. Considering the shed's contents of 1,100 explosive mines, a solid concrete structure was considered a wise approach. The specifications called for walls 18 inches thick, a concrete floor of 8 inches and, as an added measure of reinforcement, a retired streetcar cable was embedded around the entire structure near of the top of the concrete walls.[16] The building's surface was carefully finished to give the appearance of stone blocks using a process patented by Ransome the previous year.[17] Though unused since the 1930s, the building remains standing on the northeast corner of the island, directly beneath the San Francisco–Oakland Bay Bridge.

In January 1891 Ransome began construction of his most important building of this period, the Leland Stanford Jr. Museum (now the Cantor Arts Center) on the campus of Stanford University in Palo Alto, California. The museum was endowed by Jane Stanford in memory of her son, Leland Jr., who died at the age of 15. She wished for the museum to be completed by the fall of 1891, when the new school opened. The tight time constraint combined with the high cost of dressed San Jose sandstone, with which it was originally intended to be finished, prompted a decision to construct the building, and a three-story women's dorm, of concrete, faced in much the same manner as the torpedo shed. The museum was largely completed within seven months, and at half the cost of an equivalent brick-and-stone structure.[18] Wings constructed of brick and mortar were added to the building between 1898 and 1906, enlarging it significantly from its original 20,000 square feet to around 300,000 square feet. The San Francisco earthquake of 1906 destroyed all but a small section of the additions, yet did little damage to the original reinforced concrete main building. This outcome was, of course, due in part to the monolithic nature of concrete relative to brick and mortar, but a contributing factor stemmed from Ransome's inability to accurately calculate the strength of reinforced concrete. As the load-bearing capacity of the structure could only be guessed at, the amount of built-in safety factor was unknown. To compensate for this uncertainty, Ransome's buildings were more heavily constructed than necessary. Rather than risk having a beam or floor panel someday collapse under an inordinately heavy load, Ransome increased the size of beams, thickness of floors, or amount of reinforcement to the point that, in his judgment, the building could not possibly fail, even under extreme conditions. Though inefficient in the use of materials, it produced a structure able to withstand the 1906 earthquake.

By 1893 Ransome had relocated his company, now called Ransome and Smith, to Chicago.[19] He believed he would find in the East and Midwest more fertile ground for his novel system of construction and wished to escape the "severe criticism and bitter attacks" heaped upon him by those in the Bay Area who were opposed to the use of reinforced concrete.[20]

In Buffalo, New York, Ransome's system was chosen for a six-story apartment building at 24 Johnson Park designed by architect Carleton Strong. The developer, Charles Sherrill, intended to inexpensively construct this high-end apartment building by eliminating the typical cut stone exterior and substituting concrete molded to appear as stone using Ransome's patented method. The structure was promoted as the first significant building outside San Francisco built of reinforced concrete. Construction began in early 1894, but progress on the building was slow, as "many obstructions were encountered by the contractors that the use of ordinary building material would escape."[21] One of those delays resulted from the necessity of testing the building's floor construction. Small bags of gravel were dragged onto the floor of a large room until the accumulated weight amounted to eight tons, causing the floor to deflect only one eighth of an inch. Architect Strong assured observers that, as the concrete cured further, the floor could withstand three times that amount, "which is greatly in excess of necessity."[22]

Delays accelerated the developer's financial difficulties, resulting in workers and vendors going unpaid. In mid-December all those employed in constructing the building, about 100 workers, walked off the job. It subsequently came to light that Sherrill had only $3,000 in the bank when work on the $80,000 building began, but "he managed, with a shrewdness for which the man is remarkable, to raise enough money to put the building well under way." The "gloomy cement structure" remained unfinished "in doleful and tomblike prominence" until the project was taken over by new owners in 1897 and completed in October of that year.[23] Originally called the Alabama, the building opened as the Berkeley and remained so until 1911 when it was remodeled and renamed the Graystone.[24] By the late 1990s the building was vacant and run down. It was acquired in 2002 for the purpose of redevelopment by Ellicott Development Company. As the firm was beginning work on the building in 2003, a portion of the building's roof collapsed, severely injuring a worker. This mishap put the project on hold for a decade, with the building finally opening once again as the Graystone in 2013.[25]

In 1897, the United States imposed a sizable tariff on imported borax, the effect of which was that Pacific Coast Borax became the sole economical source for the US market. The chief beneficiary of the protective tariff (and the likely cause of it) was the head of Pacific Coast, "Borax King" Francis M. Smith (1846–1931). (Francis Smith was also Ransome's partner in the Ransome and Smith Company.) Almost immediately the Alameda factory built by Ransome for Pacific Coast was swamped with orders. Smith made plans to replace it with a new factory in Bayonne, New Jersey, as it was less expensive to ship the crude borax east and refine and market it there, than to refine it on the West Coast and ship the end product east. The plant was completed by October 1898 and was four stories high with a one-story wing.[26] As with Ransome's previous structures, the borax factory was, as Ransome described it, "constructed more or less in imitation of brick or stone buildings, with comparatively small windows." To give the appearance of stone, the surface of the concrete was hammered by hand or with a pneumatic hammer.[27]

The factory was initially planned to be of mill construction, but when the floor loads necessary to support the heavy tanks and processing equipment were calculated, the cost of a satisfactory brick-and-timber structure was quite high. The potential for a total loss of the building due to fire made insurance a necessity. Concrete buildings, however, were considered fireproof, and owners typically did not insure them against fire loss; only the building's contents were insured. When the expense of fire insurance over the life of the borax factory was added to the initial cost of the mill construction option, the total expenditure was nearly the same as Ransome's reinforced concrete construction, thereby tipping the decision toward the latter method.[28]

Less than four years later, the new Pacific Coast Borax factory's ability to withstand fire was tested. On April 8, 1902, an oil line burst in the single-story wing, causing a fire that spread rapidly, fed by the many flammable materials within the building. Flames consumed the wooden roof of the single-story wing, breached the partition leading to the multi-story section of the building, and swept up the elevator shaft and stairwells to the upper floors. The roof of the top floor and its supporting columns were wooden and quickly devoured by the fire, causing large tanks on the roof to fall 14 feet onto the fourth floor. Despite the enormous weight of the tanks, the fourth floor suffered only a small number of cracked beams.[29]

News of the fire was reported in over 50 newspapers across the country, all of which announced that the building had been "destroyed" or "gutted" by fire. The *Boston Globe*'s article was headlined "Fireproof Until Kindled" and stated, "A six-story cement building, at Bayonne, NJ, supposed to be fireproof, was gutted by fire last night."[30] The *Globe*'s reporter almost certainly intended "gutted by fire" to mean that the interior of the building had been completely destroyed, leaving only the exterior walls standing. The reality, however, was quite different. The contents of the building were consumed or melted by the flames, but the building itself was in good shape. The reinforced concrete floors, walls, and columns were intact and little damaged. It was claimed that the cost of repairs to the $100,000 building amounted to just $1,000.[31]

In 1900 Ransome began work on what he described as "a radical departure in the exterior construction of reinforced concrete buildings": he abandoned the practice of mimicking the appearance of traditional mill construction buildings.[32] The exterior wall was largely eliminated, leaving the bare concrete frame, and the open area between frame members was filled with large windows held in place by lightweight concrete panels below and above (spandrels and headers). The dramatic increase in window area permitted far more natural light to enter the building, a great advantage at a time when artificial illumination was in its infancy. (Ransome still considered it necessary to dress the exposed concrete by hammering its surface.) Ransome used the new system beginning in 1903 to construct factories for Kelly and Jones in Greensburg, Pennsylvania (completed 1904, demolished); United Shoe Machinery in Beverly, Massachusetts (181 Elliott Street); and an addition to Pacific Coast Borax in Bayonne (demolished).

Ernest Ransome was a brilliant inventor. He received dozens of patents on concrete construction methods and construction machinery. His reinforced concrete buildings were pioneering and his construction business was successful, but his efforts between 1884 and 1902 did not lead to wide acceptance of reinforced concrete construction. The buildings he was hired to design were built of concrete either because concrete could be used in place of stone or because the structure's contents were highly flammable or exceptionally weighty. In the former case, concrete was a cheap substitute for stone, and in the latter, the extreme requirements made the cost of concrete competitive with heavy mill construction or fireproofed steel. Aside from these atypical circumstances, Ransome's concrete buildings were generally too expensive to have widespread appeal.

One reason for the high cost was that Ransome's understanding of reinforced concrete was based on experiments he conducted and his personal experience in construction. His practical knowledge permitted him to construct buildings that met the needs for which they were intended and did not fall down. Had Ransome possessed a scientific theory of reinforced concrete construction, he could have accurately calculated the strength of beams, columns, and floors. In the absence of such a theory, to assure there could be no catastrophic failure, he designed his buildings to be far more robust than necessary. This excess margin of safety was acquired by using more steel and concrete, resulting in larger and heavier buildings, which required sturdier foundations and more labor for construction, adding further to the higher material costs.

The extent to which concrete buildings were unnecessarily overbuilt was partially revealed by a series of experiments conducted by civil engineer Leonard C. Wason (1869–1937) in 1901. Wason, a former employee of Ransome's firm, was president of the Aberthaw Construction Company of Boston, one of the few firms licensed to use the

Ransome system to construct substantial concrete buildings, including Harvard Stadium (built 1902–03). Under Wason's supervision, 14 reinforced concrete beams were tested to destruction at MIT. It was discovered that these beams "carried from 4½ to 5 times the load they were calculated to carry" using Wason's (and presumably Ransome's) formula for estimating beam strength. Despite the test results demonstrating that his formula underestimated the strength of a beam by at least 450 percent, Wason recommended it continue to be used.[33]

Ransome's construction business was successful, but he apparently put little effort into expanding it through branch sales offices. He sold the rights to use his patents to a number of contractors in several states, but it is unclear to what extent these firms were able to construct buildings without Ransome's know-how and experience.[34] One such business was the Ransome Concrete Fire Proofing Company of Cincinnati, Ohio. This firm secured a number of contracts for concrete floors and even the grandstand for the Palace of the Fans, home of the Cincinnati Reds (built 1901, demolished 1911). By April 1902, though, Ransome Concrete Fire Proofing was way behind in its payments to vendors and was being sued by several, including Chicago Pneumatic Tool Company, supplier of the pneumatic hammers used to finish the exposed surface of a concrete building. The undercapitalized firm soon went into bankruptcy. At the time of its demise, the company had over $100,000 worth of contracts on which a profit of $35,000 was anticipated, yet it did not have the cash to make payments on the $15,000 it owed and was forced to close down.[35] Clearly, there was money to be made by expanding Ransome's operations into other locations, but he was not committed to doing so.

It may be unfair to fault Ransome for not taking a greater interest in growing his business. Halbert Gillette, editor of the journal *Engineering and Contracting*, knew Ransome personally and commented after his death that "the necessity of carrying on his business often left him with but few hours to devote to inventive work. Society loses enormous benefits every year because men of genius are forced to 'earn their daily bread.'"[36] Gillette's comments suggest that Ransome's passion was for invention and that he only engineered and constructed buildings as a means to support himself and his inventive activities. In the "Personal Reminiscences" chapter of Ransome's 1912 book *Reinforced Concrete Buildings*, he describes the significant patents he received for reinforced concrete construction and the consequential buildings in which he first used them; it is clear from this history that Ransome took great pride in both the inventions and his construction "firsts."[37] Ransome was both an inventor who sought to devise new and effective methods of concrete construction, and a pioneer builder who desired to be the first to employ those innovations. Unlike Henry Ford or Joseph Boyer, Ransome did not strive to leverage his innovations into a great business.

Ransome's efforts, though, did give rise to other construction firms that grew quite large. One of Ransome's engineers, Henry C. Turner, founded his own firm in 1902, the Turner Construction Company, which grew rapidly into one of the largest such firms in the country.

4

A Breakthrough

Julius Kahn's search for a sound theory of concrete reinforcement began by absorbing the little knowledge that was available. Concrete is excellent at resisting compression, but its ability to resist stretching or tensile stresses is negligible. Tensile stresses reach their maximum along the bottom of a beam, so concrete beams require horizontal steel reinforcement bars along the bottom to bear the stress that the concrete cannot. If the steel reinforcement bar slips or pulls loose from the concrete, the beam fails. These principles were well established; William Ward had relied on them to construct his house of concrete.

As the load on a reinforced concrete beam increases, the steel reinforcement along the bottom of the beam begins to stretch. When the load is removed, the steel returns to its original condition. If the load on a beam becomes too great, the steel will eventually stretch to the point where it cannot stretch any further; it breaks and the beam collapses. To prevent this, more steel reinforcement can be added. While the bottom of the beam is under tension, however, the load also causes the top of the beam to be compressed. Concrete is able to stand quite a bit of compression, but if enough reinforcement is added to the bottom of the beam, the compression forces along the top become great enough to shatter the concrete and the beam fails. These two modes of failure,

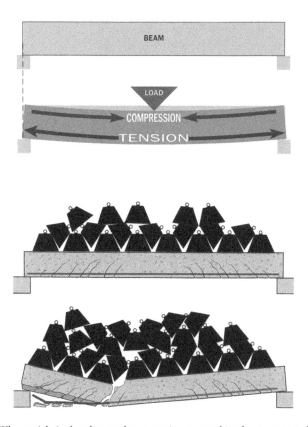

(*Top*): When weight is placed upon a beam, tension or stretching forces act on its bottom while compression forces act on its top. (*Bottom*): Concrete reinforcement methods in use around 1900 relied on steel bars placed along the bottom of a beam to resist tension stress. When weight was placed on the beam, cracks would open along its bottom. As the weight increased, the cracks would open wider, the reinforcement bar would break loose from the concrete, and the beam would fail. As the point at which failure occurred varied greatly, the safe weight-bearing capacity of beams and floors could not be reliably calculated.

tension and compression, were well-known. The possibility that the reinforcement bar could to slip or be pulled from the concrete when a beam is under a heavy load was understood as well.

What puzzled engineers and added to the mystery of reinforced concrete were the other ways in which concrete beams could fail. Sometimes cracks formed along the bottom of a concrete beam and, as the load increased, they propagated upwards, causing the beam to fail by breaking apart along a crack. There were cases where the concrete below the reinforcement bar broke off, exposing the bar and allowing it to pull loose. Unlike tension and compression failures, these types of failures seemed unpredictable.

Francois Hennebique found some success in combating these types of failures through the use of vertical "stirrups," deep, U-shaped bands of iron or steel that extended from beneath the reinforcement bar to near the top of the beam. Hennebique observed that the cracks along the bottom of the beam were not vertical, but angled toward the middle of the beam. The vertical stirrups within the beam passed across the developing cracks, impeding their growth. Placing the stirrups in the beam increased the complexity and cost of his method, but Hennebique found that the increased strength of the beam more than compensated for the cost.[1]

In the six years that Julius had worked as a civil engineer, he designed, or helped design, numerous large and complex steel structures: bridges, towers, industrial processing facilities, and materials-handling equipment. Nearly all of these structures relied for their strength on steel trusses. A truss serves the same purpose as a solid steel beam, or girder, but due to its being assembled from pieces, is able to accomplish its task using less steel than a solid component, reducing the cost and weight of the structure. Trusses are composed of one or more triangles, a shape that resists deformation, even when the connection between each of its constituent pieces is not rigid. Like a beam, the bottom of a truss is in tension (stretching) and the top is in compression. The center section of a truss is made up of pieces (called webs, posts, or diagonals) that form triangles connecting the structure's top with its bottom. Some of these webs are in tension while others are in compression.

A concrete beam is homogenous, so it would seem an unlikely candidate for comparison with a truss. Nevertheless, Hennebique had designed his reinforcement system to mimic the behavior of a simple queen post truss. He was sufficiently insightful to realize that the concrete could resist the compression stress in the top of the beam, so only the portion of the beam that was in tension required steel reinforcement. The vertical stirrups within the beam functioned in the same manner as webs in a truss. Hennebique subsequently tested beams constructed in this manner and found that they were stronger and more efficient in the use of materials. That was, however, the extent of his theoretical endeavors; Hennebique did not devise a scientific explanation that could be used to calculate the strength of such a beam. Having developed and tested a design that worked, he used it to construct buildings and, like Ransome, relied on his personal experience rather than on scientific theory.[2]

To Julius Kahn it seemed beyond question that a concrete beam reinforced with steel must in some manner function like a truss. He had a comprehensive theoretical understanding of the truss from his studies in school, honed further through extensive experience. This education and experience paid off: the 28-year-old civil engineer discovered a solution to the mystery of the steel reinforced concrete beam, and did so in a surprisingly short period of time. Julius had joined his brother's firm in early March 1902, and filed a patent application for his concrete and steel construction method on December 11, just nine months later. During the summer and fall of that year, he devised a sound theoretical understanding of composite concrete and steel construction, tested his theories in myriad ways, developed an exhaustive technical explanation of his theory, and wrote and filed a patent application. All this was accomplished while he designed and oversaw the construction of projects for Brown and Brown, Detroit City Gas, Chicago Pneumatic, and others.

Considering all the confusion and uncertainty surrounding concrete reinforcement prior to 1902, the simplicity of Julius's solution is striking. He imagined that a steel truss could be embedded in a concrete beam and the load-carrying capability of that beam would be at least as good and as predictable as if the truss were alone and not embedded. But Julius realized that he could remove all the pieces of the truss that were there to resist compression, because the concrete surrounding the steel could withstand the compressive stresses. Only the pieces of the truss that resisted tension were needed within the concrete beam.

With the compression pieces removed, Julius's truss consisted of a main reinforcement bar that spanned the entire beam along the bottom, and a series of attached web pieces or "wings" that extended upward from the main bar at a 45 degree angle. The main bar had to be relatively heavy to carry the tension stresses imposed on it, while the wings could be lighter in weight.

Before Julius could reliably and consistently calculate the load-carrying ability of the beam, he had to assure that his truss design would fail in a predictable manner. It had to always fail by having the steel main bar snap in two near the beam's center where the tensile stress is greatest. If the reinforcement bar slipped or pulled loose from the concrete,

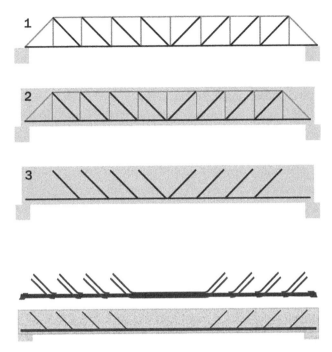

(*Top*): (1) A steel truss bridge efficiently and predictably supports weight because it resists both tension and compression stresses. In this diagram the pieces of the truss that resist tension are in black and those that resist compression are in gray. (2) Julius Kahn visualized a concrete beam with a steel truss embedded within. He reasoned that the beam would be at least as strong as the steel truss. (3) Julius also recognized that he could dispense with the sections of the truss that resisted compression because the concrete surrounding the truss would do so.

(*Bottom*): The Kahn Bar in its manufactured form. A side view of the Kahn Bar within a beam. The "wings" of the bar extended into the top section of the beam where the compression stress would hold them firmly in place, preventing the bar from moving or breaking loose from the beam. The 45 degree angle of the wings also prevented cracks from growing large enough to cause failure of the beam.

the beam would fail prematurely, before there was sufficient weight to cause the bar to snap in two. Vertical cracks that spread through the beam might also cause premature failure. If these two modes of failure could be prevented, Julius reasoned, he would be able to calculate the load-carrying ability of the beam based on the known breaking strength of the steel reinforcement bar.

In a truss, each of the pieces are firmly connected to each other at the joint where they meet. Julius reasoned that this should also be true for the truss pieces within his concrete beam. Hennebique and others assumed these rigid connections were unnecessary, as the reinforcement pieces were embedded in concrete and stresses borne by one piece would be transferred to others through the concrete that surrounded them. Julius rejected this reasoning, believing that when the steel came under stress, the adjacent concrete was likely to break away from it, thereby allowing the steel to slip.[3]

Having the main bar firmly connected to the protruding wings prevented the main bar from slipping or being pulled loose, even if the concrete around the main bar became damaged and fell off. This was due to the wings' extending upward almost to the very top of the beam where the concrete was in compression. As the weight on the beam increased, so did the compression along the top of the beam, thereby holding the wings tightly in place.

That vertical cracks appeared in a concrete beam was unsurprising—concrete has very little elasticity. When a steel-reinforced concrete beam is loaded up with weight, the steel reinforcement bar along its bottom stretches in response to the tension. The concrete, unable to stretch, develops microscopic cracks along its bottom edge. As the weight being supported increases, the cracks open farther and move upward through the beam. Unlike nearly all others attempting to solve the problems of concrete construction, Julius understood that these cracks were the result of shearing stresses within the concrete, which occur because the beam's top is being compressed while its bottom is being stretched. Different areas within the beam are pushed in opposite directions, setting up internal stresses. This is similar to a deck of cards that is squeezed from the ends: the deck bows outward and the ends of individual cards shift or shear slightly against their neighbors. Unlike a deck composed of many cards that move independently, a beam is a single piece. When the stresses become too great, the beam can break by shearing along horizontal, vertical, or angular cracks. In most cases, as the cracks that form along the bottom of a concrete beam grow in size, they curve toward the beam's middle, following a path determined by a combination of horizontal and vertical shearing stresses.

Hennebique's U-shaped stirrups reduced the problem of these shearing cracks, but their effectiveness was diminished by two shortcomings. Julius realized that maximum effectiveness in preventing the propagation of cracks could be achieved by having reinforcement pieces cross the cracks at right angles. The 45-degree orientation of the wings on his steel truss reinforcement was nearly ideal; the wings crossed at right angles the path taken by the cracks, binding the concrete together and preventing cracks from opening up. Hennebique's stirrups were oriented vertically, making them less effective. More significantly, Hennebique's stirrups were not attached to the main reinforcement bar, so they were ineffective at preventing it from slipping.

Julius was not concerned about failure due to excess compression along the top of the beam. The typical purpose of a beam was to support a concrete floor; the beam and floor were poured at the same time and comprised a single, monolithic unit. The compressive stresses were spread over such an extensive area (within the floor) that Julius perceived "it is generally impossible for [the beam] to fail in compression."[4]

Julius set out to test his theory of concrete beam reinforcement and confirm its validity. If he was correct, his tests would demonstrate that beams reinforced with his truss-like bar could only fail by having the main bar snap in the center of the beam. Julius began by building small models of wood and metal, with the wood taking the place of concrete. His workshop was the basement of the family home with tools provided by his brother Gustave. Julius next built a much larger beam. He crafted the truss from pieces of steel, cut to size and bolted together. He constructed a wooden form to contain the concrete until hard. Once the truss was placed in the form, Julius mixed the concrete and, with the help of his sister Mollie, poured it into the form and tamped it down until the truss was completely surrounded.[5] Weeks passed while he waited for the concrete to cure sufficiently for the beam to be tested. When it was ready, Julius stripped away the form and began loading the beam with weight. As he increased the weight, the beam bore it without complaint. Eventually, enough weight was added atop the beam to cause it to deform by sagging very slightly in the middle. At this point, Julius removed the weight and noted that the deformation disappeared, thus confirming that the steel, though it had stretched under the weight, had returned to its initial condition. Next he increased the weight on the beam, and the sag in the middle became more pronounced. As he had predicted—and hoped—Julius observed that there were no cracks opening up. He added more weight and, just when it looked as if the weight might topple over, the beam finally cracked in the middle, snapping the reinforcement bar in half just as Julius had predicted.[6]

The next experiment was with a full-size beam. There was, however, not enough weight available in the basement to cause it to fail. The unbroken beam was too large and indestructible to remove from the basement, so it remained there, even after the family moved from the home. Julius tried unusual experiments that would confirm his theory. He built a 14-foot-long beam containing his steel truss reinforcement, but instead of concrete, the beam was made of ice. Though unconventional, he found the beam supported a great amount of weight.[7] On a hunch, Julius molded individual blocks of concrete and placed them loose between the wings of his reinforcement bar. Though there was no mortar or adhesive of any type to hold the assemblage together, the beam could carry substantial weight. This experiment further confirmed that Julius's reinforcement bar functioned like a truss, exactly as he theorized. In a similar experiment, Julius constructed a reinforced beam with only the wings embedded in the concrete; the main bar lay outside the bottom surface of the beam, held in place by the wings. This beam performed well, demonstrating that the tension stresses in the beam were borne by the wings and transmitted to the main bar.[8] Unlike other reinforcing systems in use, the effectiveness of his main reinforcement bar was not dependent on its being gripped tightly by the concrete; the angled wings held the bar firmly in place.

Once his experiments grew too large to be carried out in his brother's basement, Julius conducted them at the Michigan Bolt and Nut Works located on Wight Street at the Detroit River.[9] The works had a nearly inexhaustible supply of pig iron that could be used to load the beams until they failed. In at least one test, the load of pig iron exceeded 100,000 pounds.[10]

Julius demonstrated to his satisfaction that his theory was correct. He had designed a beam that would always fail in the center when the maximum strength of the main reinforcement bar was exceeded. He was now able to accurately calculate the maximum safe load for any beam constructed with his reinforcement bar. As a consequence, instead of a safety factor of 10, Julius noted that structures built with his system could use a safety factor of four, the same factor as with steel structures, because the maximum strength of the beam was based on the embedded steel, not the concrete.[11] This change alone would significantly reduce the cost of concrete buildings.

Julius knew his system had the potential for widespread use as a more economical and efficient method of building with concrete; he was confident there would be demand for it, but before he could begin any marketing efforts, he had to secure a patent for his reinforcement bar. His excitement over future prospects was evident from a comment made to his sister Mollie: "If I get this patent, we'll all be on easy

A test of the Kahn Bar. Two beams, each reinforced with two Kahn Bars, supported a weight of 101,100 lbs. before failing in the middle, just as Julius's theory predicted. Julius (with arms crossed) looks supremely satisfied with the result. (Kahn System of Reinforced Concrete, General Catalog D, Trussed Concrete Steel Co., Detroit, 1904)

street."[12] At this point, Julius had little idea how successful his reinforcement bar might be, but he was certain it would earn enough to alleviate the family's persistent financial difficulties. Though the firm of Kahn and Kahn was managing well enough, its financial success was dependent on a strong economy; during the summer of 1902 the country was entering a recession.

The Kahn family had often been in financial distress. Joseph earned an adequate living as an interim rabbi, but there were often periods between his assignments when money ran short. During these periods he had started a number of businesses, including a sewing-machine dealership that did not catch on, and a cut-rate eyeglass store that had a short tenure.[13] Another business venture grew out of an idea Albert suggested for copying architectural drawings in color. He and Joseph found some reprographic equipment that, after tinkered with for the better part of a year, would do the job. Joseph partnered with a young attorney to set up a shop selling the service in New York City, but that business failed to gain a foothold and closed. Upon returning to Detroit around 1896, Joseph reopened the business as the Multi-Color Copying Company in the rear of Gustave's plumbing firm at 26 Miami Street in downtown Detroit.[14] With Mollie's help, Joseph turned the business into a going concern, earning enough money by August of 1897 for him to secure a loan to build a two-family, wood frame house on Frederick Street. But in April the following year, likely before even moving in, he advertised it for sale "at a great sacrifice for cash." Unable to sell, the family occupied it, with Joseph, Rosalie, Mollie, Felix, and Louis in one unit at 302 Frederick, and Gustave and his family in the other at 304.

In 1899 Gustave Kahn's plumbing business, established several years earlier, experienced financial difficulties. (Not long after, the business failed and Gustave took a job with the American Blower Company.) This development caused Joseph to again place his home on the market, hoping to sell it at enough of a profit to sustain the family's finances, but as before, the house went unsold. The following year Joseph accepted another position out of town and turned the Multi-Color Copying business over to Mollie, 23 years old at the time. This was a sound decision, as the business grew under her management. The profits from Multi-Color went to meet the family's financial challenges; Mollie was sending money on a weekly basis to her parents, and to Louis, to help pay for his education.[15] Also at this time both Moritz and Felix were pursuing degrees in civil engineering at the University of Michigan, probably with the financial assistance of Albert and Julius. Julius's belief that the patent would put them on "easy street" represented a hope that his family could escape their persistent money concerns.

Julius secured the services of James Whittemore, a patent attorney of the Detroit firm Thomas Sprague and Son. Whittemore may have been, for personal reasons, highly sympathetic to Julius's efforts to construct sturdier buildings. His daughter Margaret was nearly killed the previous year when an enormous chimney on the house next door fell, slicing a 10-foot gash in the Whittemores' roof and crashing into the closet of the room in which Margaret was sleeping.[16]

Julius filed his patent on December 11, 1902, in which he described the basic truss design and numerous permutations that would later form the basis for using the reinforcing bar in a wide range of applications. Four pages of sketches in the patent application showed how the bar could reinforce concrete columns, bridges, and continuous floor panels where they passed over the top of a column. Julius included sketches of trussed bars with the wings bolted, hooked, and forged onto them, methods he would use to make bars before he acquired the heavy presses needed mass produce them. To provide himself better protection against copycats, he noted in the patent text, "Although only several arrangements of webbed bars are shown here, it is understood that I may wish to use other methods of cutting the web-bars and bolting or riveting the same to the main members."[17]

Unbeknownst to Julius, as he was preparing his patent application, an extraordinary project was getting underway in Cincinnati, Ohio, that would bring a great deal of attention to the use of reinforced concrete construction. Melville E. Ingalls (1842–1914), president of the Cleveland, Cincinnati, Chicago and St. Louis Railway (the Big Four Railroad) announced in December 1901 that he would erect an office building of at least ten stories on property he had purchased earlier that year. The location on the northeast corner of Fourth and Vine streets in downtown Cincinnati he described as "the most prominent in the city."[18]

The city of Cincinnati prospered during the 19th century due to its location on the Ohio River and as a terminus for the Miami and Erie Canal, which ran between the city and Toledo, Ohio, on Lake Erie. The city's chief industry during the middle of the century was hog slaughtering, the byproducts of which gave rise to soap and candle making. As railroads began to displace water transportation, the prominence of Cincinnati as a meat-packing center declined in favor of Chicago. The soap and candle manufacturing business, however, continued to flourish in its place, resulting in the growth of one of the largest consumer products firms in the world, Procter and Gamble. After the Civil War, as railroads expanded primarily along east-to-west lines, Cincinnati's position as a gateway to the South for products manufactured in the city was threatened. As river transportation continued to decline, manufacturing firms found it difficult to market their products in southern states and to economically access raw materials sourced from the South. To address the problem, in 1869 the citizens of Cincinnati voted in favor of a proposition to construct a city-owned railroad south to Chattanooga, Tennessee; the line was completed in 1880. The following year the line was extended through leasing arrangements to New Orleans, Louisiana. As the gateway to the South, the city grew rapidly during the latter part of the 19th century. (The city still owns the Cincinnati Southern Railway and leases the line to Norfolk Southern.)

The most prominent of the city's early families was the Longworth family. Nicholas Longworth (1783–1863) left Germany and settled in Cincinnati sometime after 1800 and became wealthy as a winemaker. His youngest daughter, Catherine, married Larz Anderson Sr.[19] The couple's grandson, George Anderson (1869–1916), studied architecture at Columbia University and the École des Beaux-Arts in Paris. In 1896 he partnered with Alfred O. Elzner (1862–1933) forming the firm of Elzner & Anderson. Elzner studied architecture in Boston under renowned architect Henry H. Richardson. Elzner and Anderson thrived on business acquired through Anderson's connections with the city's elite families.[20]

Melville Ingalls was close with the Anderson family; he traveled with the son of Catherine and Larz, William P. Anderson Sr., in his private railcar and served with him on the board of directors of the Big Four Railroad, along with Cornelius Vanderbilt and J. Pierpont Morgan. Another son of Catherine and Larz was Larz Anderson Jr., and he and Ingalls were directors of Cincinnati's Union Savings Bank and Trust Company.[21] Considering the many connections between Ingalls and the Anderson family, it was hardly surprising that Elzner & Anderson were chosen as architects for Ingalls's office building.

When planning for the Ingalls Building began, the wait time for structural steel for building construction had become excessively long. Estimates for reinforced concrete construction indicated that the building could be completed sooner and at a lower cost than with steel.[22] In 1902, building a skyscraper of concrete would have been considered folly but for an unusual circumstance that prevailed in Cincinnati: the city had attracted a number of exceptional engineers with an interest in reinforced concrete. Ludwig Eid (1859–1919) was born in Bavaria, Germany, and studied engineering in Munich prior to arriving in Cincinnati in 1883. He supervised the construction of the Melan Arch Bridge in Cincinnati's Eden Park, one of the first such steel and concrete bridges in the country.[23] Christian W. Marx (1865–1950) was a professor of civil engineering at the University of Missouri, but in 1901 left to accept a position as the chair of engineering at the University of Cincinnati. As an indication of the level of interest in concrete, during 1902 the Cincinnati chapter of the American Institute of Architects established a committee to conduct tests on concrete, and heard papers on concrete construction prepared by Professor Marx and Ludwig Eid.[24] Moreover, concrete construction had by then found acceptance in the city due to its use the previous year to construct the grandstand at the ballpark for the Cincinnati Reds baseball team.[25]

When the Ransome Concrete Fire Proofing Company, builder of the grandstand, closed in 1902, an opportunity arose for better-financed concrete construction firms to enter the market. Architect George Anderson informed his brother Robert of the great potential in concrete construction, and Robert subsequently joined with his cousin William P. Anderson Jr. to found the Cincinnati Ferro-Concrete Construction Company.[26] This firm had the connections to secure the engineering work for the Ingalls Building, but neither Robert nor William had the requisite background in civil engineering. They solved that shortcoming by hiring as chief engineer Henry N. Hooper Jr. (1869–1928), a local engineer and 1894 graduate of Columbia University.[27]

By the end of May 1902, Elzner and Anderson and the Ferro-Concrete Construction Company had completed plans for the Ingalls Building. Originally envisioned as a 10- or 12-story structure, the final plans had 16 stories. By July only a small number of articles outside of the local area had made mention of the unusual project. The *New York Tribune* described it as "an experiment in construction," while a Lancaster, Pennsylvania, paper called it "the most ambitious attempt at this kind of a structure ever made."[28]

A not entirely unanticipated snag developed in August when the city building inspector, Charles A. Tooker, met with Elzner, George Anderson, and Hooper. Tooker was unwilling to approve a building permit until he could "ascertain all the principles upon which this construction is based."[29] The impasse continued for several months as Tooker attempted to acquire a firm opinion on the safety of concrete for such an unprecedented project. He sought opinions from experts across the country, but the responses were inconsistent, reflecting the widespread lack of understanding of the technology even among leading architects and engineers. Some of the responses were simply nonsensical; a "well-known architect" stated that expansion and contraction due to temperature changes during construction would doom the project.[30] Another claimed "A building erected of concrete should have a wider base than a building erected of steel. . . . The base of the Ingalls Building is out of proportion to its height." "One of the highest authorities in the country" was quoted saying "a 12 or 14 story concrete building was mere lunacy."[31] Meanwhile, excavation of the site began October 2.[32]

On November 14, the building's architects and engineers submitted a revised set of plans that included alterations requested by Tooker. Six days later, however, Tooker announced he was still unwilling to approve a permit for the building due to the lack of consensus on construction methods. Some experts advised him, for example, that "concrete construction, to be safe, should have very little water in it," while others claimed "it is better to make it almost liquid and let the water evaporate."[33] Though Tooker believed it was possible to construct a 16-story building of concrete, yet, "as nothing of the kind has ever been done or attempted in any part of the world, it is really an experiment." He felt the "responsibility of authorizing it [wa]s so great that he d[id] not think it would be right for him to assume it."[34]

Tooker's continued opposition was influenced in part by an accident that occurred the previous month in Dayton, Ohio. A nine-story addition to the Algonquin Hotel was under construction with concrete floors reinforced with expanded metal. On October 1, a section of the floor fell, injuring one worker. In announcing his refusal to issue a permit, Tooker cited this "collapse" as one of the considerations. When the owner of the Algonquin, J. Elliott Pierce, heard of this, he publicly mocked the inspector: "If Mr. Tooker's information in regard to concrete construction is no more accurate than he has concerning the Algonquin Hotel addition he has been most wondrously imposed upon. Instead of the building collapsing when it reached the second floor, a small section of the floor construction fell, because during my absence the workmen started to remove the supports before the concrete had hardened."[35]

With the foundation of the Ingalls Building nearing completion and matters with the building inspector at a stalemate, Melville Ingalls took matters into his own hands. He consulted Judge William Worthington as to legal options and then contacted the deputy mayor of the city, Charles Christie. Christie arranged for a meeting on November 24 in the mayor's office with Ingalls, Tooker, a city attorney, Judge Worthington, Elzner, Hooper, and Eid. At the meeting, Ingalls expressed a belief that concerns over the safety of concrete construction were unfounded; they were promoted as a means of preventing its widespread acceptance. The "great steel interests," he stated, could see that concrete's "general adoption would mean the loss of millions to them." Judge Worthington offered a somewhat more focused argument, asserting that the building inspector "is not required and has no authority to pass on the durability of the construction or probable safety of the proposed building," but must issue the permit if the "plans are in accordance with the rules of recognized authorities." Tooker responded that, under this interpretation of the regulations, "he ought to have the advice of a disinterested expert as to whether the plans are in accordance with the rules of recognized authorities," a point of view with which Ingalls agreed. It was decided to task Eid, a "recognized authority" on reinforced concrete, with examining and approving (or disapproving) the plans for the building.[36]

Eid had help in reviewing the plans. At the end of the first week in December, Leonard Wason of Boston's Aberthaw Construction was in town, at the request of Ingalls, to confer with Eid on the building. On Tuesday, December 9, Wason was cornered by reporters at a local club and stated that the engineers had completed their review of the plans; he provided assurances that Tooker would issue the building permit. Wason said he recommended a number of minor changes, the most significant being the method of placing the reinforcing bars in the concrete. He also made the point that a steel frame building, due to its susceptibility to rust, has a limited life, while a concrete building "is like the everlasting hills."[37]

On December 11, Tooker met in his office with Eid, Wason, Elzner, Anderson, and Hooper. The only issue in dispute at the meeting was the amount of water to be used in mixing the concrete. Wason favored a relatively fluid mixture that required little tamping, while Eid and Tooker believed a minimum amount of water produced the strongest concrete. It was agreed that concrete of both mixtures would be tested. Coincidentally, those attending the meeting had been invited to attend a test the following week in Cleveland of the floors of a Salvation Army building being constructed of concrete using the European Hennebique system.[38]

Among those from Cincinnati in attendance at the Cleveland building for the December 16 test were inspector Tooker, Eid, and Professor Marx. A beam was tested by loading weight atop until it was supporting over four times its design strength; the floor panel was loaded to three times its design strength. The maximum deflection of the beam under this weight measured less than one-half inch, whereas a steel beam under the same weight, the observers were informed, would have deflected 1¾ inches, a comparison which those present found impressive.[39]

On December 23, Ludwig Eid submitted his report to Tooker with a recommendation that the building permit be issued, which Tooker did that afternoon. The following day, formwork began on the building's already completed foundation in preparation for pouring the concrete support columns.[40] One effect of the permit issuance was to spur additional concrete building projects in Cincinnati, putting the city well ahead of others in concrete construction the following year.

The testing of concrete that had been promised during the December 11 meeting was carried out at the University of Cincinnati on Saturday, January 24, under the supervision of Professor Marx. Three blocks of concrete five inches square differing only in the amount of water used in the mixture were placed under pressure until they became crushed. The dry mixture block sustained a pressure of just over 100,000 pounds before it was crushed, while the wet mixture block crushed at around 55,000 pounds. The third block, with a mixture midway between the other two, crushed at 87,000 pounds.[41] This experiment demonstrated that overly wet concrete, though it required less tamping to remove air pockets and to assure full contact with reinforcing steel, was not as strong as concrete mixed with less water.

5

Stress and
Innovation

The year 1902 was remarkable for Julius and Albert Kahn; the next year was to be even more so. As it got underway, Julius patiently awaited approval of his patent for reinforced concrete construction and began to consider how to use the patent to create income. Complicating matters, the rapid adoption of reinforced concrete construction in Cincinnati raised the specter of competition, while the increased use of reinforced concrete floors nationally resulted in a flurry of accidents that cast a pall on concrete. As excited as Julius was at receiving his patent, the world around him was not standing still; there were plenty of issues for him to resolve before he would see any reward.

In January, Julius read an article in *Engineering News* by Captain John Stephen Sewell (1869–1940) of the US Army Corps of Engineers. Sewell, one of the government's leading construction experts, was in charge of large federal projects such as the Government Printing Office and Department of Agriculture buildings, as well as a complex of structures for the Army War College (now known as Fort Lesley J. McNair). Sewell's article, "A Neglected Point in the Theory of Concrete-Steel," highlighted a significant omission in theories of concrete reinforcement as employed by American engineers. Sewell was aware of reinforced concrete beams that failed due to cracks that began along the lower surface of the beam and propagated upward at an angle toward the beam's center. He believed—correctly—that these cracks were due to shear stresses. In Europe, Hennebique was using vertical stirrups to overcome this problem. Sewell noted, however, that Hennebique's approach was strictly empirical, based on limited experiments and educated guesses, not on scientific theory. Though generally effective, the stirrups were inefficient. "If these stirrups," Sewell stated, "are necessary, there must be some rational method of determining their proper sizes and locations. . . . No one has ever offered any analysis of this problem." Worse, Sewell pointed out, American engineers seemed to be wholly unaware of the problem of shear stresses.[1] Sewell was an advocate for concrete as "stronger, cheaper, thoroughly fireproof, and more enduring" than any other material. He observed, "At the present time, European practice is far ahead of American in the use of reinforced concrete." His hope was that a solution to the problem of shearing stresses might "be accomplished on this side of the Atlantic."[2]

Julius was thrilled to read that Sewell had come to the same conclusion about shearing stresses as he had, and he was eager to share with Sewell how the wings on his reinforcing bar would prevent the resulting cracks from propagating across a beam. Within a number of months, Captain Sewell would become an important ally, aiding Julius in marketing his reinforcing bar.

Kahn and Kahn completed the plans for the Consolidated Tool Company factory in Scotland in November 1902, and almost immediately received another commission through the efforts of Joseph Boyer. Boyer, Henry P. Joy, and others had recently incorporated the Superior Match Company. They planned to construct a factory in Detroit employing a new machine patented by a fellow Detroiter, the aptly named Henry C. La Flamboy. His machine placed matches into boxes with the head of every other match facing the opposite direction; it automated portions of the manufacturing process, reduced waste, and allowed for cheaper lumber to be used for the matchsticks.[3]

In January 1903 Superior Match purchased two acres of land in Detroit on Lawton Street adjacent to the Michigan Central Railroad tracks. By the end of February, Boyer had become president of the company, and Kahn and Kahn were working on plans for the plant. Considering that the factory was to produce 20 million matches a day, there was somewhat more than the usual concern over the threat of fire. With concrete construction having not yet arrived in Detroit, an alternate fire-resisting solution was found in the form of vitrified tile, a less porous ceramic tile that can be used outdoors. All of the building's exterior walls were constructed of vitrified tile, the floors of concrete, the windows of wire-reinforced glass, and the roof trusses of steel.[4] Ground was broken at the site in April and the structure was completed several months later. Aside from the vitrified tile exterior walls and wired windows, the building was of fairly typical factory construction, a tall, single story with a clerestory roof to admit additional light. The 120-by-200 foot structure was constructed at a cost of about $25,000.[5]

The Superior Match Company was not one of Joseph Boyer's successful enterprises. In spite of a cash infusion from Joseph L. Hudson (head of Detroit's J. L. Hudson Company department store) to acquire new machinery, by 1908 the company was out of business. The factory was sold to the Hoskins Manufacturing Company, which was relocating to Detroit from Chicago to be nearer to the automobile industry; they needed a facility that could house high-temperature manufacturing processes. The building was demolished sometime around 1998.[6]

Boyer and Henry Joy were involved in another business venture that would prove to be far more important to the Kahn brothers than the match business. In October 1902 the two men, in conjunction with a number of other investors, acquired the Packard Motor Car Company of Warren, Ohio, and planned to move it to Detroit. In January 1903, Boyer and Joy arranged with Albert Kahn to study the requirements for constructing a new automobile factory for Packard, capable of turning out three times as many cars as the Warren, Ohio, plant.[7] By June, Albert and Julius had completed plans for the plant and were taking bids for its construction on a 20-acre parcel located at East Grand Boulevard and Concord Street. A newspaper announcement of the project stated that Albert and Julius Kahn "are making a specialty of heavy factory and mill construction, paying special attention to working out the details of difficult engineering and architectural propositions."[8] The cost of the Packard job was about $90,000, making it the most desirable project yet secured by the brothers.[9]

Julius and Albert invested a great deal of effort in the design of the Packard plant in order to achieve maximum manufacturing efficiency, minimize construction and factory maintenance costs, and reduce construction time. The brothers clearly understood the importance of these considerations for factory owners, an understanding that many architects of the era lacked. A number of years later, when discussing his success as an industrial architect, Albert Kahn explained, "The plant must be economically designed. First and last, it must serve as an investment, not as a monument to the designer." "Efficiency is the watchword of the day," he continued, "directness of results, good business methods and speed in construction are the desired ends."[10] When discussing the new Packard factory with reporters, the Kahns emphasized how their firm's engineering capabilities reduced Packard's manufacturing costs by designing the buildings around the most efficient flow of materials: "In planning these buildings the skill of the engineer has been drawn upon in order that there may be no time lost in handling the material from the time that it enters at one end of the plant, in the rough, until it is turned out at the other end a finished product."[11]

Insurance was one of the largest costs of maintaining a factory, and it was reported that for the Packard plant "insurance engineering has been well taken care of in these structures." It was claimed that the buildings were so well designed that fire insurance costs were reduced by 90 percent.[12] The factory had a coal-fired power house which provided electricity to motors that, by means of overhead shafting and belts, powered the machines. Each department had its own motor, so if one department needed to shut down, other departments were not affected. Consideration was even given to the passage of employees to their workstations in a manner that was safe and eliminated distractions: the plant layout allowed workers to enter their own department without passing through any others.[13]

Concrete and wood were both used for floors in the buildings, depending on the activity to be carried out within. One of the finishing buildings contained a 50-by-50-foot reservoir in the basement. The walls and floor of the reservoir were concrete, which was a common arrangement. The floor above was concrete as well, but supported by reinforced concrete beams rather than steel. Each concrete beam contained two Kahn-type bars. Julius had not yet begun manufacturing Kahn Bars, so these were individually constructed by hand. The main bar was a 3-by-5/8-inch piece of flat steel, about 17 feet long, and the wings were 2-by-¼-inch pieces of steel, 18 inches long, bolted to the main bar at a 45-degree angle.[14] The beams reinforced with these bars in the Packard finishing building were, as far as can be determined, the first use of Kahn-type bars in the construction of a building.[15]

While the layout, provisioning, and arrangement of work areas of the Packard complex were carefully studied and planned, the buildings

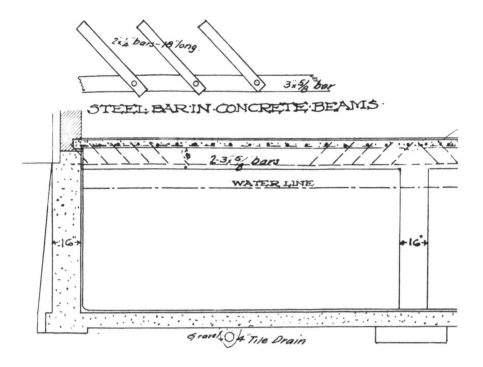

STEEL BAR IN CONCRETE BEAMS

2x¼" bars - 18" long

3 x ⅝" bar

2-3x⅝" bars

WATER LINE

16"

16"

Gravel 4" Tile Drain

FACTORY· FOR THE
PACKARD·MOTOR·CAR·CO.
DETROIT, MICH.
ALBERT KAHN, ARCHT.
JULIUS KAHN, ENGINEER.
JOB Nº 201. MAY 30, 1903.

Two sections of the architectural drawings for the 1903 Packard Motor Car Co. plant on Grand Boulevard in Detroit. (*Top*): This section shows the design of the reservoir in the basement of the finishing building. The reinforcement bars were constructed of plain steel bar stock with the pieces bolted together. Placement of the bars within the floor beams is shown by dashed lines. (*Bottom*): The Kahn brothers emphasized their firm's ability to apply the skills of both architects and engineers to the job by having both of their names on each sheet of drawings. (Albert Kahn Assoc., Inc.)

themselves were a mix of old and new technologies. As mill construction buildings, structurally they were less advanced than the concrete Kelly and Jones and United Shoe Machinery factories under construction that year by Ernest Ransome. But the Packard buildings were designed to be constructed rapidly and inexpensively, permitting the owners to achieve production quickly, at low cost. Construction of the plant began in early July 1903, the facility was turned over to the owners on September 22, and production of automobiles began in November. "Notwithstanding the unusual size of this establishment," reported one journal, "the buildings were erected in a very short time, only ninety days elapsing from the date on which the [construction] contract was signed."[16] The simplicity of the Packard structures was demonstrated by an article in Packard's in-house magazine in 1916. Beneath a photo of one of the original brick buildings was a caption stating, "On a day when there was no opportunity to put up a new building, the construction superintendent tore down one of the shops of the original plant, moved it half a mile, and set it up again."[17] By 1917, all nine of the original, mill construction Packard buildings had been replaced by concrete structures.

The Kahns' achievements with the Packard factory were genuine and provided an opportunity for Albert and Julius to promote their firm's combined architecture and engineering services, an effort that even extended to the building plans, which emphasized the collaboration of architect with engineer. The firm's other architectural drawings from the era were labeled "Albert Kahn, Architect," while the Packard drawings say "Albert Kahn, Architect; Julius Kahn, Engineer."[18] Having both architecture and engineering under one roof gave the brothers a competitive advantage, but other firms offering both services soon entered the field: in March 1903 architect Fred L. Smith joined the Detroit engineering firm of Field and Hinchman forming the architecture and engineering firm of Field, Hinchman and Smith.[19] The Kahn brothers' most powerful appeal to potential industrial customers was their understanding of and attention to production efficiency, operational costs, and speed of construction. Much of their future success resulted from remaining consistently focused on these vital concerns throughout their careers.

As the Kahns designed factories of largely traditional construction, in Cincinnati, buildings of reinforced concrete were under construction. First to rise was the Cincinnati College of Music's new theater—a

The Packard Motor Car Co. factory in Detroit as it neared completion in 1903. The firm's offices were in the two story building. To its left was the power house and the plant was to its right. The photo was taken looking north across E. Grand Blvd. (Detroit Public Library, National Automotive History Collection, resource ID: na020039)

replacement for one destroyed by fire the previous year—from plans drawn by architect Gustav Drach (1861–1940).[20] The European Hennebique system of construction was used and Ludwig Eid was contracted for the concrete work. The engineer was Austrian born and trained Leopold J. Mensch (1874–1956). The Hennebique system was well-established, but one aspect of the theater structure was unusual: the balcony was supported by two massive concrete beams over 60 feet long, claimed at the time to be the longest ever used in a concrete building. The theater was completed during October 1903 and had required less than three months to construct.[21]

Drach used the Hennebique system for another Cincinnati project, a fireproof, six-story storage warehouse. Construction of this massive, brick-clad, reinforced concrete structure began in March 1903 and required 18 months to complete. This unusual and attractive structure remains in use to this day at 706 Oak Street.[22]

Macdonald and Kiley Company, a Cincinnati manufacturer of men's shoes, had been in business only since 1901, but was so successful that they built a new factory during 1903. The Ferro-Concrete Construction Company erected the four-story, reinforced concrete building, 44 by

140 feet in size. One extraordinary aspect of the structure was its extensive windowed area, described at the time as "almost like a glass house, being one continuous run of windows around the entire building." The area between columns, and from floor to ceiling, with the exception of an eight-inch brick spandrel (between the floor and window sill), was filled with double hung windows, making it the first concrete "daylight factory" in the world.[23] (It was completed before Ernest Ransome's daylight factories for Kelly and Jones and United Shoe Machinery.) The former Macdonald and Kiley factory at 2060 Reading Road is now an office building, though the refaced exterior belies the building's age.

Leopold Mensch was the engineer and contractor for an impressive manufacturing building constructed for the Pugh Printing Company in Cincinnati, designed by the architecture firm of Dittoe and Wisenall. In March 1903 the architects announced that building plans were nearly complete. For reasons that are unclear, construction contracts were not let until April of the following year. The building opened in June 1905 and was described at that time by *Cement and Engineering News* as the "largest reinforced concrete building in the US." Today it is the Park Place at Lytle, a condominium building.[24]

During 1902 the American Book Company purchased the homestead of Larz Anderson Sr. (grandfather of George, Robert, and William Anderson) with the intention of building a new factory for their Cincinnati operation. In February, as plans for the new building were being prepared, a massive fire tore through downtown Cincinnati and destroyed much of the company's existing plant and equipment. Building contents that were not burned were ruined by water, including a substantial inventory of books. Numerous other buildings were destroyed as well, and at one point wood for the concrete forms on the Ingalls Building was threatened, saved only by the quick work of firemen who flooded the exposed planks with water.[25] In the wake of the blaze, American Book was committed to a fireproof structure for their new building; they selected Elzner and Anderson as architects. Unfortunately, when bids were received for construction, the cost was higher than the company was willing to pay, so the architects were ordered to revise the plans. To achieve the necessary cost savings, Elzner and Anderson substituted concrete for the stone that would typically have been used on the building's exterior, including the window sills, coping, string courses, decorative surrounds, and cornice. The combined office and factory building, described at the time as "mammoth," occupied one-half of a city block. Though no longer home to the American Book Company, the attractive building remains in service on the northeast corner of Cincinnati's Third and Pike Streets.[26]

April 1903 brought the announcement that Cincinnati's John Van Range Company was to build a four-story factory and showroom on the southwest corner of Fifth Street and Broadway. The architecture firm for the reinforced concrete building was Samuel Hannaford and Sons. This was surprising, because at a meeting of Cincinnati architects just six months prior, when Alfred Elzner denounced mill construction buildings as "firetraps," Samuel Hannaford rose to defend the method. Construction on the range factory began around May and was completed mid-summer the following year.[27]

In October, architect Jacob J. Rueckert was taking bids for a seven-story building to be occupied by the George Bieler and Sons Company and used for producing their Brookfield Rye whiskey. Contractors were asked to bid on three construction methods: reinforced concrete, steel, and a steel and mill hybrid. The building's owner, Louis Hauck, made the decision to go with concrete. Instead of using copper to construct the building's three, 2,500-gallon whiskey and water tanks, concrete was used instead, a first for the whiskey industry.[28]

These buildings, all begun in 1902 and 1903, represent an astonishing degree of innovation. Aside from the sheer volume of consequential, reinforced concrete structures, there were specific achievements: the longest reinforced concrete beam in the country, the largest concrete building, and the first daylight factory. Each of these was accomplished by different architects and engineers, using a variety of reinforcement systems and customized reinforcing methods. Yet, the confidence and courage of those who designed, built, and financed these pioneering buildings has been largely overlooked. Attention has focused on the Ingalls Building—the first concrete skyscraper—but not on the broader context of Cincinnati's technological advances in concrete construction from which it arose.

The broad shift to concrete in Cincinnati demonstrated the advantages concrete already held over steel in cost and lead times, even in the absence of a greater scientific understanding of the method. The decision to build fireproof structures in the city during 1902 and 1903 was largely motivated by concerns over the loss and damage to businesses resulting from fire, and by the rapidly increasing cost of fire insurance. But the choice of concrete rather than steel in Cincinnati was due to the presence of an unusual number of architects, engineers, and entrepreneurs with an understanding of the technology and a willingness to make use of it.

Nevertheless, the Ingalls Building was a noteworthy achievement for concrete construction. The building was largely completed between December 24, 1902, when the building permit was issued, and December 31, 1903, when the first tenants moved in. W. H. Ellis and Company, headed by William H. Ellis, was the contractor for the building. The company won the contract as lowest bidder, though the fact that William Ellis's daughter was married to Robert Anderson, head of the Ferro-Concrete Construction Company—engineering firm for the building and subcontractor for concrete work—may have had something to do with it. Nevertheless, William Ellis was a competent and clever builder who devised a number of labor-saving devices to speed work on the building. One of those inventions was a movable platform used for working on the building's exterior. It was suspended on cables from a framework extending through and anchored to a window opening, allowing it to be raised and lowered from inside. The suspended platform eliminated the need for a scaffold to be built up around the building.[29]

The Ingalls Building had been a topic of local interest through 1902, but by early spring 1903 William Ellis reported that "architects and civil engineers of the East are watching the progress of the Ingalls Building in this city with great interest." Experts from Boston, St. Louis, and New York had visited Cincinnati to see the building and examine the plans. "These experts," stated Ellis, "are convinced, after studying the plans and inspecting the work, that it is just as safe to erect 25 stories of concrete as it is to build one story."[30]

By early May 1903, roughly 80 percent of the building had been leased. The largest tenant, occupying five floors, was the Queen and Crescent Railway, a line that included the city-owned Cincinnati Southern Railway. One half of the 13th floor was reserved by the architecture firm of Elzner and Anderson.[31]

In May 1903 the journal *Fireproof* grudgingly admitted the building, which had reached the 8th floor, was "of more than ordinary interest." The author went on to snivel that the stone used in the concrete was "not screened or washed," and that the wires set in the concrete to attach the exterior facing were "badly rusted." "It would appear to be a decided mistake," *Fireproof* declared, "to use anchors of that kind with-

The Ingalls Building in Cincinnati, Ohio, the world's first concrete skyscraper, around 1903. (Library of Congress, Detroit Publishing Company photograph collection, control number 2016795003)

out having these wires dipped into a non-corrosive paint." (When the building was renovated in 2020, the exterior required no major attention to the anchors.) Their final judgment on the structure: "When the time lost in concrete construction is added to the cost of the building, it will be found that standard steel and tested fireproof construction is decidedly cheaper and better."[32]

A more comprehensive article appeared on May 23 in *Engineering Record* and included an extensive technical description of the building's design and method of construction, accompanied by numerous illustrations taken from the building plans. Contrary to the claim by *Fireproof* as to cost, *Engineering Record* reported that "preliminary comparative estimates and designs for skeleton steel construction and for reinforced concrete construction indicated that the latter was somewhat cheaper."[33]

In July, as the building reached the 12th floor, more articles appeared. *Engineering Record* highlighted other advantages to concrete construction. There were no obstructions surrounding the building caused by trucking and the large cranes required to hoist steel. The Ingalls Building had, stored in its cellar, adequate supplies of concrete and other material "to keep the work in progress for several weeks, thus affording considerable advantage in security against interruptions from labor troubles."[34] *Engineering News* carried an impressive, eight-page write up containing nearly enough detail to recreate the building, even to the point of describing specialized wheelbarrows that had "two wheels to prevent tipping over" and sides of equal height so the contents could be leveled off to assure identical volumes in each load.[35] As an indication of how widespread interest in the building had become, the July edition of the German publication *Beton und Eisen* (Concrete and Iron), reprinted the entire May 23 *Engineering Record* article. The article appeared in English and was accompanied by German-language commentary criticizing the slow pace of technological advance in European concrete construction, a problem the journal attributed to overly conservative regulation by authorities and an aversion to experimentation.[36] On July 26, the *New York Tribune* ran a five-paragraph article headlined "A Concrete Skyscraper." It described the building as "an experiment in construction" and explained to the uninitiated: "The process followed in the erection of the Ingalls Building is known as 'reinforced concrete.'" Relative to steel, the article pointed out, concrete was lower in cost, more permanent, and permitted work to proceed on the lower floors to make them ready for occupancy even before the upper floors were poured.[37] The article ran in more than a dozen newspapers nationally.

On Saturday, August 29, 1903, the roof of the Ingalls Building was completed, and an enormous American flag was raised atop the building in a ceremony lead by Melvin Ingalls and William Ellis. It was reported that the roof could have been completed and the ceremony held the day before, but superstitions about Friday being an unlucky day resulted in the completion being held over to the next day.[38]

On the afternoon of December 30, fire struck downtown Cincinnati's Koch and Braunstein Building at 22 East Fourth Street, across the street from the buildings that had been destroyed by the February fire. The fifth floor of the building housed the offices of architects Elzner and Anderson, just days away from moving to their new offices on the 13th floor of the Ingalls Building. The firm suffered water and smoke damage to many of its architectural drawings. The following day, the architects became the first tenants to occupy the Ingalls Building.[39] Two months later, fire tried once more to vent its rage against the architects. A worker in the Ingalls Building was using a gasoline lamp to illuminate a shaft in which he was installing wires, when, for reasons unknown, the lamp exploded. The worker hurled the lamp out into the hallway where it came to rest against the door of Elzner and Anderson's office, burning the paint off it.[40]

The design of the steel reinforcement used in the Ingalls Building is largely based on the Ransome system, as applied by Henry Hooper and the Ferro-Concrete Construction Company. The floors are reinforced by twisted square steel bars in two layers at right angles to each other. The girders supporting the floors are reinforced with steel rods and twisted steel stirrups—by this time Ransome, like Hennebique, had come to appreciate the value of using stirrups (or "U-bars") to counteract shearing stresses. The columns contain vertical, round bars to carry compression loads, surrounded at intervals and tied to rectangular hoops that prevent the bars from buckling outward. Smaller twisted bars are placed nearer to the surface to handle tension loads that occur when the building is exposed to wind. The joint between the girders and columns is strengthened by reinforcement bars that extend through the beam and column at a 45-degree angle and are embedded within the concrete corbel beneath the girder where it meets the column.[41]

Alfred Elzner offered his judgment on the Ingalls Building in a June 1904 article for the *Architectural Record*. While conceding that the building took a "little longer" to erect than a standard steel cage type, the cost was "probably somewhat less." He predicted that, for the next building of the kind, "not only the cost, but also the time required for completion, would undoubtedly be considerably reduced." The design of the building's overly large columns, Elzner stated, was "controlled by a spirit of conservatism," and "the columns might readily be made much smaller." "The sizes of concrete structural members have not yet been reduced to the most economical basis, and it may, and undoubtedly will, require some little time, since it is a comparatively new field of engineering."[42]

Engineer Leopold Mensch offered a similar appraisal in his 1904 publication *Architects' and Engineers' Hand-book of Re-inforced Concrete*

Constructions. He claimed the "wasteful amount of steel and concrete" used in the building was necessary to "overcome the objections of city authorities," though it resulted in "probably the strongest high building ever erected in this country." Nevertheless, in spite of the wasted material, "a notable economy over the ordinary type of steel skeleton construction was obtained." Looking ahead, Mensch declared that, for hotel and office buildings, the cost of concrete construction "will be found to be from 25 to 40 percent lower than for steel construction."[43]

6

Seeking Profit

Julius Kahn spent much of spring 1903 working with Albert on the plans for the Packard plant. The construction contracts for the factory were awarded near the end of June, and Julius departed on a trip out East to gather feedback from engineers on his reinforcement method and possibly find a way to bring it to market. On June 27, Julius met in New York City with a prominent, retired engineer by the name of Abbot who offered a great deal of encouragement. After carefully examining the drawings and test results that Julius brought with him, Abbot said that this method of concrete reinforcement was "the best thing he had ever seen." He was impressed as well by the research Julius had done on shearing stresses as a cause of premature beam failure and thought Julius's solution of angled wings extending from the main bar as a means to resist them was "the most practical he had seen." Yet, it was Abbot's advice on the business side of matters that was most significant. Julius anticipated that he would license firms throughout the country to produce and sell his bars, but Abbot told Julius "it would be a great mistake to establish agencies everywhere for manufacturing them." "You ought to manufacture the bars yourselves and sell them, keeping whatever profit there is entirely in your own hands." He explained that manufacturing the bars would require only a modest, upfront investment.[1]

In the afternoon, Julius paid a visit to his former employer, the Brooklyn Navy Yard, and met with civil engineer C. A. Wentworth. The feedback he received here was encouraging as well, with Wentworth concluding that Julius had "accomplished what all others had tried with their corrugated and twisted bars." Wentworth recognized that Julius had "proven there is a truss capable of taking care of shear," and most important, that its strength could be calculated. He asked Julius to let him know once his reinforcement bar was available as "there would be no question about his using it."[2]

Over the course of his meetings in the East with firms that manufactured steel reinforcement and fireproofing materials, Julius found nearly every one of them keen to manufacture and sell his bar. Having observed during his time in Japan the underhanded and insincere manner in which business was conducted, Julius had acquired a reluctance to accept at face value the promises made by those who wished to engage him in a business venture. These firms wished to manufacture the bars and pay Julius a royalty, but in light of his misgivings about the integrity of some business people, he foresaw having "an endless job" trying to determine how many bars they actually sold and collecting the correct amount of royalties.

Julius wrote to Albert that he had made up his mind about how to bring the bars to market—Abbot's words of advice had had an immediate effect on his decision. He relayed to Albert the suggestion from Abbot that they produce the bars themselves, concluding, "I really think this is the only way to do it." He explained his feelings to Albert: "The majority take fearful advantage of you. They listen to all your good ideas merely for the purpose of seeing how they can get around [the patents] and improve on them." Citing as an example, Julius wrote, "Take the N. Y. Expanded Metal Co., they seem most anxious to manufacture my bar, perfectly enthusiastic about it, and yet, for some reason or other I feel like a little fellow in their hands and if I gave them the exclusive right to manufacture the bar, I would be quickly squeezed out." Julius's concerns were sufficiently alarming that he considered foregoing additional meetings. "I am almost inclined to think that I should do better now not to see any other concerns in the reinforced concrete business, but come home and get into it myself. I feel we are just educating them." Julius was reluctant to share with other firms the principles of his reinforcing system and explained to his brother, "They'll find some way of getting around me and doing the same thing in a way just sufficiently different from mine so as to not infringe" [on the patent]. "I am so fully convinced in my system that I hate like furies to let anyone take hold of it but ourselves." "I just feel that as soon as I give the privilege to any-one to make the bar I will be out of it to a large extent."[3] These were not unreasonable fears. Julius was a young engineer from Detroit with little in the way of financial or legal resources with which to take on a patent fight. An unscrupulous business could exploit his ideas for years while a legal battle costing thousands of dollars worked its way through the court system.

While in New York, Julius conveyed to Albert an amusing obser-vation about work habits in the city. "Few of the business men of New York seem to come to their office at all on Saturday," he wrote. "They seem to live out in the suburbs and, owing to Saturday being only a half day, they don't deem it worthwhile coming in at all." He also took a jab at architects: "These men all consider themselves extremely important and divine. . . . I kind of dislike being cut short by men who consider themselves so important." Having decided he would no longer meet with architects, Julius concluded, "I don't think that there will be much trouble to get them to use [the bar] through advertising."[4]

On July 1, 1903, Julius was in Washington to meet with Captain John Sewell, whom he had contacted after reading Sewell's article on the need for dealing with shearing stresses in beams. The meeting went so well that Sewell referred Julius to his superior, Major Abbott in the office of the Chief of Engineers, who also became enthusiastic about the system. Abbott assured Julius that, once his bar became available, he would "be delighted" to approve any requests by officers within his department who wished to employ it.[5]

Julius had been working on a new innovation that, combined with his reinforcement bar, would permit construction of lighter-weight concrete floors. At that time, the standard method of constructing con-crete floors was to support the floor with concrete beams; the floors and beams were monolithic as they were poured at the same time. This system worked perfectly well, but it had disadvantages. Constructing the forms for the beams and floors was complicated, time-consuming, and required a great deal of lumber. In the completed building, the ceil-ing, rather than being flat, was crosshatched with beams. Julius had the idea of filling the space between the beams with lightweight, mostly hollow, terra cotta tile blocks. These blocks would have no structural purpose, as they would merely fill the space between the reinforced concrete beams. This method would greatly facilitate construction: instead of building individual wood forms for each beam, the entire floor could be constructed on a flat platform of wood. The blocks would be set on the platform in rows, end to end, with reinforcement bars placed in the space between each row of blocks, and the sides of the blocks functioning as the form for the concrete beam, eliminating the need to build wood forms. The entire exterior perimeter of the platform would be enclosed in a wooden form up to the level of the top of the floor; then concrete would be poured over the entire assemblage, creating the beams and floor in one piece. The resulting floor would be lighter in weight and require less concrete than a solid concrete floor. It would also be flat on its underside as the beams were contained within it, providing a flat ceiling for the story below. This ceiling could be easily finished by applying a coat of plaster. An added advantage was that the flat ceiling reflected light much better, an important consideration in an era when the primary source of illumination was natural light entering through the windows.

During one of his meetings in New York, Julius had shown preliminary sketches of this block-and-beam idea to an engineer and had been told that it would be difficult to manufacture the custom designed terra cotta blocks. Prior to traveling to Washington, Julius reworked the design so as to reduce the manufacturing issues. He shared this new iteration with Sewell, who encouraged Julius, telling him the "terra cotta scheme is just right."[6]

As a consequence of his meetings with those who would likely use his bar, Julius began to see how he could turn his invention into a successful business. He would purchase from the mills rolled lengths of steel with the proper profile for his bar: a thick center section with thin flanges along the sides. He would set up a manufacturing operation to complete the manufacturing process by shearing the flanges to turn them into wings, and then market the completed bars directly to contractors and construction firms. In addition, he also anticipated that his firm would "do the work" by establishing a construction company, perhaps with his brother Moritz as its head. "A little later when our capital allows," he wrote to Albert, "I think we ought to establish branch offices at the various larger cities."[7]

Julius returned from his trip with a more fully developed concept of the physical form his bar would take. His initial patent covered the underlying concept of an embedded truss with attached wings, but the

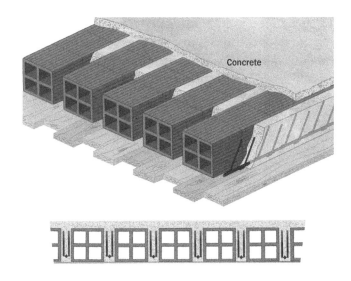

Construction of the Kahn floor. Boards formed a flat platform on which the floor could be constructed while the concrete set. Hollow terra cotta blocks were laid in rows leaving room between them for the Kahn reinforcement bars. Once the bars were in place, concrete was poured, forming the beams and floor simultaneously. The completed floor was lighter than a solid concrete floor and featured a smooth ceiling—free of beams—along its lower face.

numerous sketches that accompanied the patent were intended more as an effort to lay claim to different means of executing the truss rather than illustrating a production-ready form. Among the options were flat, steel plates having wings variously in the middle, on one side, or on both sides.[8]

Julius filed a third patent application on August 14, 1903, illustrating the final form of his reinforcement bar as well as a revised version of his terra cotta block floor. (Julius applied for a second patent prior to leaving on his trip East which did not mention concrete, but demonstrated that his truss system could also work with precast blocks, bricks, or any other solid body that could fit between the wings of his bar.[9]) The reinforcement bar was shown in two versions. The first was a single bar with a cross section shape of round, square, or diamond, and having flanges extending on both sides which, when cut and bent up, became the wings. The second version had two somewhat smaller bars with a single flange between them for the wings. In the end, Julius selected the single bar with a diamond-shaped cross section to manufacture, most likely because it permitted twice as many wings as the two bar version. The diamond shape may have been less expensive to roll than the square or round shape, or it may have facilitated cutting the wings. The terra cotta blocks for floor construction shown in the patent were those that Sewell had judged were "just right." They were designed to reduce the amount of concrete in each beam to the bare minimum, but to achieve that, the blocks required curves and flanges.[10] The expense of producing the block may have been greater than the cost of the concrete saved and the slight savings due to the reduced dead weight of the floor; consequently, the final production version of the block was eventually revised to a simple rectangle.

On August 18, 1903, Julius's first patent was granted and he moved quickly over the next few months to implement his business and marketing plans. Within a matter of weeks, Kahn and Kahn secured their first job using reinforced concrete, a storage shed for the Great Northern Portland Cement Company of Baldwin, Michigan. Great Northern had begun manufacturing cement in June 1903 and was rapidly expanding their production capacity. Julius and Albert were hired by the firm to design a large storage shed for cement, to be constructed of reinforced concrete. The structure, roughly 200 by 100 feet in size, was the first reinforced concrete building constructed using the "Kahn System of Reinforced Concrete" and likely the first reinforced concrete building of any kind in Michigan.[11] While Great Northern had been established on the farsighted premise that demand for cement would increase dramatically, it turned out that making cement from the local marl was uneconomical, particularly in light of falling cement prices. The plant shut down in April 1906 for lack of sufficient coal and by the end of the year was in receivership. The cement shed, though derelict, remains standing and is clearly visible on satellite view maps about 2.5 miles south of the town of Baldwin, Michigan.[12]

A far more significant commission arose around the same time as a result of the meeting Julius had with Captain Sewell. Sewell was in charge of constructing the US Army War College at Washington Barracks, District of Columbia (now Fort Leslie J. McNair), and wished to use the Kahn Bar. To confirm the performance of the bar, he invited Julius to Washington to observe the Army engineers conduct tests on his and other reinforcing methods for concrete beams and floor slabs. Both Julius and Albert traveled there and watched as ever greater loads were placed on concrete test panels until they failed. The panels reinforced with twisted steel bars (Ransome system) exhibited cracks opening up along the bottom of the beam and progressing upward and

Though it was never fully completed, the Great Northern Portland Cement Warehouse was the first reinforced concrete building in Michigan and the first in the world built with manufactured Kahn Bars. It was constructed in 1903 on James Rd. south of Baldwin, Michigan. (Courtesy of Dalton Smith)

in toward the beam's middle. As these cracks grew larger, the concrete surrounding the reinforcing bars fell away. All of these panels failed due to shearing stresses. When the Kahn Bars were tested, the panels held up under a greater load, and when failure finally occurred, it was due to the main reinforcing bar snapping in two near its middle, just as expected.[13]

The Army War College was a large project that encompassed 20 buildings, the most substantial of which is the imposing War College Building (now Roosevelt Hall) designed by the New York architecture firm of McKim, Mead, and White. At the north end of the parade ground are two barracks buildings, nearly as large as the War College Building which they face. Sewell contracted with Julius to design the floors and provide reinforcement bars for these two barracks buildings and also the band barracks.[14] The War College Building's design was finalized the following year, and Sewell used Kahn System reinforcement bars throughout for floors, roof, and beams, the floors being constructed using the system of terra cotta blocks and bars devised by Julius and slightly modified by Sewell.[15] For a number of larger girders, Sewell used heavier reinforcement bars built up the same way as the bars for the Packard finishing building, by attaching individual pieces of steel to a main bar at a 45-degree angle rather than shearing the wings from flanges.[16]

Sewell's influence was instrumental in securing additional government business for Julius, including 10 buildings at the US Naval Academy at Annapolis and 20 buildings at the US Military Academy at West Point. More important than the value of the government business was the enhanced credibility the Kahn System accrued due to its approval and use by the highly regarded US Army Corps of Engineers and Captain Sewell, "a military engineer of recognized authority and independence."[17]

More than any other qualified individual of the era, John Sewell recognized the significance of Julius's achievements. A lengthy article on reinforced concrete written by Sewell in 1906 states, "Two very important advances have been made in the United States; one of them is the attachment of the web reinforcement to the horizontal reinforcement, so that they are firmly fastened together. . . . The other is the plan of arranging the tensile web members at an angle of forty-five degrees, so as to parallel the tensile web stresses." The importance of these advances, wrote Sewell, "would not have been so clearly recognized as it is now, but for their development by Julius Kahn, of Detroit, about three or four years ago, and their subsequent commercial exploitation."[18]

On Wednesday, October 7, 1903, Julius founded the Trussed Concrete Steel Company.[19] The firm's name was derived from the truss he invented to create "trussed concrete" beams and floors; the company itself being in the business of manufacturing steel products. (The company was often referred to as "Truscon," a shortened version of its name.) Julius was the majority stockholder in the company; to raise cash to finance the new firm, he brought in partners. Albert Kahn invested $10,000, as did Day Krolik, Albert's brother-in-law. Herman Krolik, brother of Albert's father-in-law, invested $27,000. Ralph M. Dyar, secretary of the Wellston Portland Cement Company, provided $10,000. Joseph Boyer, who had brought so much important business to Albert and Julius, chipped in $5,000 and became vice president of the new firm, bringing with him a great deal of business experience.

George W. Patterson Sr., assistant dean of the college of engineering at the University of Michigan (for whom Albert had designed a home the previous year), invested $2,000 on behalf of his young son. In lieu of a cash investment, Julius signed over to the company his patents, valued at $100,000, and became the firm's president.[20]

Based on information Julius had gathered from mills and manufacturing firms, he estimated that he could purchase steel rolled to his specifications for 1.3 cents per pound and his company could shear the wings onto the bar at a cost of 0.2 cents per pound. He believed the market would support a price of 3.5 cents per pound, giving the firm a per-pound gross profit of 2 cents.[21]

Truscon's first office consisted of a small room in downtown Detroit's Union Trust Building. It was sparsely equipped with a roll top desk, a typewriter, and two chairs: one for the bookkeeper and another for the stenographer. On a typical day, Moritz and Felix Kahn would be at work in the office as well as Ralph Dyar, while Julius was out conducting tests or arranging the firm's first sales, often with Albert's help. When the company hired its first engineer, Maurice Goldenberg, there was no room for him in the office, so a temporary workspace was found for him in Albert's architecture firm, located in the same building. Goldenberg received his training at the Massachusetts Institute of Technology, where he graduated with a BS in architectural engineering. After a short stint with the American Bridge Company, he was hired by Truscon. Julius told him, "We have the most perfect reinforcing bar known. . . . The opportunities [in concrete construction] are wonderful. We will be one of the greatest concerns of the United States one day. You just stick to it and grow with us." Reflecting on this first conversation with Julius, Goldenberg later stated, "The sincerity with which this was said, together with the personality of the man dominated me completely. I was fascinated and deeply impressed."[22]

Julius's marketing campaign was kicked off by the publication of an article he had written on his theory of concrete reinforcement. The nearly three-page article included photos of tests and illustrative drawings, and appeared in four widely read engineering journals between October 15 and 17, 1903: *Engineering News*, *Engineering Record*, *Railroad Age*, and *Railroad Gazette*. The article described tests Julius had made on concrete beams reinforced using twisted steel bars of the Ransome type; "without one exception" the beams failed due to shearing stresses. He described the importance of resisting such stresses and mentioned Sewell's previous article that made the same point. Julius explained that the solution required having both horizontal and vertical reinforcement. Beams reinforced in this manner, he wrote, could only fail in the middle with the main bar snapping in two, and he backed up that assertion with descriptions and photographs of tests he had performed. As the strength of a beam reinforced in this way was entirely dependent on the strength of the main bar, he asserted, it is "subject to close calculation in the same manner as a steel I-beam or truss." As a consequence, a concrete beam "need no longer be subjected to a factor of safety of ten; the ordinarily adopted factor for steel, four, is sufficient."[23]

The tone of the article was scientific and factual, devoid of any effort to directly promote the Kahn System. Though "Kahn Bar" appears in a number of the article's captions, the sole reference to his company was in the final paragraph: "The above systems of concrete re-enforcement which have been described are controlled by patents granted and now pending by the Trussed Concrete Steel Co." Julius appreciated that a successful effort to market his system depended on educating engineers and architects on the scientific principles upon which it was based. Once the necessity for resisting shearing stresses was acknowledged, it was a short path to seeing the Kahn Bar as the most efficient and economical method of doing so. The article accomplished more for Julius, at no cost, than many thousands of dollars of advertising could have.

Julius took the copy from the article and used it as the basis for a catalog, *Kahn System of Reinforced Concrete*, illustrated with numerous photographs of experiments on reinforced concrete floors and beams.[24] One photo shows the floor in a War College barracks building supporting a test load of 26 tons with no deflection.[25]

The nearly 80-page catalog contained technical information on the use of Kahn Bars, including tables showing their safe load-bearing capacity in various applications. There were explanations and illustrations demonstrating how the Kahn Bar could be used for bridges, culverts, tunnels, retaining walls, and reservoirs, each of which was accompanied by a detailed drawing showing exactly how the reinforcement bars should be placed within the structure. As a sales tool, the catalog would have been highly effective with its target audience: engineers, contractors, architects, and construction departments of municipalities and corporations. To be effective, though, the catalog had to be in their hands. Julius relied on the inexpensive, but effective strategy

This diagram, showing how Kahn Bars could be used for beams, floors, and columns, appeared in the 1904 Kahn System catalog. (*Kahn System of Reinforced Concrete*, General Catalog D [Detroit: Trussed Concrete-Steel Co., 1904])

of using the free publicity available through technical publications. He sent a copy of his catalog, accompanied by a brief description of its contents, to the journals, which printed announcements or short blurbs using the supplied copy. A typical example appeared in the November 19, 1903, issue of *Iron Trade Review* alerting readers to "a catalogue of the product controlled by the Trussed Concrete Steel Co. of Detroit." The single-sentence description stated, "Some noteworthy illustrations show very clearly the increased strength obtained by the addition of suitably formed steel rods to concrete beams and columns and the value of vertical reinforcement in concrete work."[26]

Julius's attention was required at this time on so many aspects of his business efforts it's no surprise that he nearly arrived at his wedding unprepared for the nuptials. He had met Margaret Kohut during the time he was working in New York City, and the two planned to wed in that city on December 24, 1903. With so much work to do, Julius delayed leaving Detroit for New York until the day of his wedding, finally getting around to purchasing a ring for his bride on his way out of the city.

The Ingalls skyscraper brought beneficial attention to the nascent concrete construction industry in 1903; unfortunately, the last three months of the year saw a cascade of construction calamities that aroused fears about concrete's safety. The year had begun with two dramatic collapses of concrete buildings under construction, the first occurring in February at a seven-story bank and office structure of the Lawrence Savings and Trust Company of New Castle, Pennsylvania. The shoring holding up the concrete roof was removed too soon, allowing it to collapse through each of the floors below, killing one man and injuring others, including the building's architect.[27] The second accident occurred on March 28 at the site of the Johnson Service Company building in Milwaukee. The Ransome method of reinforcement was used to construct the floors, beams, and columns of the building's interior, while the self-supporting exterior walls were of brick. It was a hybrid structure, essentially a mill construction building in which the wooden floors, beams, and columns were replaced by reinforced concrete. A 55-by-18-foot section in the front of the building had just been poured when it suddenly fell, taking with it the floors below and a portion of the brick front wall. Fortunately, no one was injured. It was later determined that the floor below, which supported the shoring for the newly poured floor, had been overloaded and gave out under the excess weight.[28]

One interesting aspect of this incident is that it was the president and founder of Johnson Service Company, Warren S. Johnson, who provided *Engineering News* with a detailed explanation as to its cause. Johnson's grasp of the technical aspects of reinforced concrete suggests that he was deeply involved in selecting the material to construct the building, the first concrete building in Milwaukee.[29] The structure was completed without further incident and the Johnson Service Company (renamed Johnson Controls in 1974) occupied the structure until 2021.[30]

As autumn 1903 arrived, the pace of concrete construction accidents picked up, beginning with a pair of county courthouses. In October, a portion of the third floor of the La Crosse, Wisconsin, courthouse collapsed as the concrete was poured, an accident due to insufficient shoring. The following month, a section of floor in the Marshall, Illinois, courthouse suffered the same fate when the shoring was removed. An investigation revealed that the failure was due to "inexpert designers and too great a desire for cheapness" on the part of the county. As the year drew to an end, accidents became rife. On December 2, four sections of floor in the Carnegie Library, under construction in Binghamton, New York, fell when the shoring became overloaded. Two days later, the concrete roof being poured on the nine-story Bellefield Apartments in Pittsburgh collapsed and fell onto the freshly installed floor below, causing it to give way and allow the mass to crash all the way to the basement, killing one worker. The contractor was in a hurry to get the building under roof and, lacking an adequate number of boards available for shoring, had used shorter boards spliced together. The spliced shoring pieces failed.[31]

The following week a rather bizarre failure occurred in the four-story brass shop of the J. L. Mott Iron Works in Trenton, New Jersey, one of five buildings under construction for the company. The contract with the construction firm required that each floor of the 300-by-50-foot building be tested by loading them with sandbags to twice the weight they were designed to sustain under normal use. The building was constructed with self-supporting exterior brick walls and concrete floors supported by the brick walls and, down the center of the building, a girder supported by a row of concrete columns—another hybrid structure. On the morning of December 8, a 41-by-17-foot section of the third floor was being tested. All but ten sandbags making up the 180-ton test weight had been placed, when suddenly a loud cracking sound was heard. Thomas Delaney was on the second floor, underneath the test section, monitoring the instrument which measured the floor's deflection. The loud noise attracted his attention to the floor above, which he saw was beginning to crack and fall; he and two other workers sprinted to safety just as the mass of concrete and steel hurtled past, carrying down with it the section of the second floor on which they had just been standing. The wreckage then slammed onto the first floor, where at that moment, two workers had the unbelievably bad luck to be passing through. They were killed instantly. A guard had been posted to keep people out of the building while the testing was in progress; one of the men killed, an employee of the contractor, had been warned to stay clear just five minutes prior to the accident.[32]

The cause of the collapse, it was later determined, was the inadequate and improper anchoring of the concrete floor's reinforcing rods to the brick walls of the building. According to one technical journal, the accident demonstrated that a span "submitted to a test equivalent to the weight of two locomotives on the third floor of a building, must have upon the brick wall a bearing surface of more than 12 inches in order to obtain a sufficient anchorage of the steel rods to the walls."[33] The building was subsequently completed and serves today as a nursing and rehabilitation center.[34]

In Corning, New York, a three-story, concrete retail building for the Wing and Bostwick Company was under construction. The building's architects, concerned that the concrete work be properly carried out, required the contractor to conduct a load test of each floor of the building and replace any work found to be substandard. The first floor had been tested and found to be well constructed; but the architects had reason to believe that the work on the upper two floors was being carried out unsatisfactorily, and they anticipated that the floors would fail the load test. It turned out that the load test was unnecessary. At four in the morning on December 15, a watchman on the third floor of the structure was shocked to see a portion of the concrete roof fall. Shock turned to alarm and the watchman "made record time in descending, barely reaching a place of safety when the rear wall and from twenty to thirty feet of the roof and . . . floor space on the three floors crashed into the cellar." The architects attributed the collapse "to the fact that the reinforcement of the concrete in the part which failed was almost entirely omitted."[35]

The Norman Street School was the first school in Boston constructed with a steel frame and concrete floors so as to make the five-story building fireproof. The concrete floors were supported by steel I-beams. On December 15, as the school neared completion, an 11-by-25-foot panel of the fourth floor gave way, taking out the floors below as it fell. The cause of the failure was traced to the concrete mixture: the stone used was too large and improperly mixed. While not a particularly dramatic or lethal incident, it received publicity in industry journals due to its unusual cause.[36]

These failures provided ample opportunity for those opposed to concrete construction to argue that the technology was flawed and dangerous. For Julius, the timing couldn't have been worse—just as he was starting up his business, the pitfalls of concrete construction were in the spotlight. He was angry that so much work was carried out by unqualified individuals and that engineers and architects were far more lax in their design of concrete structures than with those of steel. Julius wrote a three-page article denouncing the lack of professionalism; it was published January 1904 in multiple architecture and engineering journals.[37] "The writer has given this subject considerable study," he stated, "and he cannot bear to sit by quietly and allow, what he considers a most beautiful field of construction, to be ruined by the incompetence of men who so largely work therein."[38]

Julius had personally observed the shortcomings he denounced. Less than two years earlier, Albert had described to Julius the method by which the strength of the Palms Apartments concrete floors had been calculated: "By guess. There are no scientific data." Now Julius condemned those who constructed "by guess": "Where men have lacked such technical [engineering] knowledge, they have invariably entrusted the work to concerns who specialize in concrete, and who have been paving or sidewalk contractors before." "Anyone who entrusts this construction with them is certainly guilty of gross negligence." Referring to the Wing and Bostick job, Julius wrote that "the concern which supplied this reinforcement . . . had made fences its main business before." After discovering that steel fencing was being employed as reinforcement for concrete, the firm "plunged deeply into the field of reinforced concrete and hesitated at no constructions, no matter how difficult."[39]

Julius characterized recent failures due to improper shoring and improper material or mixing as obvious cases of gross incompetence that were "entirely inexcusable." But, "in the majority of cases," he wrote, "the causes were of a different nature": "insufficient and improper reinforcement." Most contractors working in the field were conscientious, but as few "possess a scientific knowledge of the materials with which they are dealing, their work at its best is mere speculation." The problem, Julius explained, was that the maximum strength of a beam depended on the strength of the reinforcement bar. But, as beams typically failed due to shearing stresses, well before the maximum strength of the bar was reached, "calculations for the beam have therefore been made for the wrong place in the beam." Not only were the calculations inaccurate but the lack of reinforcement against shearing stresses made such beams dangerous; beams that fail due to shearing stresses do so suddenly and without warning, as was the case with the notable failures reported in 1903. Beams that fail due to the breaking of the reinforcement bar, as with the Kahn Bar, give adequate warning by displaying significant sag accompanied by visible cracks along the bottom surface.[40]

To emphasize that proper reinforcement was the primary safety consideration, Julius wrote that "even the poorest mixture of concrete . . . would carry large loads before failure." He cited examples of structures that he had constructed where the shoring was "removed with perfect safety at the end of three days." "The concrete had not set to sufficient hardness to carry heavy strains," but "had sufficient hardness to carry 300 or 400 pounds per square inch in compression and, therefore, the safe load." Julius concluded the article by citing the example of a 14-foot beam of ice he had constructed using his system: "The beam stood up like a rock under loading. Is this sufficient proof," he asked, "that proper reinforcement has something to do with the safety of concrete structures?"[41]

The article prompted letters from readers of *Engineering News*. For the most part, these letters provided abundant evidence—albeit unintentional—supporting Julius's contention that many in the field lacked a scientific understanding of how steel reinforcement worked. One letter from a Chicago engineer exemplified the amateurish and unscientific approach to concrete reinforcement, arguing that "cracks are due to a slipping of the metal in the concrete and are not due to a shear," a problem he claimed was easily solved by placing additional reinforcement at the end of the bar, a conclusion arrived at because it "seemed rational."[42]

The most acerbic response to Julius's article came from engineer Albert L. Johnson of the St. Louis Expanded Metal Company, which marketed his Johnson corrugated reinforcement bar. Johnson's response was pompous and dismissive: "The fact that Mr. Kahn should take the trouble to develop, however carelessly, the shearing stresses in the vertical section, merely indicates that he has no real knowledge of how or where the maximum shearing stresses in such beams are developed."[43] The journal provided copies of the letters to Julius so his response could be published in the same issue. He took the opportunity to not only refute Johnson's assertions, but to market the Kahn Bar: "As for the Kahn bar being essential to success, not a single mention of it was made in the article in question. But since Mr. Johnson attacks it, let us consider his objections." Julius offered, among other explanations, photographs of tests he had made on three otherwise identical beams reinforced using plain bars, Johnson's bars, and his own trussed bars. The photos showed the first two failed under a weight of about 3,000 pounds by "vertical and longitudinal shear" near the ends, while the Kahn beam failed under a weight of 4,800 pounds by "the steel parting as usual near the center."[44]

The exchanges continued into April with Julius finally taking the gloves off in his response: "It will be very interesting to trace the evolution of Mr. Johnson's ideas from his various statements in engineering publications. [In] the catalogs issued by the Expanded Metal Co., prior to 1903 . . . shear is not even mentioned." However, Julius pointed out, Johnson wrote a letter to *Engineering News* in response to Captain Sewell's 1903 article on shearing stresses stating, "The writer has recently inserted a discussion of the shearing stresses at the end of the beam in a new catalogue that his company has now in press, which will tell when shear bars are necessary, and . . . an increase in capacity of 50% can safely be depended upon by their judicious use . . . but no rule is given practically or theoretically for the determination of the number of shear bars that would be required and the method of arrangement." "From this," wrote Julius, "we are led to infer that in 1903 Mr. Johnson recommended placing vertical bars in his concrete, but practically acknowledges lack of knowledge as to their correct placing."[45] Johnson responded once again, but by this point, Julius had more pressing matters: filling orders for his reinforcement bar.

7

Growth

Julius's decision to manufacture his bar rather than licensing other firms to produce and sell it was due to his concerns over patent infringement and the collection of royalty payments, but his concerns did not end there. He understood that, once his bar was on the market and meeting with success, others would likely attempt to make and sell similar bars. While his patent would discourage ethical manufacturers from selling copycat bars, less scrupulous firms might seek a way around the patent and enter the market as competitors. Julius anticipated that the most effective means of mitigating this threat was to expand his organization so rapidly that it became dominant nationally within a very short time. One strategy was to establish local sales representatives in numerous cities. In addition to the Trussed Concrete Steel office in Detroit, the firm opened offices in New York City and Toronto, Canada, and by March 1904, had agents representing the firm in Baltimore, Buffalo, Cleveland, Chicago, Louisville, Milwaukee, and St. Louis.

The company's New York office was opened by Julius's brother Moritz, who like Julius attended the University of Michigan and was a civil engineer. His prior work experience was not extensive; after graduating in 1903, he worked briefly for the American Bridge Company in Detroit before joining Truscon and moving to New York. In

1905, Moritz was sent to London, England, to establish the first European office of the company. His fellow employees in the London office described Moritz as a typical "American; dynamic, cigar smoking and highly informal," a curious observation considering that his parents were Germans who, after immigrating to America, barely had time to unpack their bags before Moritz was born.[1]

Julius hired his brothers Gustave and Felix, also a civil engineer, as sales representatives for the company. In 1906 Gustave established Truscon's Canadian manufacturing subsidiary in Walkerville (Windsor), Ontario, and by 1909, was also serving as vice president of the Canadian Cement and Concrete Association. From 1914 until his retirement in 1929, Gustave served as Truscon's vice president of sales.[2] Felix joined the company after graduating from the University of Michigan, then relocated to San Francisco in 1907 to head the Truscon office there as the city rebuilt from the earthquake and fire of 1906. In 1913 Felix left Truscon to partner with Alan MacDonald in the engineering and construction firm of MacDonald and Kahn. This firm became quite successful and was responsible for many significant projects, including the Mark Hopkins Hotel and the Hoover Dam. One of the firm's most exotic projects was the design of a concrete transport ship. Concrete was sought as a substitute for steel in an effort to speed construction of desperately needed ships to supply the British during the First World War; both steel and steelworkers were in short supply at the time. The war ended, however, before any concrete ships were ready to serve.[3]

Trussed Concrete Steel's Cleveland, Ohio, agent was Julius Tuteur, a successful entrepreneur who, like Julius, was a German Jewish immigrant. Tuteur had invented a steel joist hanger and established the Duplex Hanger Company of Cleveland in 1894 to market the hanger and other building materials. Benjamin Rose, one of Cleveland's leading real estate developers and owner of the Rose Building (built 1900, the largest office building in Ohio at the time), was having plans made in early 1904 to construct a three-story office building. Tuteur sold Rose on steel-reinforced concrete, who then hired Truscon to design and construct the concrete work.[4] Cleveland's building code, however, did not allow for multi-story concrete structures. Rose and Tuteur had sufficient political clout to have the building code, under revision at the time, amended to include provision for "trussed concrete construction." Title X of the Cleveland building code, sections 10 through 21, dealt exclusively with trussed concrete construction, the language of

The Kahn family around 1906. *Front row left to right:* Mollie, Joseph, Rosalie, Paula; *back row:* Felix, Gustave, Julius, Albert, Moritz, Louis. ("Albert Kahn [*back row, 3rd from right*] with his parents and 7 siblings, ca. 1900; HS13331" Albert Kahn Family Papers. University of Michigan Bentley Historical Library)

which was almost certainly authored by Julius Kahn as it was nearly identical to the language contained in his patent applications. There was, however, one significant restriction imposed on concrete buildings: a limit of either four or six stories in height, depending on the type of structure.[5] Rose's new building, located on the northwest corner of Erie (now Ninth) Street and Bolivar Road, was completed prior to the end of 1904, and was likely the first constructed by Truscon outside of Michigan.[6]

In Chicago, Truscon was represented by Knapp Brothers, a firm that aggressively marketed the Kahn System for fireproof structures that could be built at lower cost than steel frame buildings. In April 1904 the Iowa School for the Deaf in Council Bluffs was destroyed by a massive fire. Knapp Brothers secured the contract to replace the wrecked building with a much larger structure and an adjacent hospital building, both of which were constructed of concrete reinforced with Kahn Bars. (The school continues to operate from these buildings.)[7] Knapp

Brothers also used the Kahn System to construct the Carnegie Library in Sterling, Illinois, and the Werner Brothers Storage building in Chicago, both completed in 1904 and in use to this day.[8]

During 1904 Trussed Concrete Steel added additional sales agents in Pittsburgh and Erie, Pennsylvania; Kansas City, Missouri; Louisville, Kentucky; Oklahoma City, Oklahoma; and Seattle, Washington, giving the company a presence from coast to coast. The Seattle agent, International Fireproof Construction Company, secured the first contract for a Kahn System building on the west coast, a three-story concrete building for a local laundry company.[9]

In most cases the motivation for using the Kahn System was its lower cost relative to steel frame construction for buildings needing to be fireproof; the Cedar Rapids, Iowa, public library stands as an example. In January 1904 the city's board of library trustees adopted plans to construct a new library building at a cost of $75,000, paid for with funds donated by Andrew Carnegie. A newspaper article described the proposed structure: "The floor and roof construction and all partitions will be of some form of fireproof construction, using steel and iron for all structural parts." Upon learning of the planned construction, the sales representative for Truscon convinced the architects that the building could be completed sooner and at a lower cost by using the Kahn System instead of structural steel. When informed that the cost of the building could be reduced by about $700, the trustees accepted the substitution. In May, as the library was being built, the local paper carried a large article headlined "The Library Building and the Kahn Concrete-Steel Truss," describing in great detail the theory behind the Kahn System. Drawings accompanying the article showed cross sections of the floors with Kahn Bars in place.[10] This type of publicity did much to alert construction professionals and the general public to the existence of the new technology. A similar article on the Kahn System appeared in the February 20 issue of *Scientific American*, the most widely read technology-oriented periodical in the country. The article described "a new system of reinforcement" developed to overcome the weaknesses in previous systems. It noted that the Kahn System was being used to erect army barracks in Washington, DC, and was to be used as well at the naval academy. From the information contained and the wording of these two articles, it is nearly certain that they were authored by Julius with the intention of providing publications with readymade content that was accurate, persuasive, and contributed to Truscon's marketing efforts.[11]

Trussed Concrete Steel Company ad from *Municipal Engineering*, December 1904. Just over a year since its founding, the company had sales agents in 14 cities in addition to the home office in Detroit.

Similar articles continued to appear in technical publications as well. Following the opening of his Toronto office in March 1904, Julius managed to place a half-page article on the Kahn System in the *Canadian Engineer*. The article concluded with the name and address of the firm's representative and the suggestion that interested parties could view the bars being installed at a building under construction in Toronto.[12] In June, the journal *Concrete* devoted a full page to a test made on a concrete beam by the contractor building the library in Cedar Rapids. A photo accompanying the article showed a weight of 100,000 pounds supported by a single concrete beam reinforced with two 1¼ inch Kahn Bars.[13]

An unusual building constructed with the Kahn System during 1904 was the small arms ammunition storehouse at the Frankford Arsenal near Philadelphia. The arsenal, established in 1816, developed and manufactured small arms and artillery munitions for the US Army (until its closure in 1977).[14] The contract to construct the 212-by-60-foot storehouse was awarded to Cramp and Company as low bidder; they elected to substitute reinforced concrete for the steel frame originally specified by the government.[15] The building had exterior walls of self-supporting brick, while the floors, columns, and beams inside were of concrete, and reinforced with Kahn Bars.

The floors of the two-story building were designed to support a rather high live load of 425 pounds per square foot. The Army was skeptical that reinforced concrete was capable of supporting this amount of weight and insisted on testing a mock-up of the beams and floor to be used in the building. When the test was made, the mock-up easily supported 425 pounds. More weight was added until the floor panel was supporting 162,000 pounds—more than 2,000 pounds per square foot—with a deflection of only 7/16 of an inch. At this point, the test was discontinued, as it was clear "the floor slab would easily have a safety factor of 4." The commanding officer of the arsenal, though satisfied with the results of the test, suggested the load be left in place. After 20 days, however, there was no further deflection.[16] The girders that were to support the floor beams were tested separately and carried a load of 216,000 pounds—three times the live load they were designed to support—with a deflection on only 3/32 of an inch. Conducting these tests was no easy task. Placing the load of 216,000 pounds of lead blocks weighing 100 pounds each required eight men working two eight-hour shifts. The cost of the lead used was $15,000, nearly half the cost of the building itself.[17]

In Detroit, the Kahn System had yet to be used in constructing a building, but that was about to change. The American Arithmometer Company of St. Louis, manufacturer of the Burroughs adding machine, saw such rapid growth in sales during 1902 and 1903 that it had outgrown its existing factory. William Burroughs, founder of the company, had died in 1898 and Joseph Boyer was now the company's president. In early 1904, Boyer made the decision to relocate the firm from St. Louis to Detroit and build a new factory there. Boyer acquired land on the southwest corner of Second Avenue and Amsterdam Street (across Amsterdam from the Chicago Pneumatic plant) and asked Albert Kahn to draw up plans for a factory and headquarters building nearly twice the size of the firm's St. Louis plant.[18]

The layout of the factory was straightforward, with a large, single-story machine shop 320 feet long and 126 feet deep. A smaller second story above the shop held the company's offices. Other departments were contained within a wing off the rear of the building, the second floor of which was a gymnasium for the employees. The machine shop and portions of the rear wing had a sawtooth roof to admit natural light. The machine shop was also illuminated by suspended arc lights, and each machine had its own incandescent bulb.[19]

The floors and roof of the factory were constructed using the system devised by Julius of reinforcement bars sandwiched between hollow terra cotta blocks. The beams supporting the second floor offices were of concrete reinforced with Kahn Bars. However, rather than fully adopting concrete construction and using reinforced concrete columns, the roof and second-floor office section were supported by cast iron columns and the exterior brick walls. This hybrid construction reflects a rather timid commitment to reinforced concrete, surprising in light of the number of buildings under construction or already completed using the Kahn System by April 1904, when the plans for the factory were drawn.[20]

Nevertheless, both *American Architect* and *Engineering Record* published illustrated articles on the building, viewing it as sufficiently innovative to merit such coverage. Or so it would seem. The *American Architect* and *Engineering Record* articles were identical, save for minor edits, suggesting that the copy actually originated in the marketing department of Julius's firm. The "hollow-tile and cement construction" of the floors "has proved itself thoroughly satisfactory in every way, light in weight, easily and quickly installed, and comparatively inexpensive," the articles crowed. As for the roofs, "Fireproof roof construction has always been somewhat of a problem; ... The form adopted proved not only less expensive, but entirely free from all condensation, an objection so common in most concrete construction." Both articles noted that the details of the building's construction were "designed by the Trussed Concrete Steel Co., the manufacturer of the trussed bar and contractor for the work in this building."[21]

While preparing for its move to Detroit, American Arithmometer encouraged its roughly 400 St. Louis–based employees to remain with the company, promising to relocate them and their families to Detroit. As construction of the new factory wound up around the beginning of October 1904, the company chartered a train to carry the employees, their families and possessions, and the machinery of the plant to their new home. A welcoming party headed by Detroit's mayor William C. Maybury and the president of the Board of Commerce, J. L. Hudson, met the train as it crossed into Michigan. The train pulled into Detroit's railroad station at 9:40 p.m., and Detroiters who had gathered to watch the spectacle greeted the 465 passengers with a round of cheers. A receiving committee guided the new arrivals to dedicated streetcars that transported them to prearranged housing accommodations. The new factory was in operation by the end of October.[22]

In St. Louis, the departure of American Arithmometer was barely noticed, as that city was host to the 1904 World's Fair, a massive enterprise that attracted nearly 20 million visitors (the US population in

1900 was 76 million). Manufacturers from around the world displayed their wares, including the American Association of Portland Cement Manufacturers, which had its own building equipped with a state-of-the-art testing laboratory.[23] Outside of this building were exhibits by firms marketing reinforcement systems for concrete. According to one journal, "The most extensive individual exhibit of reinforced concrete structures was of the Kahn system."[24] Six beams, 17 feet in length, were displayed along with a section of Kahn floor and reinforced concrete columns. The quality of the display earned a gold medal for Truscon from the fair's organizers.[25]

Displays at trade shows and articles in publications increased awareness of the Kahn System and the scientific principles upon which it was based, but Julius understood that interest in his system could only be converted into sales if he could successfully remove impediments to its use. The greatest obstacle faced by those wishing to build with concrete was the lack of trained engineers capable of designing a reinforced concrete building. It was clear to Julius from the outset that his firm could not merely offer reinforcement bars for sale but would have to provide engineering services as well. He could have made such services available for a fee, but decided instead to build the cost into the price of the reinforcement bars and make the engineering service available at no charge.[26] This accommodation made reinforced concrete construction available to any architect, engineer, or contractor, regardless of their lack of experience with concrete construction. The architect would submit drawings for a building to Truscon's engineering department. The engineers calculated the required floor strengths based on the building's proposed use and then created detailed plans for the concrete structural elements—floors, columns, and beams—showing the location of each reinforcement bar. The bars required for each floor were shipped together to the construction site, and each bar was tagged so that its location could be found on the detailed engineering plans.[27]

The small number of construction firms with experience building with reinforced concrete was another impediment to the sale of Kahn Bars. One of the great advantages of concrete was that much of the work could be carried out by unskilled laborers, but only when constantly overseen by well-trained individuals experienced with reinforced concrete. To overcome this obstacle, Truscon offered to provide its customers with a qualified supervisor to manage the concrete work. In October 1904 the company established the Concrete Steel and Tile

Construction Company to handle construction work. The incorporators were nearly the same as those of Truscon, with the addition of architect George D. Mason, Albert's former partner.[28] Over the next several years, Concrete Steel and Tile would construct many of the most consequential Kahn System buildings.

As 1904 drew to a close, the number of buildings completed or under construction using the Kahn System was small but significant. In its first year of operation, Julius's company had established a presence from coast to coast through a network of sales agents in major cities. The frequent publication of articles, letters, and catalog announcements, provided by the company to industry journals, brought awareness of the Kahn System to engineers and architects. The Trussed Concrete Steel Company had achieved a national presence and was well poised for growth in 1905.

Ransome's method of construction was at the same time beginning to receive wider attention, aided by the few construction firms having experience with the system, such as Turner in New York and Aberthaw in Boston. In 1904 Ransome constructed the Kelly and Jones factory in Greensburg, Pennsylvania, the first of his concrete factories to dispense with the appearance of a mill construction building and employ a full concrete frame with maximum window area—a daylight factory. Ernest Ransome was the architect and engineer of the building, and his construction firm was the contractor. This was followed by the similarly designed factory complex for the United Shoe Machinery Company in Beverly, Massachusetts, completed in 1905 and composed of three buildings, each 60 feet wide by 522 feet long and four stories high. The concrete work was engineered by Ernest Ransome, and the contractor was the Fosburgh Company of Boston.[29] In Brooklyn, the Robert Gair Company had plans drawn for a brick-and-timber structure of six stories, the maximum height permitted under the building code for mill construction. The contractor, Turner Construction, convinced Gair to switch to reinforced concrete, which resulted in a building that was slightly higher in initial cost, but had lower fire insurance and maintenance costs. As a bonus, by avoiding code restrictions, the building was made eight stories high. Construction was begun in the fall of 1905 and completed in 1906.[30]

All three of these projects received favorable and detailed coverage in industry journals; a newspaper article on the Gair Building claimed, "Builders and insurance men all over the country are watching with interest."[31] Taken together, these projects demonstrated that large industrial buildings could be economically constructed using the Ransome method. As impressive as these buildings were, though, there was a considerable obstacle to replicating similar structures on a widespread scale. The engineering work on two of these buildings was carried out by Ernest Ransome personally and the Gair Building was engineered by Henry Turner, who worked ten years for Ransome prior to founding Turner Construction in 1903.[32] To construct a building using the Ransome method required hiring for the concrete work Ransome's firm or one of the few firms, like Turner, licensed to employ the method.[33] Given the limited number of individuals qualified and licensed to construct a building using Ransome's system, it wasn't foreseeable that there would ever be a vast number of buildings constructed using the method.

Ransome was in the business of selling engineering and construction services. Julius, however, saw himself in the business of selling steel reinforcement bars, the worldwide market for which was nearly unlimited. By the end of 1905, the path taken by Julius permitted his firm to surge past Ransome's in sales and recognition for achievements in reinforced concrete construction. The two most significant concrete structures erected that year were both constructed with Kahn System reinforcement, the Blenheim Hotel in Atlantic City and the Farwell, Ozmun, Kirk and Company warehouse in St. Paul, Minnesota.[34]

The Blenheim Hotel was significant for a number of structural and aesthetic achievements, not the least of which was its claim to be the largest reinforced concrete building in the world.[35] The hotel was built by Josiah White, owner of the Marlborough House, a large hotel constructed in 1900 of iron, stone, and timber. In April 1902, a massive fire swept through Atlantic City destroying 11 hotels, including the Luray, also owned by White. In the wake of the fire, Atlantic City required that all new hotels be of fireproof construction. As a defense against the possibility of fire, the Marlborough House established its own fire department, equipped with a custom-built fire engine that could fit on the building's elevators.[36]

The Marlborough House was quite successful, and White believed the market would support another luxury hotel, which he planned to build on the adjacent property. (The new hotel was called the Blenheim, but once opened, White's two adjacent hotels were known collectively as the Marlborough-Blenheim.) White required the architect of the Blenheim, William L. Price, to have the hotel completed prior to the 1906 summer season. A second condition imposed was that construction noise be kept to a minimum so as not to disturb the guests of the Marlborough. It would have been difficult to meet these requirements had the building been constructed with a steel frame, as a series of strikes and strike threats in the steel industry threatened delays and the racket produced by riveting the steel members would have made the nearby guest rooms in the Marlborough uninhabitable. Consequently, Price sought quotes on both steel and Kahn System reinforced concrete construction and was pleased to find that the concrete option would cost $126,000, nearly $100,000 less than steel. More importantly, work could be started immediately, while the wait for structural steel would delay the project at least four months.[37]

Construction began June 12, 1905, and was largely complete a mere five and a half months later on December 1. The hotel was 600 feet long and 125 feet wide, eight stories high with a dome that reached 12 stories, and contained 250 guest rooms. Roughly 550 tons of Kahn reinforcement bars were used in the building.[38] The architect viewed the Kahn hollow-tile floor as the most "significant feature of the construction," as it greatly reduced the time required to erect the building and reduced by more than 7,000 tons the weight of the floors the building had to support.[39] A clever innovation was the use of Kahn Bars to support the building's numerous balconies as cantilevered extensions of the main floors. This permitted the balconies to extend up to six feet from the exterior wall without any additional means of support.[40]

The Blenheim's concrete construction resulted in substantially reduced expenses for fire insurance. The premium was reported to be "less than one-third of the lowest rate ever fixed before on a building of like size in Atlantic City" and resulted in an annual savings of $18,000.[41]

The entire exterior of the structure was concrete, the space between columns having been filled in with terra cotta blocks and covered with a thin layer of concrete. The appearance of the Blenheim was notable in that it was "frankly treated as concrete" rather than manipulated to look like stone or hidden beneath a decorative layer of brick.[42] Price added an enormous, concrete dome to the building and had it covered with gold and green terra cotta. Other eye-catching terra cotta accents were added in the same colors, complemented by rows of orange and red tiles. The building's exterior was enlivened by numerous balconies, bay windows, and vertical buttresses that provided texture and depth.

The Blenheim Hotel on the Atlantic City Boardwalk, ca. 1908. (Library of Congress, Detroit Publishing Company photograph collection, control number 2016795897)

After more than 70 years of successful service, the Marlborough-Blenheim was demolished in 1978 to make way for Bally's Atlantic Hotel and Casino. The former Marlborough House was easily razed with a wrecking ball, but the concrete Blenheim required stronger measures: the building had to be imploded.[43]

Farwell, Ozmun, Kirk and Company of St. Paul, Minnesota, was a successful hardware and consumer products wholesaler. The firm occupied a building constructed in 1893 after a fire destroyed its previous home. By 1905 the company required larger quarters for its growing business, and the company's architect, Louis Lockwood, planned a large mill construction building. Representatives from Truscon intervened and convinced the firm to construct a concrete building, which could be had at a cost of just 7.5 percent more than the proposed timber-and-brick structure.[44]

Work was begun on the concrete frame of the Farwell, Ozmun, Kirk and Company building (now the Ramsey County Government Center East Building) on June 1, 1905, and the roof was completed by the end of November that year, an impressively rapid pace of construction considering that the nine-story, 450,000-square-foot building was said to be the largest concrete warehouse in the country.[45] As the building was going up, a 10-story, steel-frame office building was being erected for Security Bank in nearby Minneapolis. A newspaper article on June 17, 1905, reported that construction of the bank was delayed due to the "inability to get steel columns." "Steel mills in the east will not stop rolling beams to roll columns," the article explained. "Now, they are rolling beams and they will continue to roll beams until they get through." Nearly 13 months later the paper reported that the building was finally "nearing completion."[46]

Due to the nature of the products to be warehoused in the Farwell building, the floors were designed for a relatively high safe load of 500 pounds per square foot. They were tested by loading one section with pig iron to a weight of 1,500 pounds per square foot, which produced a deflection of only 1/64 of an inch. A photograph taken of this test shows two men casually leaning against an eight-foot-high pile of iron weighing 156,000 pounds. The photo was published in the *Engineering Record* along with a letter from Truscon's chief engineer, Maurice Goldenberg, asserting that concrete beams tested in place in a completed structure produced results quite different from those obtained when testing a single, isolated beam in the laboratory. "With a load of 1,500 lb. per square foot on this floor, the stress on the steel would be considerably in excess of the elastic limit," considered to be the ultimate strength of a beam. "Nevertheless," noted Goldenberg, "there was no apparent effect upon the [floor] slab." Among the reasons for this, Goldenberg stated, is that beams in the laboratory, isolated from floor slabs and other structural members "will very likely fail by compression" (crushing of the concrete in the top of the beam). For beams in structures, "failure by compression is almost unknown."[47]

Not long after the building was occupied, its fireproof construction was tested. On the evening of March 31, 1906, a fire started on the sixth floor, growing large enough to set off the automatic sprinklers, which doused the flames. The building was unharmed, though $600 worth of merchandise was damaged, mostly by water. The fire appeared to be the work of unintentional arsonists: it was claimed that rats gnawing on matches caused them to ignite and set fire to tableware wrappers.[48]

The Blenheim Hotel and Farwell buildings demonstrated that the Kahn System was well suited to large and complex projects, particularly when rapid completion was a concern. The ensuing publicity inspired increased confidence in the method's economy, speed of construction, and application to widely varied requirements.

The year 1905 also saw significant success for Truscon's affiliated firm, the Concrete Steel and Tile Construction Company. In Brooklyn, New York, the Hanan & Son shoe company sought to increase its factory space by constructing a new building that would adjoin its existing five-story, brick-and-timber factory. The new building, of reinforced concrete, was engineered by Truscon and constructed by Concrete Steel and Tile. In order to blend the appearance of the new building with the existing structure, its exterior was clad with bricks of the same color. Unlike the older building, though, the bricks are merely a curtain wall, supported by the same concrete beams that support the building's floors. Typically, a curtain wall of this type was applied in order to completely hide the concrete frame of the building, but in this case, a small section of the beam was molded to extend even with the bricks over each window, thereby presenting the appearance of a stone lintel—an unusual adaptation made for aesthetic purposes.[49] The building remains in use today at 220 Water Street.

One of the earliest uses of reinforced concrete for railroad buildings was the roundhouse for the Grand Trunk Railway in Mimico (Toronto), Ontario, Canada, constructed by Concrete Steel and Tile in 1905 with the Kahn System. Roundhouses were used for performing maintenance on locomotives, work that involved flammable materials and open flame. Concrete offered a cost-effective, durable, and fireproof building far more suitable for the type of work performed than the brick and timber typically used. According to *Engineering Record*, the Grand Trunk's concrete roundhouse "attracted considerable attention from railroad officials." Indeed, articles appeared in numerous journals and even newspapers announcing the construction of a concrete roundhouse. Interestingly enough, the architect of this innovative structure was Walter S. Painter, who replaced Albert Kahn as George D. Mason's partner in 1902 when Albert left to join with Julius.[50]

During construction of the roundhouse, a test section composed of a roof panel, supported by girders and four columns, was constructed adjacent to the roundhouse, the purpose being to "inform definitely the officials of the railway the exact strength of the roundhouse." This extra section was left in place six months to allow the concrete to cure while the roundhouse was completed.[51] On July 26, 1905, the section was tested by piling gravel on top of it, held in place by a framework of boards. When the weight of the gravel reached 500 pounds per square foot, far in excess of the 75-pound safe load, the deflection in the girders was only half an inch and the floor slab had a one-inch deflection. At 850 pounds, cracks became visible near the center of the girders. More gravel was piled on, and by 4:00 p.m. its weight amounted to just under 300,000 pounds, or 1,260 pounds per square foot; the girders were deflected four inches and the floor, six. Given the ominous sagging of the floor and girders, no further weight was added, and by 6:00 p.m. the girders and floor had each deflected another two inches. The day's work having lasted longer than anticipated, and with dinner in the offing, a rope was thrown over the test section and tightened with the intention of expediting the final collapse, but this failed to have any effect. Before long, though, the supporting columns began to gradually buckle outward and the test section settled slowly to the ground.[52]

The test demonstrated the legitimacy of Julius's contention that the Kahn Bar was exceptionally safe under conditions of excessive overloading. The test section's extreme deflection and the appearance of cracks provided an obvious warning of impending failure; when the end came, there was no sudden collapse, but rather a slow settling. The test also demonstrated the cleverness of Truscon's marketing: the test was described in detail in *Engineering Record*, *Cement Age*, and *Railway and Engineering Review*. The article in *Railway and Engineering Review* was authored by civil engineer F. F. Weld, who noted that concrete's "freedom from corrosion and its fireproof qualities make it especially adapted to [roundhouse] construction," and "a great saving in time can be effected by using the concrete-steel construction." It was not mentioned, however, that Fred F. Weld was not a journalist but the chief draftsman for the Trussed Concrete Steel Company.[53]

In Elgin, Illinois, Alfred B. Church had caught the eye of the Kane County board of review, which sought to increase county revenue in 1903 by taxing his extensive stock holdings—as the stepson of the late Gail Borden, inventor of condensed milk, he was quite wealthy. Church was so infuriated by the county's money grab that he "quit Elgin forever" and moved to the East Coast. One of Church's business interests was the Elgin-based Star Watch Case Company, a manufacturer of high-quality watch cases. In 1904 fire destroyed the company's factory, providing Church with an opportunity to fulfill an earlier vow that he would move his businesses from Kane County as well. Church decided to relocate Star to Ludington, Michigan, a town on the shore of Lake Michigan that, due to the area's bustling lumber industry, had excellent port facilities and railroad connections.[54]

Considering the rough treatment meted out by flames to the previous factory, Church wanted his new one to be fireproof. He hired Detroit architects Edward Van Leyen and Edward Schilling to design the factory. Construction on the concrete factory began in April 1905 and was completed in early fall. The Fruechtel Construction Company of Saginaw, Michigan, was the general contractor and the concrete work was subcontracted to Concrete Steel and Tile, which used Kahn System reinforcement for all beams, columns, and floors. This was the first factory building in Michigan constructed entirely of concrete.[55]

Wristwatches became widely used during the First World War, as soldiers needed a durable and easily referenced timepiece to coordinate operations. After the war the popularity of wristwatches boomed, and Star was one of the few firms able to transition from manufacturing pocket watches to the newer style. The factory expanded in 1919, and by World War II the firm had more than 500 employees. The highly skilled workforce, accustomed to manufacturing small products to extremely tight tolerances, was engaged during the war to produce waterproof, stainless steel watch cases for the military, as well as compass cases, small arms, and even parts for the Norden bombsight. Unfortunately, the US government prohibited the manufacture of civilian watches during the war, thereby providing an opportunity for the Swiss, unburdened by war production, to gain a foothold in the American watch market. After the war, domestic manufacturers were unable to regain market share lost to Swiss and, later, Japanese companies. In 1982 Star Watch Case, the manufacturer of cases for Elgin, Gruen, Longines-Wittnauer, Hamilton, Waltham, Omega, and many others, closed its doors; the factory complex at 306 South Rath Avenue was later demolished.[56]

Julius's company had, by the end of its second year in operation, achieved spectacular success. Nearly 1,000 structures throughout the country had been completed or were under construction using the Kahn System.[57] Architects with no previous reinforced-concrete experience were comfortable specifying the system because the concrete engineering was performed by Truscon. Contractors could confidently take on the construction of concrete buildings knowing that the concrete work could be overseen by Truscon's associated construction firm.

Though Truscon ran a handful of advertisements during 1905 to promote its system, the extensive coverage provided by trade publications was likely more effective. In the six months from July through December 1905, *Engineering Record* ran seven articles on various concrete structures built with the Kahn System.

There were developments on the home front for Julius as well. His wife Margaret gave birth to the couple's first child in February 1906. On the day of the birth, according to Margaret, Julius "went about like a Tom-boy, full of laughter and mischief, and when people came to congratulate him, he pulled himself up until he looked twice as tall and twice as broad—a great big proud father!"[58] The child, Gisela, would grow up to become the first woman inducted into the United States Chess Hall of Fame and the first American woman to earn a chess master's rating. Gisela learned chess in 1938 at age 32 while sailing from France to New York. She won her first US women's chess championship in 1944, eventually winning nine times by 1969.[59]

Given the close relationship between Albert and Julius Kahn, it's surprising that Albert was not in the forefront of reinforced concrete construction in Detroit. Albert could have designed the first all-concrete factory in the state, but surprisingly he was unwilling to forego cast iron columns in favor of concrete for the 1904 Burroughs plant (or was unable to convince Joseph Boyer to do so). Other architects in Detroit were ahead of Albert in reinforced concrete construction during 1905: George D. Mason had three concrete buildings underway that year, including two large hotels, and John Scott had a seven-story cold storage building going up. All four of these structures used the Kahn System.[60] The following year, however, the situation changed dramatically, as Albert's relationship with Truscon resulted in a complete transformation of his architecture business.

8

Big Changes
for a Big Industry

No industry was more greatly impacted by the advent of reinforced concrete building technology than motor vehicle manufacturing, and for good reason. Automobile manufacturing prior to 1900 was essentially a cottage industry, but that changed quickly. Though domestic production of 11,000 automobiles in 1903 was barely measurable among the nation's industries, the leading manufacturers, Oldsmobile, Cadillac, and Ford, in their efforts to respond to rising demand were already pressing up against the limits of mass production technology. As they implemented methods to increase output and efficiency, it became clear that one significant impediment to increasing production was the obsolete design of the buildings that served as factories. The state-of-the-art manufacturing building of 1902 was the mill construction design dating from the 18th century, somewhat improved by the addition of sprinkler systems and automatic fire doors. Most consumer-product manufacturers at the time were little hampered by such structures, but automobile production required a large assembly area and heavy machine tools.

Aside from the incompatibility of high volume production of vehicles in the cramped quarters of mill construction buildings, automobile manufacturers had two overriding concerns in their factories: The

The chassis painting department of the Carter Car Motorcar Company of Pontiac, Michigan, in 1905. The cramped workspace within this typical mill construction factory is interrupted by numerous timber columns and poorly illuminated by the limited number of windows. (Detroit Public Library, Burton Historical Collection, EB01a034)

ever-present danger of fire was the first, particularly as highly flammable solvents, paints, fuels, and lubricants were used in the manufacture of vehicles. The second was the need to construct buildings rapidly. As manufacturers saw the number of orders for the coming production season grow beyond current capacity, they would scramble to have additional factory space constructed. This may seem like a failure to perform proper business planning, but in the industry's early years, while total output increased rapidly, the demand for individual brands fluctuated significantly. Domestic production of motor vehicles was 131,000 in 1909, a 1,200 percent increase over the number produced in 1903.[1]

The hazard of producing automobiles in buildings constructed primarily of wood and brick became evident early on. After the Olds Motor

Works factory on Jefferson Avenue in Detroit burned to the ground in 1901, the city of Lansing, where the company had a second plant, gave Oldsmobile 56 acres of land and a cash payment as an incentive to move its operations to that city. The money was later returned with the explanation that having two factories was "good insurance." "If one should be destroyed by fire we could take care of our most pressing orders at the other."[2]

Next to Oldsmobile, the second-highest-volume producer of motor vehicles in 1903 was the Cadillac Motor Car Company, located on Amsterdam Street in Detroit. In January 1904 a gasoline fire started in a car at the factory. Disaster was averted as firemen immediately extinguished the flames—the fire station was conveniently located next door.[3] The respite was short-lived, however; on April 13 the cap on a riveting machine blew off, allowing hot oil to spray about, causing a fire that, fed by varnish and gasoline, spread quickly. The fire burned through sections of the main factory and partly demolished a nearly completed new wing being added to the plant.[4] Though the fire caused no deaths, a number of workers suffered harrowing experiences. Margaret Overbeck "had to be dropped out of a third story window" to escape the flames.[5] At the time of the fire, Cadillac had a backlog of orders valued at $3 million. The company figured that if it could return to full production within 30 days, about $500,000 worth of those orders would be lost.[6] Cadillac did not wish to risk another fire and planned to rebuild using fireproof construction. The method selected by its architects, Rogers and MacFarlane, was steel frame enclosed in terra cotta tile. Cadillac also had its existing, undamaged structures rebuilt, making them fireproof as well.[7]

Oldsmobile and Cadillac learned the hard way that the life expectancy of traditional mill construction buildings might be short when vehicle manufacturing took place within. One of the few firms to anticipate this problem from the outset was the Thomas B. Jeffery Company of Kenosha, Wisconsin, manufacturer of the Rambler automobile. The company began operations in a former bicycle factory of typical mill construction, then in 1903 it added a large, single-story building they claimed was fireproof. With its floor and walls of concrete, and with iron interior columns, the structure was more resistant to fire than traditional factories. But the wooden beams supporting the roof were far from fireproof.[8] The building was designed by Kenosha architect Charles A. Dickhaut, who had other buildings with concrete floors to his credit. Dickhaut's architecture and engineering expertise was largely self-taught. After attending the Chicago College of Technology for two years, he returned to Kenosha around 1888 and opened his own architecture practice. He met an untimely death at age 45 when in 1908 a flour storage building he had designed, of concrete reinforced with wire and pipe, collapsed while he and others were removing the shoring. The coroner's inquest found that the "the accident was wholly due to faulty and incorrect construction."[9]

After its Detroit factory burned to the ground, Oldsmobile rebuilt and continued to manufacture in Detroit.[10] The 1901 fire destroyed some of the company's patterns, a serious and costly loss, as the patterns were the master forms or models on which individual vehicle parts are based. To minimize the chance of this happening at its Lansing factory complex, in 1904 Olds hired the firm of Field, Hinchman and Smith, Engineers and Architects (later known as Smith, Hinchman and Grylls) to design a standalone, fireproof pattern-storage building. For the two-story structure, the firm specified brick exterior walls, steel supporting columns, and Kahn System reinforced concrete floors and roof.[11] The floors and roof were constructed by Truscon's Concrete Steel and Tile Construction Company. This was the first reinforced concrete building constructed within an automobile factory complex.

In major cities, many early automobile owners stored their vehicles in large garages. The inconvenience of not having the vehicle located at their home or apartment was mitigated by the fact that most of these early adopters had chauffeurs to fetch their cars. The hazard of housing, fueling, and servicing many gasoline-powered vehicles within buildings constructed of wood in a densely populated area was obvious and, by the end of 1903, it was becoming common to construct these garages of noncombustible materials with concrete floors. In Boston, less than two years after constructing its first auto garage, the Massachusetts Automobile Club ran out of room to store its member's cars. It built a three-story addition of stone, brick and terra cotta, with concrete floors.[12] In New York City, the Automobile Club of America initiated construction in 1905 of an eight-story garage and clubhouse supported by a steel frame encased in concrete. The floors were of reinforced concrete and constructed by Truscon's Concrete Steel and Tile Construction Company.[13]

In May 1905 the E. R. Thomas Motor Company of Buffalo, New York, announced that it planned to erect a new, three-story automobile factory on land behind its current building at 1200 Niagara Street. The new plant, it was noted, would be constructed entirely of reinforced concrete. The building's architect was Sydney H. Woodruff, better known now for having erected the 1923 "Hollywood" sign in Los Angeles.[14] Besides the Thomas plant, Woodruff was in the midst of designing reinforced concrete industrial buildings in Buffalo for Jacob Dold Packing and the Buffalo Lounge Company.[15] Plain round bars were used for reinforcing the concrete in the Thomas factory. Construction progressed slowly; by mid-September the building was only up to the second floor.[16] Impatient to utilize the additional space to meet an order backlog, some Thomas autoworkers occupied part of the unfinished building the first week of December, even as concrete was being poured nearby.[17] When it was finally completed in February 1906, the Thomas plant was an L-shaped building, three stories tall with a half basement and about 60,000 square feet of space.[18] The building remains in use to this day by the Rich Products Corporation.

Meanwhile in Detroit, Cadillac needed additional space at its factory on Amsterdam Avenue. On July 29, 1905, Cadillac head Henry M. Leland visited the office of architect George D. Mason and discussed with him the construction of a new building on property adjoining the existing plant. By August 23, Mason had worked up a cost estimate for a reinforced concrete factory building and presented it to Leland. Five days later, Leland once again visited Mason's office to review the plans and receive a detailed explanation of concrete construction.[19] Leland's openness to reinforced concrete was most likely due to his having watched from his office window the construction of the nearby Burroughs factory in 1904 as well as the new, three-story, fully reinforced concrete Burroughs factory building under construction at that time just 400 feet from the Cadillac plant. Both had been engineered by Truscon and erected by Concrete Steel and Tile, the same firms that Mason proposed for the construction of Cadillac's new factory. Leland likely appreciated that, aside from being lower in cost, using concrete instead of structural steel would permit construction to begin immediately, avoiding the wait for steel beams and columns to be fabricated and transported from the mill.

On the evening of September 6, Leland phoned Julius Kahn to agree to the Truscon contract and give the go-ahead to begin work. The following morning, excavation began at the building site and Truscon placed a large display ad in that day's classifieds seeking "laborers and

This photo shows the Cadillac automobile plant at 450 Amsterdam Street in Detroit under construction on October 23, 1905. The first-floor concrete has been poured and the forms removed. The second-floor concrete has been poured and the forms remain in place. Workers on the third floor are building the wooden forms and installing Kahn Bars in preparation for pouring the floor and support columns for the roof. Numerous vertical boards (shoring) support the floors until the concrete cures sufficiently to support its own weight. The building was completed less than three weeks later. (Detroit Public Library, Burton Historical Library, resource ID: MR0353)

teams for excavating."[20] On September 10, a single paragraph appeared in the *Detroit Free Press* announcing that George Mason was constructing an addition to the Cadillac plant at a cost of $75,000.[21] The first Kahn Bars were delivered to the site on the 11th; on the 20th, two weeks after Leland had agreed to the contract, the first concrete was poured. The *Detroit Free Press* published an article on the new factory on October 16 accompanied by a photo showing that construction of the third (and final) floor had begun. According to the article, 150 men were at work on the structure; a Cadillac spokesman was quoted saying, "We hope to occupy the building early in December."[22] A construction photo taken November 4 shows all the concrete work completed and the bricks going up on the building's exterior.[23] Another photo, dated November 19, 1905, shows the completed building.[24]

The new Cadillac factory, located at 450 Amsterdam Street, was the world's first reinforced concrete automobile factory—the first structure constructed entirely with the transformative, new building technology for an industry that would itself become not only transformative but the nation's largest manufacturing field. The building is three stories high (plus a full basement), contains over 94,000 square feet, and was completed in 67 days, an incredible achievement.[25] Cadillac operated from the building until 1946, when it was sold to the Westcott Paper Products Company, which occupied the building until 2021.

As Concrete Steel and Tile finished with the Cadillac building, its workforce was redeployed to the Packard Motor Car factory to build a small addition designed by Albert Kahn's firm. At the time, the Packard plant was composed of the one- and two-story mill construction buildings designed by Albert and Julius two years earlier. Packard No. 10, as the new building was called, was small, just over 17,000 square feet on two floors, suggesting that its construction was intended to convince Packard head Henry P. Joy that concrete was a viable alternative to traditional construction.[26] Work on the site began around November 13, 1905, and the building was likely completed during January 1906.[27] Many sources claim that this building, Packard No. 10, was the first reinforced concrete automobile plant, which clearly it was not. More significant is the common but erroneous claim that Packard No. 10 represented a revolutionary and highly influential innovation that paved the way for future concrete factories. On the contrary, there was almost no media coverage of the building at the time it was constructed, and Albert Kahn's firm thought so little of the job that no photos were taken of its construction.[28]

With the large Cadillac factory completed, Julius recognized the enormous potential market represented by the rapidly growing vehicle manufacturing companies. With sales offices throughout the country, Truscon was perfectly positioned to secure work constructing automobile factories.[29] Newspaper reports on the auto companies made marketing easy; construction of new automobile factories was important news, with coverage typically beginning early in the planning process, allowing Truscon to get its salespeople in the door from the outset to promote the advantages of concrete over other construction methods.

Truscon's aggressive pursuit of factory construction for automobile manufacturers paid off handsomely in 1906, as the firm secured four substantial auto plant projects. The first was for the George N. Pierce Automobile Company of Buffalo, New York, manufacturer of the Pierce-Arrow. An article in the *Buffalo Evening News* on January 2, 1906, stated that the Pierce firm had acquired 15 acres of land to build a new automobile factory complex.[30] Then on January 24, the *Buffalo Times* ran a larger article headlined "Great New Plant for Pierce Co." that quoted the company treasurer: "As to the nature of the building, etc., we have not yet decided, except that we expect to have a practically fire-proof structure."[31] By this point, Truscon was attempting, without success, to convince Pierce of the superiority of concrete construction. To design its plant, the auto company had hired the architecture and engineering firm Lockwood, Greene and Company of Boston. Lockwood had extensive experience designing mill construction buildings, but none with reinforced concrete and, according to Albert Kahn, "It was utterly impossible to convince this firm of the advantages of reinforced concrete."[32]

Fate intervened, however, at 11:30 on the night of February 25 when a fire broke out in the four-story building on Main Street that was home to portions of the Pierce Company's automobile and bicycle manufacturing operations. By 1:00 a.m., the building, including its sprinkler system, was "a smoking ruin." The loss was estimated to be close to $100,000, but according to the local Pierce sales manager, the most serious impact was the inability of the company to meet orders. "The fire did put us back considerably," he stated. "The department destroyed was where we tested all the motors."[33] Truscon, previously rebuffed by Pierce, was hired on April 15 to convert the Lockwood Greene factory design to reinforced concrete. Albert Kahn was brought in as "associated architect" to work as an equal partner with Lockwood Greene, a step taken due to, in the words of the Pierce building committee, "his experience in concrete construction and in automobile plants."[34] Kahn's work designing the Packard factories and concrete Burroughs buildings was viewed by Pierce as complimenting Lockwood Greene's lack of experience in those areas. The Concrete Steel and Tile Construction Company was hired to build the 325,000-square-foot factory complex at a cost of $300,000.[35] The first spadeful of earth was turned at a ceremony on April 26, 1906, and within six months the buildings were complete.[36]

In Detroit, the Packard Motor Car Company, pleased with the way No. 10 turned out, was now sold on concrete as a superior material for its auto factory. In the spring of 1906, the company was ready to add to its complex and planned a large building of around 90,000 square feet that, when completed, brought Packard's total factory space to 310,000 feet. Construction began the first week of April, and the building was completed within two and a half months. The new addition extended from the end of Building No. 10, the end wall of which was opened up so the interior space between the two structures was continuous and unobstructed. (Although contiguous, the new addition was treated by Packard as two buildings, Building No. 11 and Building No. 12.) The addition cost $90,000 and, as before, Albert Kahn was the architect, Truscon the engineering firm, and Concrete Steel and Tile the contractor.[37]

Around the time the Pierce Company's old plant in Buffalo was going up in flames, Arthur L. Garford of Elyria, Ohio, was making city leaders hot under the collar with his threat to move his auto parts manufacturing firm to Cleveland. The Garford Company was formed in May 1905 when a group of investors headed by Garford acquired the Cleveland and Elyria plants of the Federal Manufacturing Company. Garford converted these plants to manufacturing automobile parts and the business was so successful that by February 1906 the factories were booked through the end of the year and had to turn away business. To increase production, Garford planned to build a much larger factory that would combine the operations taking place in the two plants. Garford preferred to locate in his hometown of Elyria, but the new plant was projected to employ 1,500 workers, far more than could be accommodated by existing housing in the city of 10,000. Without a substantial increase in the number of homes, Garford would be forced to build his new plant in Cleveland. The issue was resolved when a number of investors came forward with commitments to construct new homes and Garford made the decision to build his plant in Elyria.[38]

Garford chose to build a concrete factory and awarded the engineering contract to Truscon. Presumably as a result of Truscon's influence, the company selected Albert Kahn as the architect. To handle construction, the Detroit-based Vinton Company was selected. Plans for the 100,000-square-foot plant were ready by the end of March, and the building opened early the following year.[39]

The final factory in the quartet of 1906 auto plants engineered by

An ad for the Kahn System from the February 15, 1907, issue of *Concrete* shows a photo of the E. R. Thomas automobile factory, completed by Concrete Steel and Tile the prior year in Buffalo, New York.

Truscon was the E. R. Thomas Company's building number 4 at its complex in Buffalo. Less than six months after the 60,000 square foot Sydney Woodruff–designed building was completed, the company was cramped for space and sought to have another building of roughly 60,000 square feet. For this new factory, Thomas chose the Kahn System, a decision likely motivated by a desire to have the building erected more expeditiously than had been the case with the earlier concrete building. They also accepted Truscon's recommendation that Albert Kahn be selected as architect of the plant. Construction began early in June and was completed by September.[40]

These four factories represented a total of 575,000 square feet of reinforced concrete construction. This was, as far as can be determined, the vast majority of all new factory space constructed for the automobile industry during 1906.

Albert Kahn's close working relationship with Truscon resulted in a profound change in the nature of the architect's business. Truscon's dominance of the reinforced concrete industry and its network of nationwide sales offices facilitated the firm's capture of nearly all the major reinforced concrete construction of automobile factories during the pivotal year of 1906. Given Albert's previous experience as architect of other Truscon concrete factories and as architect of Packard's automobile plants, when Truscon recommended to Pierce, Garford, and E. R. Thomas that Albert be hired to design their factories, they had good reason to do so.[41]

Prior to 1906, Albert Kahn had designed around 200,000 square feet of automobile factory space, all of it for Packard Motor, and less than 20,000 of it being concrete construction. During 1906, Albert added to this track record 90,000 more square feet for Packard and a whopping 485,000 more as a result of the Pierce, Garford, and E. R. Thomas jobs brought to him by Truscon. He ended the year having designed nearly 600,000 square feet of automobile factory space for four manufacturers in three states, all of it of reinforced concrete.[42] By virtue of this experience, Albert became the leading architect of concrete factories in the United States and unquestionably the most experienced architect of automobile manufacturing facilities.

The dramatic impact these commissions had on Albert Kahn's business can be appreciated by comparing the nature and quantity of architectural jobs recorded by Kahn's company in the years prior to and after 1906. In 1905, Albert's firm listed 23 commissions, of which 14 were residences, or alterations to residences, and four were factories; all located in Detroit. For 1906, his firm recorded 27 jobs, with six being residences and seven being factories—the first year in which the number of factory jobs exceeded residential. All were located in the Detroit area except the Pierce, Thomas, and Garford jobs. The numbers for 1907, however, demonstrate that the firm had achieved a transformative shift in its customer base. Out of 56 total commissions, 13 were for residences and 19 were for factories or factory additions. Most of these factories were automotive related, including the Brown-Lipe Gear Company of Syracuse, New York, for which Albert designed a five-story plant constructed by Truscon and Concrete Steel and Tile. A notable non-automotive job from 1907 was the eight-story Mergenthaler Linotype Company factory in New York City, also constructed by Truscon and Concrete Steel and Tile.[43]

Among the last entries on the list for 1907 was the first job for the Ford Motor Company: a new plant in Highland Park, Michigan, which would soon to be the largest manufacturing facility in the world. A Los Angeles newspaper explained the reason for Kahn's selection as architect: "Albert Kahn, well known as the successful architect of the Packard plant, the Thomas plants at Buffalo and Detroit, the Garford plant and the Pierce, is the architect selected for the new Ford factory."[44] Kahn's firm completed plans for the facility by mid-1908, and the contract for its construction was awarded to the B. M. Zadeck Construction Company of Chicago during August. The massive building—four stories high, measuring 865 feet long and 75 feet wide—was completed in July 1909.[45] Truscon ran advertisements at the time gloating that Ford received 20 bids from contractors for constructing the plant and the five lowest bids all specified the Kahn System. Moreover, the lowest bid for steel frame construction was $65,000 more than Zadeck's bid of $250,000 using the Kahn System.[46]

An unusual feature of the new Ford plant was the type of windows used. Concrete factory buildings typically had banks of three or four double-hung windows installed side-by-side between the support columns. These large, double-hung factory windows were cantankerous in operation and required regular maintenance. The Ford plant was one of the first buildings in the United States to install a new window type that was composed of a steel frame supporting individual panes of glass. The frame was built up from pieces of rolled steel into which notches were cut so that the horizontal and vertical pieces snapped together forming a strong structure. Sections of the frame were hinged and could be opened to allow for ventilation. These windows were manufactured by the Crittall Manufacturing Company in England under the brand name "Fenestra." The first major building in that country on which they were installed was the Lots Road Power Station in Chelsea, constructed 1902–04. Albert Kahn's chief designer, Ernest Wilby, became aware of Fenestra windows and suggested they be used on the Ford Highland Park building. Seeing great potential for this product in the United States, in 1908 Crittall licensed Detroit Steel Products to manufacture and sell "Detroit Fenestra" windows. (The Detroit factory was not yet set up at the time the Ford plant was built, so the window frames were imported from England.)[47]

The Fenestra windows were a great improvement, allowing more light to enter the building, improving ventilation, reducing installation costs, and nearly eliminating maintenance. Within a short time Detroit Fenestra windows were adopted for other buildings, but their dominance of the marketplace didn't last long. In April 1909 Julius Kahn and Thomas H. Kane, manager of Truscon's Youngstown works, filed a patent for a steel window frame. The frame system designed by Kahn and Kane was composed of I-beam shaped rolled bars held together by special bolts. The bars had only small holes punched through their centers, an approach that did not weaken the bar, as did the notches cut through the bars in the Detroit Fenestra frames. Kane further improved the Truscon frame system by inventing an inexpensive and easy-to-install metal fastener to securely hold the glass panes within the metal frame.[48]

Truscon's "United Steel Sash" was first marketed in 1910 and quickly surpassed Detroit Fenestra as the market leader. Detroit Steel Products sold nearly 60,000 square feet of Fenestra window frames to Ford for the Highland Park plant, but that record was surpassed in 1910 when Truscon sold over 80,000 square feet of frames to the Dodge Brothers for their new plant in Detroit and then 95,000 square feet to the Bush Terminal warehouse in New York. Not long after, the United Shoe Machinery Company of Beverly, Massachusetts, replaced all the double-hung windows in its immense factory, constructed by Ernest Ransome in 1906, with United Steel Sash windows.[49] Steel window frames were significant in that they were the technological improvement that brought multi-story, reinforced concrete factories to the pinnacle of development. They also paved the way for the next major development in factory design: single-story buildings almost entirely enclosed by windows.

An ad for Trussed Concrete Steel's United Steel Sash windows from the May 1911 issue of *Western Architect*. Truscon became the country's largest manufacturer of steel sash windows and the window division was the firm's largest and most profitable.

In the long run, steel window frames proved to be one of Truscon's most important products. At the company's 25th-anniversary banquet in 1928, Milton Clark, head of the Steel Window Division, pointed out, "Only a few years ago we were the smallest division of the company. Today we are the largest, not only in volume of sales, but in margin of profit." United Steel Sash was also the leading manufacturer of steel window frames in the country.[50]

Truscon leveraged its success with automobile factories in a clever and cost-effective manner. Throughout 1906 the company ran a series of full or nearly full page ads in trade journals, business magazines, and association publications. Many of these ads stated within the copy that "four of the largest automobile plants in the world are now in process of construction" using the Kahn System, but the featured subject of the ad was typically a non-automotive Truscon building such as the Farwell, Ozmun, Kirk warehouse, the US War College, the Marlborough-Blenheim Hotel, or even the reinforced concrete Chandler Walker residence in Windsor, Canada. To reach auto industry decision-makers, Truscon's strategy was to bombard automobile industry journals with announcements about concrete factories under construction and photographs of the buildings going up. To fill their pages, the journals used this information to produce numerous brief articles on Truscon's work, sometimes accompanied by a photograph of the bare concrete frame of the building, a surprising sight to those accustomed only to mill construction factories.[51] Once the factory was completed, Truscon provided detailed construction information and photographs to *Engineering Record* and, in the cases of the Cadillac, Packard, and Pierce jobs, was rewarded with multipage, illustrated articles that described the method of construction and particular advantages gained by using reinforced concrete.[52] The article on the Pierce factory concluded with a statement of incalculable advertising value: "The buildings were erected in six months by the Concrete Steel & Tile Construction Co. of Detroit. This was about one-third the guaranteed time for either mill construction or steel."

The importance of rapid construction was illustrated in one of the few Truscon advertisements that featured an automobile factory. This ad appeared in January and February 1907 in trade publications and in a number of general-interest magazines as well (*Sunset, The World Today,* and *Everybody's Magazine*). Headlined "From Burned Ruins to Finished Factory in Forty Days," the ad described how architect George D. Mason, Truscon, and the Concrete Steel and Tile Construction Company achieved "a record in fireproof construction made possible by the Kahn System of reinforced concrete."[53] The "burned ruins" to which the ad referred was a section of the Anderson Carriage Company factory located in what is now Detroit's Russell Industrial Center. The structure was of mill construction and only five years old when destroyed by fire.[54] (At the time of the fire, Anderson Carriage had begun manufacturing automobile bodies. The following year, the firm initiated production of its own vehicle, the Detroit Electric, eventually becoming the 20th century's largest domestic manufacturer of electric vehicles.) In a blow to those claiming that sprinkler systems alone could protect brick-and-timber structures from fire, the office building of the Wilson Body Company, adjacent to Anderson Carriage, was also destroyed. The building had a typical fire-suppressing sprinkler system fed by a water tower on the roof. Flames leaping from the Anderson plant ignited the wooden water tower, causing it to rupture and leave the sprinkler system with no ammunition to fight the fire. The flames worked their way down from the roof through the entire building.[55]

On the heels of the "burned ruins" ad came a five-page article by

George J. Seymour in *Cement Age* titled "Another Reinforced Concrete Speed Record." Seymour described in detail how the concrete Anderson Carriage factory was constructed and included photographs of both the exterior and interior. He endorsed concrete construction for accomplishing "what would have taken steel or brick and wood men two or three times as long to complete," and noted that the speed was achieved "without detracting in the slightest from the utmost stability, strength and rigidity" of the structure.[56] The construction contract signed by Anderson on October 4, according to Seymour, committed Concrete Steel and Tile to complete the north half of the building within 40 working days (by November 21) and the remainder, 40 working days later (January 10).[57] Seymour didn't indicate whether these deadlines were met, stating instead that the north half of the building was under roof by October 23 and the south half by November 7. Dated construction photographs show that, although the north half of the factory was not completed within 40 days, the entire structure was finished sometime between December 3 and 11.[58] Erecting a three-story, 80,000 square foot factory in two months was a stunning achievement.

Another strategy employed by Truscon to leverage its automobile factory successes for marketing purposes was unleashed in April 1907: the firm issued a booklet titled *The Typical Factory* describing the construction of the Pierce automobile plant. It was available at no cost to anyone mailing a request on business letterhead. Truscon sent sample copies to numerous trade journals serving the construction and automotive industries. Included with these sample copies was a description of the booklet's contents written so as to appear to be a review. Quite a few journals took advantage of this readily available content. The articles often commended the fine quality of the expensively produced book, conveying clearly that it was not just a cheap promotional piece. More importantly, these write-ups praised the quality, size, and low cost of the concrete Pierce factory and the speed with which it had been constructed.[59] At least one publication lauded the fact that structural work for the entire complex "was completed in approximately six months' time, or exactly one-half the time required by contractors using the ordinary methods."[60] It hardly mattered whether a prospective customer sent for the booklet, these articles effectively conveyed Truscon's marketing message: reinforced concrete offered manifold advantages over traditional construction.

The following year, another booklet on the factory was published,

The Anderson Carriage Company factory building was an 80,000-square-foot factory constructed in just two months. It was located in Detroit's Russell Industrial Center. (Detroit Public Library, Burton Historical Collection, MR0273)

this one issued by the Pierce Company: *The Factory Behind the Great Arrow Car*. Virtually identical descriptions of the book were published in at least four different trade journals beginning in August 1908. The articles began: "Although published with an entirely different object in view, the illustrated book, entitled 'The Factory Behind the Great Arrow Car,' presents a remarkably strong argument in favor of reinforced concrete, the material used throughout this plant." The balance of the write-up contains a concise inventory of the many advantages of concrete construction. Here again, an effective marketing message for Truscon was contained within what appeared to be a review. The fact that the articles appeared in construction industry journals (*Cement Age*, *Concrete Age*, *Industrial Magazine*, and *Canadian Cement and Concrete Review*) rather than auto-related publications suggests that the booklet's content was provided by Truscon rather than the Pierce Company.[61]

It's worthwhile to consider the impact reinforced concrete construction had on automobile manufacturing by eliminating the constraints imposed by obsolete mill construction factories. The article that appeared in the *Canadian Cement and Concrete Review* discussing *The Factory Behind the Great Arrow Car* does a fine job of listing some of the advantages of concrete construction: It has greater strength than brick, so the distance between supporting columns can be much greater, allowing for considerably larger workspaces and assembly areas uninterrupted by structural columns. Compared with brick, concrete buildings permit substantially more window area. Reinforced concrete floors have greater rigidity than wood or even steel floors, reducing vibration which both hinders the machining of parts to tight tolerances and causes greater wear and tear on the machines themselves. Unlike wood floors, concrete floors do not decay or wear, are germ-proof and waterproof, and will not easily absorb flammable liquids.[62] Interestingly, the *Canadian Cement* article does not mention the two most significant advantages of concrete construction: buildings of concrete don't burn, and concrete factories can be constructed far more rapidly than either timber or steel factories. Perhaps by 1908 these two features were well-known and it was more productive to mention the less obvious characteristics of the material.

9

Fatal Mistakes

Construction accidents involving reinforced concrete received far more media attention than those involving other methods. The journal *Engineering Record* highlighted this preoccupation in an editorial: "The collapse of a steel flooring system during the erection of a New York building . . . is not particularly interesting except as it illustrates that other forms of construction other than reinforced concrete must be executed with careful attention to details in order to prevent such accidents."[1] Any accident involving concrete typically sparked calls for greater regulation, limits on the height of concrete buildings, and even outright prohibition of concrete structures. Those with vested interests in other methods of construction seized on any accident to denounce concrete as unsafe, while manufacturers of competing concrete reinforcement systems condemned as inherently flawed the method employed at the accident site. There was significant risk for the Trussed Concrete Steel Company, as a serious accident involving a building constructed with its system would be seized upon by those attempting to blunt concrete's replacement of steel, brick, and timber, and by Truscon's competitors hoping to increase market share at Truscon's expense.

The rapidly growing number of reinforced concrete buildings under construction required an ever increasing number of laborers, most of whom had no experience with concrete. This placed an enormous burden on foremen and supervisors to oversee every aspect of construction: the proper proportions of material in the concrete mixture, the construction of forms, setting up of shoring, placing the reinforcement bars, tamping the concrete mixture into the forms, and keeping the shoring in place until the concrete was adequately cured. With so many Kahn System buildings under construction it was only a matter of time until a serious construction site accident occurred.

The first mistake came on the morning of September 6, 1906, in Elyria, Ohio, at the site of the Garford automobile factory, under construction by the Vinton Construction Company of Detroit using the Kahn System. Workers were removing shoring from a single-story section of the building when a wall and part of the roof gave way, killing three workers and injuring others.[2] Upon receiving news of the accident, Julius set out for Elyria, arriving the following day accompanied by Truscon engineers Maurice Goldenberg and W. H. Dillon.[3] G. Jay Vinton, head of the Vinton Company, also arrived to participate in the investigation. The building's architect was Albert Kahn, but, as the building was well outside the Detroit area, construction oversight had been subcontracted to a supervising architect based in Cleveland.[4]

The three men killed in the Garford accident were Italian nationals.[5] The building boom in the United States attracted laborers from around the world, most of whom spoke little or no English, adding further complexity to the challenge of employing inexperienced workers. One of the bricklayers on the job had 10 years of experience in England, but the Garford building was his first job after having arrived in the United States less than a month earlier.[6]

While Vinton was one of the largest construction firms in the city of Detroit, and had worked on a number of jobs designed by Albert Kahn and George Mason (the Palms Apartments, and Belle Isle aquarium and horticulture building), the firm's experience with reinforced concrete construction was limited; the Garford building may have been its first.

The cause of the collapse was apparent from the start, in part because it occurred as workers were removing the shoring. The concrete in the columns supporting the roof was not sufficiently cured to support the roof's weight unaided by the shoring. The Vinton Company's lack of adequate oversight brought about the accident, and the firm was quick to accept responsibility; within two months, Vinton had agreements in place to compensate those injured by the collapse and the families of those killed.[7] This rapid settling of claims had the added benefit of bringing to an end the coroner's inquest into the three deaths, as he had difficulty securing testimony from witnesses.[8]

The Garford factory was completed without further incident and was used by the company for less than 10 years, by which time the firm had been absorbed by Willys-Overland. The building, at the corner of Clark and Prospect Streets, presently serves as the global headquarters for the Ridge Tool Company, manufacturers of the Ridgid brand of hand tools.

The next mistake occurred two months later on November 9 in Long Beach, California, at the site of the six-story beachfront Bixby Hotel. Workers were pouring concrete to form the roof of the large, H-shaped building when the section in which they were working collapsed into the basement. Ten workers were killed immediately and another succumbed to his injuries two months later.[9]

A banner headline in the following day's *Los Angeles Herald* screamed "Nine Workers Killed in Bixby Disaster," accompanied by a list of nine dead, 26 injured, and 11 missing.[10] An architect, Octavius Morgan, whom the article asserted was an "authority on reinforced concrete work on the coast," immediately attributed the disaster to the Kahn System, used to construct the building's floors and structural beams. Morgan claimed the collapse was due to the use of Kahn "hollow tile floor slabs" rather than "solid concrete," and challenged "the Kahn people to prove their claims that their mode of floor construction is superior."[11] The article's next paragraph quoted the Bixby Hotel's architect, John C. Austin: "The accident was caused by an error in judgment on the part of the contractor," who removed the shoring on the fifth floor too soon.[12] A syndicated article on the collapse that appeared in the *San Francisco Chronicle*, and at least half a dozen other papers, reported that "a representative of the architectural firm says that the accident undoubtedly was due to the fact that the floors in the building were of reinforced tile, which evidently could not stand the weight of the structure."[13] This erroneous report was likely a misguided attempt at summarizing the comments of Octavius Morgan, whom the reporter mistakenly believed was the building's architect. The *Los Angeles Times* article on the disaster stated, "The reinforcing being used [for the floors] is a patent held under the name of Kahn Bar system. There is a division of opinion as to the stability of floors thus constructed. Five of them gave way yesterday in the Bixby Hotel."[14]

FIG. 1. VIEW OF HOTEL BIXBY, LONG BEACH, CAL., UNDER CONSTRUCTION OF REINFORCED CONCRETE.
(View Taken from Sea Front Oct. 25, 1906.)

FIG. 2. VIEW OF HOTEL BIXBY AFTER COLLAPSE OF NOV. 9, 1906.

The Bixby Hotel before and after the collapse of November 9, 1906. (From *Engineering News*, November 29, 1906)

In an effort to subdue the overheated condemnations of the company's floor system, Truscon's Southern California representatives, Heber & Thayer, released a statement carried the same day by the *Los Angeles Herald*: "We do not care at present to express our opinion as to the probable cause of the failure. . . . The design for that portion of the structure in which the Kahn system of reinforcement was used (namely, floors and beams) was . . . in accordance with the formulae used by them in the design for hundreds of buildings throughout the United States."[15] Heber & Thayer extended an invitation to any "disinterested and competent engineer or architect [to] call at our office and check over this design."

Witnesses at the scene disagreed as to whether the top floor fell first causing those below to yield under the weight of falling debris, or whether one of the columns on a lower floor failed, precipitating a collapse of the structure above. A carpenter at work on the fourth floor stated, "The top came first. When it struck the lower floors there was a decided vibration as if the upper floors were forcing the others down as they struck."[16] The building's contractor, on the roof when the building fell, reported that, "the center of the building seemed to sink for about 12 feet. There was no perceptible sound of impact. It went down in the shape of a bowl."[17]

Determining the cause of the accident was complicated because much of the fallen structure had been moved and broken up in the frantic effort to free victims from beneath the debris.[18] The Truscon-designed floors and beams were eliminated from suspicion early in the investigation, as the same design had been successfully employed in hundreds of buildings, and subsequent tests of the floors in the Bixby demonstrated they were properly installed and capable of supporting more than six times the weight for which they were designed.[19] The concrete was found to be of good quality and the foundation, it was determined, had not moved or sunk.[20] This left two possible causes: the premature removal of shoring on the fifth floor or the failure of a structural support column. The columns did not use Kahn Bars; their steel reinforcement was designed by the building's architect and, as investigators discovered, the amount and method of reinforcement was inadequate.[21] Moreover, there was evidence that placement of the reinforcement bars and pouring of the concrete columns had, in some cases, been carried out carelessly.[22]

Ultimately, an investigation by the coroner concluded that the collapse was precipitated by the removal of shoring on the fifth floor before the concrete was sufficiently cured to support the added weight of the concrete roof, a conclusion accepted by nearly all who studied the collapse.[23] While the architect's substandard design for reinforcement of the columns did not cause the accident, it may well have permitted a more extensive collapse than might otherwise have occurred.

Though cleared of any responsibility for the accident, Truscon sought to aggressively counter any concerns about its system and, specifically, any reservations raised by newspaper reports on its use of hollow tile in concrete floors. To achieve this, Truscon took out a nearly quarter-page ad in the Sunday *Los Angeles Times* on November 25. The ad included a photograph of the Bixby Hotel floors being tested by piling hundreds of bags of sand on which nine men were seen standing, accompanied by copy pointing out that the test load was "six times the load for which these floors were designed."[24] A second photo shows the underside of one of the floors and the caption explains that "the concrete joists spanning between the girders carry all the load." Addressing directly the purpose of the hollow tiles, the copy stated: "The rows of hollow tile are merely used to fill the spaces between the joists, which would ordinarily be vacant and unattractive. As far as strength is concerned, all of the tile may be removed without any injury to the construction." To demonstrate how widely employed was the Kahn System, the ad noted that it was used in "five million dollars' worth of building per month" in the United States, and listed five substantial buildings in the local area being constructed with the Kahn System.

Despite the calamity, work resumed on the hotel later in November, and it opened for business in March 1908 as the Hotel Virginia.[25] The hotel only remained open for six months before the proprietors closed it down. The developers had assumed that the city of Long Beach would grant them a "table license" to serve wine in the hotel restaurants, but the temperance-oriented city government refused to do so.[26] "We have tried to conduct the hotel as a temperance hotel," said the hotel's manager, "and have failed of making expenses."[27] The Virginia remained closed for seven months until a compromise was worked out with the city. By 1933 the hotel had passed its prime and was to be razed to make way for parking; wrecking of the building began in late February. A week later, Long Beach was struck by a severe earthquake that, according to one report, "took the job out of the wreckers' hands."[28]

The third mistake occurred a mere 12 days after the Bixby Hotel collapse, and its impact on Truscon was more serious. On the morning of November 21, 1906, the two-story Emulsion Building under construction for the Eastman Kodak Company near Rochester, New York, partially collapsed, killing four men. According to witness accounts, the construction foreman, William Costello, examined the concrete in the roof of the nearly completed building and directed that the shoring be removed.[29] Shortly after the shoring was taken out, "there was a creaking, grinding noise, and then without further warning the roof and the floor of the second story in the northeast corner of the building began to sag. Next came a crash and the entire floor fell."[30]

The building had no architect per se; its general layout and interior arrangement of space were established by Eastman Kodak's internal engineering department, and these requirements were submitted to

Truscon, whose engineers determined the exact design and construction specifications for the reinforced concrete structure.[31] Erection of the building was carried out by Truscon's Concrete Steel and Tile Construction Company, of which Costello was an employee. Given this division of responsibility, it was clear from the outset that Truscon, either as designer of the building or as contractor, would shoulder blame for the accident.

On the day following the collapse, the city coroner had foreman Costello arrested and charged with second degree manslaughter and criminal negligence.[32] Julius Kahn was in Cleveland at the time of the accident and immediately set out for Rochester. Engineer Francis Wilson from Truscon's Detroit office and James Costello (brother of William), in charge of Truscon's Buffalo projects, arrived in the city as well.

On November 23, two days after the accident, the coroner began his inquiry by calling witnesses from Kodak, Truscon, Concrete Steel and Tile, as well as a number of construction workers employed at the site by other firms. The coroner was assisted on technical matters by civil engineer John Y. McClintock, county engineer and former Rochester city engineer. In the course of the inquiry, it came to light that some of the construction had been carried out in an inconsistent and shoddy fashion, particularly as to the placing of reinforcement bars and pouring of concrete. Inspection of the wrecked structure, as well as the building's intact sections, revealed instances of reinforcement bars improperly placed, including bars visible on the surface of the concrete, rather than embedded within. Some columns had sawdust, wood shavings, and leaves along their bottom joint with the column below, a consequence of failing to clean out the wooden form after it was assembled by carpenters. Some of the concrete was found to be of poor quality, having been carelessly mixed or containing sand contaminated with dirt. Columns showed evidence that the vital task of tamping the concrete to fill voids and remove air bubbles was improperly performed.

Most significant was the discovery that one of the columns brought down by the collapse had been constructed differently than specified; the plans showed "column 47" was to have been 18 inches square up to four feet above the main floor and then 12 inches square from that point to the roof. There should have been eight reinforcement bars in the column, four Kahn Bars and four ¾-inch round rods. Investigators examined the fractured remains of the column and found it was 12 inches square for its full length and contained only the four Kahn

Bars. The adjacent column 46, however, contained eight bars where only four were shown on the plan, prompting speculation that the four bars required in column 47 had instead been carelessly placed in the nearby column.[33]

Questioned during the inquiry about the size of the column, Truscon employee Albert Schuett, a 25-year-old engineer and 1903 graduate of the University of Michigan, stated that he had been consulted about column 47 by foreman Costello who asked if it would be satisfactory to construct the column 12 inches square all the way up. Schuett stated that he "thought twelve inches was the proper size," but that he "had no authority to authorize the change." "Costello had the authority," Schuett said, "and I suppose he gave the order after hearing my opinion."[34]

County engineer McClintock concluded that the collapse was caused by the failure of column 47. In his report to the coroner, he stated that the column, as constructed, was incapable of supporting even the dead weight of the floors above. As the concrete in column 47 was three weeks old, McClintock thought there had been sufficient time to allow it to harden adequately, so taking down the shoring later would not have prevented the collapse.[35]

The inquest concluded on December 14, and the coroner issued his report on December 20. That same day the coroner had the assistant manager of Eastman Kodak, Perley S. Wilcox, arrested on a charge of criminal negligence; his bail was paid by George Eastman.[36]

The coroner's report was damning for both Truscon and Concrete Steel and Tile. It stated in part: "I find the Concrete Steel & Tile Construction Co., of Detroit, guilty of criminal negligence in submitting the working drawings, not in conformity with the agreement with the Eastman Kodak Company and allowing pressures upon these columns beyond any safe limit." The coroner charged Costello with criminal negligence for allowing concrete to be poured without proper tamping; placing an inadequate number of reinforcing rods; and "by gross and culpable negligence" permitting debris and contaminants to remain in the concrete forms. Beyond these charges, the coroner stated several "conclusions of fact," the first of which being, "The Kahn bars, and similar bars, with sheer members attached, are not suitable for columns, because of difficulty in properly tamping the concrete."[37]

Perley Wilcox of Eastman Kodak received equally harsh treatment in the report: "I find Perley S. Wilcox . . . an educated engineer and experienced in the construction of buildings, to be guilty of gross and culpable negligence . . . by permitting column 47 to be constructed far weaker than was called for in the original plans made under his direction"; and "in not removing work which was obviously defective." Throughout the inquest, Wilcox and other Kodak engineers asserted that they had no familiarity with concrete construction and were, therefore, entirely reliant on Truscon and Concrete Steel and Tile to inspect and judge the quality of the work. The coroner, however, made a point of quoting from the construction contract that "the owner shall have power to cause any improper, inferior or unsafe work to be taken down and altered" at the contractor's expense.[38] Apparently the coroner felt that Wilcox, in light of his training and experience, was obligated to inspect the structure and object to what the coroner believed were obvious defects in construction.

Eastman Kodak responded to the coroner's report by hiring two leading engineers, Christian W. Marx of Cincinnati and Edwin Thacher of New York, to make their own investigation into the collapse. In their report on the cause of the accident, the two engineers maintained that premature removal of shoring was to blame: "The failure was due to the fact that the supports under girders and floor construction were removed too soon for that season of the year." Had it been "left undisturbed for a period of at least four weeks longer," there would have been no problem. In contrast to the coroner's findings, Marx and Thacher stated that "the concrete throughout was of good quality." They disagreed with engineer McClintock's assertion that column 47 was improperly designed, offering a series of calculations that relied on somewhat different assumptions than McClintock's, and concluded that the load on the column was only 60 percent as great as McClintock claimed.[39]

Marx and Thacher also oversaw a test of the building carried out by two Eastman Kodak engineers on a column "constructed the same as was column 47."[40] The column withstood a weight 12 percent greater than that for which it had been designed. The roof and mezzanine were tested as well and found capable of supporting several times the weight for which they were designed.[41] The difference of opinion between McClintock and the team of Marx and Thacher as to whether the shoring was removed too soon, and the disagreement in calculating the dead load on column 47, while significant, could be viewed as professional differences of opinion. The observation by Marx and Thacher, however, that "the concrete throughout was of good quality" is surprising in light of the harsh criticism of the work by McClintock and the coroner.

Fireproof magazine published the observations of yet another engineer who visited the building two days after the collapse. He found in the columns "a fairly good quality of concrete, with the exception that the sand seemed to be a class of bank sand instead of torpedo, which should have been used." A sample of concrete secured from a floor, however, was found to be "an exceedingly poor quality of concrete" that "should not go into any class of concrete work." He was unable to locate any columns containing sawdust and woodchips.[42] These observations were inconsistent with those of both McClintock and Marx and Thacher.

So the cause of the calamity remained uncertain, at least in the narrow sense of whether the shoring was removed too soon or whether column 47's improper construction was to blame. In a broader sense, though, the cause was not to be found in column 47 or the shoring of the roof, but in the relationship between Truscon and Eastman Kodak. For its part, Eastman Kodak was in the midst of a substantial increase in production capabilities to meet rapidly increasing demand for Kodak film products; they had at least eight buildings under construction by Truscon at the time of the collapse.[43] Truscon had planned to dedicate an engineer to oversee construction at each building, but the number of buildings going up outgrew the number of engineers available. Shortages of lumber and sand of the appropriate quality and type caused delays. Unskilled laborers and skilled workers with appropriate experience were both in short supply. As a consequence, the buildings rose more slowly than Truscon had promised. Eastman Kodak's Perley Wilcox responded by browbeating Truscon's foremen in an effort to speed up the work.

Three weeks prior to the collapse, William Costello notified Julius Kahn that he wished to be relieved from the project due to conflicts that had arisen between himself and Wilcox, differences that Costello stated were personal. Julius sent a telegram to Truscon engineer Francis W. Wilson asking him to intervene with Costello and convince him to remain on the job, which Wilson was able to do.[44]

Eastman Kodak's hectoring to speed up construction was not limited to Truscon's workers at the site. John Mullen, Truscon's onsite superintendent, had been at the building every day, but the home office transferred him to Detroit a week prior to the accident due to "some difficulty with the Eastman people."[45] Henry F. Porter, an engineer who worked on the Eastman Kodak project until several weeks prior to the collapse, described what led to Mullen's transfer: "An inordinate desire for haste possessed the owners and hence the necessarily slow progress begat growing impatience." Finally, a week prior to the collapse, Truscon, "yielding to the clamors of the owners, instituted a change in superintendents."[46] According to Porter, the new superintendent was "a good executive and expert brick mason," yet "was practically ignorant of the requirements for good concrete work." Though he came to the Eastman job from a previous, successfully completed Truscon project, Porter said that his work there had been characterized by "hasty, careless installation."[47]

Even after the collapse, Eastman Kodak continued to press for accelerating the pace of construction. In the first week of January, Kodak reassigned the construction contract from Concrete Steel and Tile to the Frederich Company, a local construction firm. The reason given by Kodak for the change was, "The construction company was not pushing the work as rapidly as we desired. We thought the buildings ought to go up faster, and we told the construction company as much."[48]

In February 1907 the criminal cases of William Costello and Perley Wilcox were heard by a grand jury, which declined to indict either man.[49] This was most fortunate for Kodak as they promoted Wilcox in 1920 to president of Tennessee Eastman Corporation, then placed him on Kodak's board in 1935, and in 1945 elected him chairman of the board. As for those who were killed and injured by the collapse, Truscon and Kodak jointly settled with the families and survivors.[50]

While Wilcox's impatience may have been a factor leading to the collapse, responsibility for the safe and proper construction of the building resided entirely with Truscon. Overwhelmed with more work than it could properly handle, Truscon allowed supervision of critical aspects of concrete construction to be performed by unqualified individuals. Porter argued that Truscon fell prey to its own advertising, which stated, "The system of reinforced concrete is sufficiently simple to permit of its use by the ordinary, everyday contractor without previous experience in reinforced concrete."[51] This was an untrue and dangerous claim, yet the company's performance on the Eastman Kodak Emulsion Building suggests that some in the firm had come to believe it. From the beginning of concrete construction with the Kahn System, it was recognized as essential that the unskilled laborers employed to construct buildings be constantly and carefully overseen by properly trained supervisors with adequate experience in reinforced concrete. The Emulsion Building's second superintendent lacked the necessary knowledge and experience, thereby bringing about the circumstances likely to precipitate a serious accident. Truscon changed their advertising after the Kodak accident to include the statement: "Perfect safety when in the hands of experienced men exercising care in handling the details and giving proper attention to the requirements of the design."[52]

Truscon's public response to the Kodak accident appeared in the form of a lengthy letter by the firm's chief engineer, Maurice Goldenberg, which appeared in the March 16, 1907, issue of *Engineering Record*.[53] Goldenberg did not mention the Eastman Kodak accident by name, but referred to recent "so-called 'failures' in reinforced concrete structures." He stated that these accidents were not due to shortcomings in concrete as a method of construction, but rather "the lack of care and attention on the part of the individual in the handling of details" during construction, echoing the firm's new advertising copy. Goldenberg recited the sobering statistic that of 1,358 workers belonging to the Bridges and Structural Ironworkers' Union in Chicago, 156 were killed or disabled during the previous year while constructing bridges or steel frame buildings—reminding readers that lives are lost in all forms of construction, not just concrete.[54] He emphasized a unique and advantageous feature of concrete construction: if there is any serious defect in design or construction of a concrete structure, it will collapse when the shoring is removed. Structures built of other materials, however, can harbor weaknesses that only become apparent when the structure is placed under stress, most likely after it has become occupied.

Goldenberg took issue with the practice of referring to accidents during construction as a "failure of a reinforced concrete structure" as it implied that the structure, once completed, "did not meet the requirements for which it was planned" or "proved a 'failure' structurally," which, to his knowledge, had never occurred. To demonstrate the "unusual strength and rigidity" of reinforced concrete relative to other construction methods, he cited two examples, the first being the Bekins Building in San Francisco that survived both the earthquake and subsequent fire. The second example was the extraordinary case of a six-story reinforced concrete building in Tunis, Tunisia, which, over the course of several hours on April 22, 1906, tipped to a 25-degree angle due to the subsidence of marshy soil beneath one side. A building constructed of any other material available at the time would have collapsed under similar conditions, but the monolithic concrete structure suffered no damage whatsoever. To restore the dramatically leaning building to level, the high side was loaded up with thousands of tons of sand bags and some of the soil adjacent to the foundation was removed. Within a short time the building righted itself, though it sat about 16 feet lower than before the subsidence.[55] The former grain warehouse remains in use to this day at the corner of Rue Ali Darghouth and Rue Aberrazak Cheraibi in Tunis.

One issue Goldenberg did not address was the "finding of fact" in the coroner's report that Kahn Bars were not suitable for columns due to the difficulty in tamping concrete around the attached shear members. This issue was taken up in the editorial section of *Concrete and Constructional Engineering*, which pronounced that each method of concrete reinforcement had its strengths and weaknesses. The Kahn System, it noted, was particularly well suited to beams and, while less ideal than the European Considère system for columns, was perfectly satisfactory when installed properly.[56] (It was essential to place Kahn Bars properly when constructing beams in order for them to withstand the tension across the bottom of the beam. The primary force on columns, however, is compression, which concrete is quite capable of withstanding. The reinforcement bars placed in columns are not as essential to extracting maximum strength as they are in beams. Consequently, even though the tamping of concrete in the column caused the wings of the Kahn Bar to be somewhat compressed against the bar, the strength of the column was not seriously affected.)

In early 1907 Truscon issued the *Hand Book of Instructions Regarding Material and Workmanship for Superintendents and Inspectors of the Kahn System of Reinforced Concrete*. The book provided "the most minute instructions covering every phase of concrete work from the erection of the falsework to the removal of the forms."[57] Clearly the intention was to more widely disseminate standards or "best practices" established by the company's engineers so there would be less reliance on the individual judgment of supervisors in the field. But it also reinforced the company's new emphasis on the need for "exercising care in handling the details."

The three construction accidents of 1906 had little impact on Truscon's sales, most likely due to the company's safety record, which was exceptionally good: the Eastman Kodak collapse was the sole case in which the firm was at fault for causing a serious accident. Nevertheless, the accident resulted in Truscon winding down its construction subsidiary, Concrete Steel and Tile. In the short time Concrete Steel and Tile had been in operation, it performed the essential service of constructing Kahn System buildings where no other capable contractors were available. By early 1907, however, the number of construction firms competent to erect Truscon-engineered structures had increased dramatically. Truscon's focus was on designing and manufacturing steel products, and it had never sought to nurture Concrete Steel and Tile into a large firm; in fact, the subsidiary frequently operated at a loss. Maurice Goldenberg, a director of Truscon, once said, "That company and its large volume of business was a veritable gold mine of experience, but a gold brick, financially."[58] The last major project for Concrete Steel and Tile outside of Michigan was the 1907 Mergenthaler Linotype building in Brooklyn. In Detroit, the last significant projects for the firm were the Grinnell Brothers Building on Woodward Avenue (1908) and two buildings for the Hammond, Standish & Company slaughtering firm (1908–09).[59]

10

Bridge to the Future

Aside from buildings, the Kahn System was used to construct many other structures, including coal breakers, stadiums, culverts, dams, storage bins, retaining walls, tunnels, and, most importantly, bridges. Of these, architectural historian Carl W. Condit wrote that Julius "Kahn's success is revealed . . . by the number of reinforced-concrete bridges for which he was responsible. Many of these involved novel forms such as long-span simple girders and cantilever girders that appear to have been introduced by Kahn himself."[1]

The chief mode of transportation for both freight and people in 1900 was the railroad, which operated over 200,000 miles of track in the United States (the present interstate highway system has less than 50,000 miles). Tens of thousands of bridges were required to carry tracks over obstacles. Due to the necessity of building large numbers of bridges capable of sustaining the weight of locomotives, railroads were in the forefront of bridge design during the 19th century. Early bridges were constructed of stone or timber, each having distinct disadvantages. Stone, while extremely durable, was quite expensive, and constructing stone bridges in remote locations was challenging. Wooden bridges were cheap and readily constructed but required constant maintenance and were easily damaged or destroyed by fire, often by brush fires started by embers thrown from the locomotives.

During the 1800s iron began to be used for bridges, becoming more common in the 1840s as improved truss designs emerged. In the 1870s the cost of steel fell dramatically as the Bessemer and open-hearth methods of production matured, causing iron to be largely displaced by steel for railroad bridges.[2] One of the difficulties inherent in steel bridge construction was the available means for fastening the steel sections together. The most common method was to pass a pin through holes in the sections, but these sometimes worked loose due to the vibration and flexing caused by passing trains. Riveting systems came into use in the late 1800s, though the early ones were bulky and difficult to use. This problem was eventually solved by the invention of the pneumatic riveting hammer, a tool that could be operated by a single worker to drive rivets through the steel members of a bridge, simplifying construction.[3] The pneumatic riveting hammer was invented by Joseph Boyer, the same Joseph Boyer who moved his machine shop to Detroit in 1900 and subsequently secured for Albert and Julius Kahn some of their most important industrial projects.

While far more ideal than timber and less expensive than stone, steel has its own disadvantages, chief among them is the necessity for maintenance. To resist the destructive progression of rust, steel must have a protective coating (typically paint) which must be constantly renewed, otherwise rust can quickly erode structural integrity. Metal fatigue is another problem: repeated flexing of the structure, due primarily to traffic, results in weakening, cracking, and failure of steel members.

As a consequence of steel's maintenance concerns, concrete offered the potential for a less expensive and longer-lasting alternative. The first concrete bridges were simply stone bridge designs with concrete substituted for stone; but whereas stone bridges were constructed by piling stones to form a self-supporting arch, the concrete versions were typically one solid mass of concrete. These bridges had no metal reinforcement, though sometimes an embedded light metal mesh reduced cracking. The earliest known bridge of this type in the United States was a pedestrian bridge completed in 1872 in Brooklyn's Prospect Park, the Cleft Ridge Span. It was constructed of concrete with the ornate features cast in place, as constructing the bridge of stone as originally planned would have been exceedingly expensive. Not until 1893 was another solid concrete bridge built in the US, this one carrying Pine Road over Pennypack Creek in Philadelphia. For railroads, bridges of solid concrete became common as their

Ernest Ransome's 1890 concrete bridge in Golden Gate Park carries Kennedy Drive over a walkway near the conservatory. The surface of the concrete was treated to give the appearance of stone. (OpenSFHistory/wnp37.02636)

greater mass could better absorb the stresses caused by fast-moving and heavy locomotives.[4]

As with concrete buildings, Ernest Ransome was an early pioneer in reinforced concrete bridges. In 1890 Ransome was working on the Yerba Buena Island torpedo shed and the Leland Stanford Jr. Museum, both of which had exteriors treated to give the appearance of stone rather than concrete. That same year, Ransome was the contractor for two bridges in Golden Gate Park, the Alvord Lake Bridge, a 20-foot span carrying Kazar Drive over a walkway, and a similarly styled bridge carrying Main Drive (now John F. Kennedy Drive) over a walkway directly opposite the entrance to the park's conservatory. Ransome was almost certainly selected as contractor so that the bridges could have the appearance of expensive stone with the much lower cost of concrete. These were the first reinforced concrete bridges in the United States, and possibly the first in the world.[5]

The next development came in 1894, when a modest bridge with a span of 20 feet was built over Dry Run Creek, southeast of Rock Rapids,

Iowa.[6] The bridge was constructed by Fritz von Emperger of the Melan Arch Construction Company. Emperger was the American representative of the Melan system of bridge building, invented and patented by Viennese engineer Josef Melan. The system used heavy I-beams embedded within the concrete to strengthen the structure. Though considered a type of reinforced concrete, it could more accurately be described as concrete-reinforced steel—the bridge contained nearly enough steel to get by without the concrete. Nevertheless, the system worked and represented an improvement over solid concrete. Its chief disadvantage was its excessive and inefficient use of steel.[7]

Later that year Emperger began work on a second and larger Melan bridge in Cincinnati's Eden Park. This 70-foot span is 34 feet wide. Embedded within the concrete structure are 11 I-beams, 9 inches in height and 36 inches apart. Construction bids ranged from a low of $7,130 for the Melan system to just over $12,000 for stone construction. It is notable that the city sought bids for both stone and concrete, but insisted that if concrete was used, it not be made to appear to be stone, as that would constitute "an architectural lie." In order to improve the appearance of the bare, gray concrete, a yellow tint was added to it when mixed. The bridge opened in 1895 and remains in service with slight alterations.[8]

While functional, these bridges were constructed for light duty; the first heavy-duty reinforced concrete bridge is the often overlooked West Grand Boulevard Melan railroad bridge in Detroit, constructed from 1895 to 1896. When completed, it carried seven railroad tracks of the Michigan Central Railroad over two lanes of Grand Boulevard and two sidewalks. While the 50-foot span was slightly shorter than the Eden Park bridge, its width of 109 feet was exceptional. Embedded within the concrete bridge are 41 steel ribs (built up from individual pieces) that are two feet deep at the base and one foot at the top of the arch. So much concrete was used in the bridge, due to its great width, that it was claimed to be the largest monolithic structure in the world as well as the largest Melan arch construction. The exposed vertical faces of the bridge were clad with courses of first-quality stone masonry, likely due to the status of Grand Boulevard as an important street along which large, stately homes had been built. The bridge continues today performing much the same as it did when built, though the four stairways that once led from the sidewalk to the bridge surface have been clumsily bricked closed at the top and the bridge face bears the scars of vehicles attempting to squeeze through an opening not quite tall enough to accommodate them. While the bridge attracted a fair amount of attention when it was constructed, its significance is now recognized only on a handful of websites dealing with historic bridges, one of which describes it as "among the oldest surviving concrete bridges in North America."[9]

Over the ensuing years, variations of the Melan design were developed and patented. The systems were employed to build street bridges throughout the country, but little changed in the technology of bridge construction until 1904, when an unusual bridge designed by architect Peter J. Weber was constructed in Chicago's Jackson Park. Weber was born in Germany in 1863 and moved to Chicago in 1891, working at various times for the architecture firms of Adler and Sullivan and Daniel Burnham. He also helped design buildings for the World's Columbian Exposition—held in Chicago's Jackson Park—and later opened his own firm. In 1903 Weber submitted the winning entry for a contest to design a bridge carrying South Lake Shore Drive over the waterway connecting Jackson Park's Outer Harbor with its South Lagoon. To give his entry a cost advantage over stone or a Melan-type structure, while still offering the ornate exterior its highly visible location required, Weber selected the Kahn System of reinforced concrete. South Bridge, as it is officially known, is clad in pink St. Cloud granite and adorned with carved stone animal and human faces, which gave rise to its nickname, "Animal Bridge." Truscon was the contractor in charge of constructing the 46-foot reinforced concrete span, the first bridge built using the Kahn System. It was completed in 1904. In 2003 the bridge was completely reconstructed and all the original concrete and steel structure was removed. The exterior stone cladding was retained and replaced on the completed bridge, replicating its original appearance.[10]

In Indiana, the fast-growing city of Wabash was an early adopter of emerging technologies. Its population increased by almost 35 percent from 1880 to 1890 and then grew nearly 70 percent more by 1900. Wabash was the first city in the world to be illuminated at night using electric lights. Seeking to replace the city's expensive gas lights, in 1880 two of its residents became aware of the "Brush Light," a form of arc lighting invented by Charles F. Brush, an electrician in Cleveland, Ohio. As an experiment, Wabash placed four of the arc lights atop the city's courthouse and found they provided sufficient illumination such that "the small type of an ordinary newspaper could be read with ease."

"Receding from the light its power diminishes, although for all practical purposes for which it is intended the light is sufficient for one mile from the place it is situated."[11] The experiment was judged a success, so the city purchased the Brush Lights and was soon besieged by officials from other cities seeking information on the system; its hotels were "filled to overflowing with strangers who come to Wabash to see the marvel of the 19th century."[12]

Wabash County began constructing bridges of concrete in 1902 and the following year abandoned steel bridges altogether due to their short lifespan and tendency to fail.[13] In the city of Wabash, the bridge carrying Ferry Street over Charley Creek had been condemned in 1902. As bridge construction was the responsibility of the county commission, the Wabash city council sought to have them build a replacement. The commission refused to grant funds for the bridge due to the fact that, according to the city council, none of the commissioners lived in Wabash, though the city council's insistence on an expensive $15,000 structure may have been an issue. Wrangling between the city and the county ensued until August 1904, when the council took matters into its own hands and awarded a construction contract to a firm that offered to erect the bridge for $9,555. This effort to outflank the county commissioners failed, however, as it was subsequently determined that the city had no authority to appropriate money for a bridge. Nevertheless, this effort finally goaded the county into budgeting the sum of $8,000 for a new bridge, an amount they knew was more than $1,500 less than the lowest bid received by the city. In October the county sought bids for construction but received no satisfactory offers. A second effort in late December was also unsuccessful. Finally in February 1905 the county accepted a bid from John A. Ross of Frankfort, Indiana, to construct a reinforced concrete bridge at a cost of $7,100 using the Kahn System.[14]

The Ferry Street Bridge (also known as the Charley Creek Bridge) was completed during 1905 and is 240 feet long with two 75-foot arches. Most exceptional is the parabolic design of the arches. This is likely the first concrete parabolic arch bridge in the United States and possibly the first in the world of a type that would become popular during the 20th century.[15] The Sixteenth Street Bridge over Piney Creek in Washington, DC, is often credited as being the first parabolic arch bridge, though ample evidence demonstrates it was not: it was begun after the Ferry Street Bridge and not completed until 1906.[16] The editors of *Engi-*

neering News may have caused the confusion when they reported late in 1905, "It is claimed, and we suspect rightly, by the engineers [of the Sixteenth St. Bridge] that this is the first parabolic concrete arch in America."[17] But two weeks later *Engineering Record* reported, "A concrete arch bridge . . . has been commenced at Washington to carry 16th St. over Piney Creek. Like the Charley Creek bridge recently completed at Wabash, the arch rib is parabolic, but, unlike that bridge, it will be of concrete without reinforcement."[18]

A significant amount of press coverage accompanied the completion of the Ferry Street Bridge because of its reinforced concrete construction. The *Manufacturers' Record* referred to the "modern concrete bridge" as "a striking example of reinforced-concrete work as applied to bridges." "This bridge is built entirely of concrete reinforced by the Kahn trussed bar, a form of construction that produces a bridge combining beauty of line, durability, economy and ease of construction." A brief description of the use of the reinforcing bars concluded with the comment that "the erection and placing of these steel members was found to be very simple."[19] *Engineering News* ran an article on the bridge accompanied by detailed illustrations showing placement of the reinforcement bars and the design for the formwork and shoring used to construct the concrete arch. The high level of interest in the bridge may be surmised by the quantity of letters referencing it in subsequent editions of that journal over the next three months.[20]

The Ferry Street Bridge continues to carry traffic over Wabash's Charley Creek and is a candidate for the National Register of Historic Places. It was rehabilitated in 1985 in such a manner as to retain its historical character.[21]

Another parabolic arch bridge constructed in 1905 using the Kahn System is a striking footbridge over a ravine in Milwaukee's Lake Park. The park was planned by Frederick Law Olmsted's firm of Olmsted, Olmsted and Eliot in the 1890s and executed over the following years. The Lake Park Ravine Road Footbridge is of the ornamental type often constructed in parks to serve the dual purpose of carrying traffic and adding visual drama to the landscape. In this respect it is similar to the two Ransome bridges in Golden Gate Park and the Melan Arch Bridge in Cincinnati's Eden Park.

The architectural design for the bridge has in later years been credited to George B. Ferry and Alfred C. Clas of the Milwaukee firm of Ferry and Clas, though a contemporary account states, "The design was prepared by the contractor, and the contract let after some slight modifications had been made with reference to the architecture." At the time of the bridge's construction, Clas served as one of Milwaukee's park commissioners, a position he could not legally hold had he been hired by the commission as architect of the bridge. Nevertheless, the records of the park commission include numerous payments to Clas for architectural services, so the city and park commission apparently choose to overlook the conflict of interest.[22]

The bridge was engineered and constructed by Milwaukee's Newton Engineering Company, two of whose founders, Ralph and Alfred Newton, attended the University of Michigan's engineering school around the same time as Julius Kahn. Newton Engineering was selected as contractor on the basis of its low bid for construction, which, at $6,246, was a mere $46 less than the next lowest bid. The bridge was completed around the middle of October 1905. During construction, drainage problems hampered the foundation work, and as a result Newton requested an additional $664 from the park commission to cover the extra costs. This led to a dispute between park commissioner Clas and Newton, with Clas claiming the "bridge was a poor piece of work" and refusing to pay until "certain alleged defects" were remedied. In the end, Newton Engineering was paid the extra compensation they sought.[23]

Upon its completion, the Lake Park Bridge received attention due to its picturesque appearance, reinforced concrete construction, and unusual parabolic arch. In 2016 the bridge was again in the spotlight, as years of neglect had resulted in sufficient deterioration to require its closing. Milwaukee County, the owner of the bridge, considered options that included repair, replacement, and demolition. In an effort to save the bridge, the preservation group Lake Park Friends stepped up with a campaign that raised over $900,000. Public pressure eventually tipped the balance toward repairing the bridge. In 2020 the county committed $500,000 to the project and a federal government program offered $2 million, but then the COVID pandemic caused construction costs to spike, putting the repair $1 million over budget. The county could not delay the project, as the federal grant of $2 million was contingent on beginning work during the first half of 2021. To cover the shortfall, the Milwaukee County Board of Supervisors authorized an expenditure of $1 million from county emergency funds. The repaired bridge should be good for the next 50 years, as some of the money raised by Lake Park Friends was set aside to address the bridge's future maintenance needs.[24]

Perhaps the most impressive and innovative bridge designed by Julius and his firm was the massive concrete viaduct built in Richmond, Virginia, for the Richmond and Chesapeake Bay Railway. The *Dallas Morning News* described the viaduct as "one of the most remarkable pieces of monolithic concrete construction."[25] A trade journal called it "a novel railway viaduct which resembles a large many-legged monster towering over housetops. . . . The special points of interest in the structural details are the large girder beams and the use of concrete beams as struts."[26] Julius Kahn wrote that the viaduct was "the largest structure of its kind and, at the time of its construction, was probably the boldest undertaking of its kind ever attempted."[27]

The railway was founded in 1905 by Frank Jay Gould, son of the disreputable railroad titan Jay Gould. The initial segment of the railway was to run south from the city of Ashland 15 miles to a terminal northwest of downtown Richmond. To reach the terminal, the tracks would have to descend from high ground into a heavily built-up valley and cross major streets and the tracks of another railroad. To avoid having numerous street crossings and a steep grade as the track entered the valley, it was decided to carry the railway on a massive viaduct 2,800 feet long and varying in height from 18 to 70 feet above street level.

Constructing the viaduct of steel was considered and rejected due to the high initial cost and ongoing maintenance expenses. In its place, a timber trestle with steel girders spanning the streets and tracks was planned. Timber was already being delivered when Gould, who was touring Europe, saw a trestle constructed of concrete in Spain and ordered that quotes be sought for a concrete viaduct. A number of firms throughout the country were asked to propose a design and specify a cost; the offer selected was Truscon's. Work on the viaduct was begun in late May 1906 and was completed in early January 1907.[28]

Truscon's design for the viaduct consisted of a series flat concrete girders (not arched) ranging in span from 20 to 80 feet—these were the "novel forms" referred to by Carl W. Condit in his aforementioned description of Julius Kahn's achievements. The girders were supported by A-shaped, concrete trestle legs. The entire structure appeared far too delicate to withstand a strong wind, much less the weight of a locomotive. Yet Truscon's contract required that the viaduct be tested by loading it with twice the amount of weight for which it was designed.

The Richmond and Chesapeake Bay Railway viaduct is seen here being tested on June 25, 1907, using a 50-ton locomotive and two gondola cars loaded to 40 tons each. The maximum deflection of the girders was carefully measured and was less than 3/16 of an inch. (The Valentine, Richmond, VA, PHC0047)

The test was delayed due to the slow delivery of the oak railroad ties required to place the track. Finally on June 25, 1907, the test was conducted with a 50-ton locomotive and two gondola cars loaded to 40 tons each. The deflection of the girders under this weight was measured at numerous points and the maximum deflection recorded was less than 3/16 of an inch. Railroad bridges are subject to additional stress arising from the motion of concentrated loads passing over them. For this reason the viaduct was also tested by bringing the locomotive and cars to a sudden stop, a test the viaduct easily passed.[29]

By the fall of 1907 the line was operating four electric cars transporting passengers and freight between Richmond and Ashland. An overhead wire provided power to the cars' electric motors, permitting them to reach speeds of up to 90 miles per hour. It was anticipated by Gould that the line would bring produce into Richmond from farms, and carry commuters encouraged by the availability of speedy transport to locate in suburban areas along the line. He also intended to extend the line east from Ashland to the Chesapeake Bay, but a lack of financing frustrated that plan.

The Richmond and Chesapeake Bay Railway was one of many such electric interurban railroads that became popular around 1900, particularly in the Midwest. The cars were self-propelled like trolleys, but more heavily built and significantly faster. The interurban routes typically connected cities within a regional area; the Detroit United Railway, for example, connected the cities of Detroit, Pontiac, Port Huron, Farmington, and Trenton in Michigan. As seemingly useful as the interurban was, most lines succumbed by the 1930s to competition from personal automobiles, trucks, and rubber-tired intercity bus lines. Unlike many of the interurban systems, however, the Richmond and Chesapeake Bay Railway was unable to turn a profit even during the peak years of interurban popularity and shut down in December 1917. A statement released by the officers of the company explained that, with no profit, those who financed its construction received no return on their investment and had incurred substantial interest charges on loans. "The discontinuance of the service will no doubt subject the former patrons of this road . . . to inconvenience," the statement read, "but they must realize that the service which they have heretofore enjoyed has been at the expense of those who made the original investment in the property, and who have borne the burden during the entire period through which the service has been rendered without remuneration."[30]

The line was eventually sold and service reestablished in 1919 as the Richmond-Ashland Railway Company. It operated until 1938, at which point the rails were torn up and sold for scrap. The viaduct survived until 1958, when part of it was demolished to make way for a school. By 1965 the viaduct was gone, and all that remains of the railway are the car barn and terminal, now restored, on West Broad Street.[31]

The city of Asheville, North Carolina, in the fall of 1909 sought to have the county commissioners allocate funds to construct a bridge across the French Broad River to connect the city with West Asheville. The commissioners had only $70,000 available for the project, an amount they knew to be insufficient. Nevertheless they invited contractors to submit bids for a concrete bridge of their own design, provided the total cost was less than $70,000. To their surprise, the commissioners received eight bids at or below the $70,000 maximum and awarded the contract to the lowest bidder, Charles B. Clark and Company of Baltimore, which had submitted plans prepared by Truscon.[32]

Excavation for the bridge began in February 1910. Good progress was made until September when record high flooding of the French Broad River washed away the form work for the second arch before the concrete could be poured, causing a three month delay. The bridge was opened on February 21, 1911.[33]

The West Asheville Bridge, or "Concrete Bridge" as it came to be called, was 931 feet long and 35 feet wide with 19 spans carrying it across the river, a street, and four railroad tracks. All but two of the spans were flat girders; the other two were open arches, each having a span of 145 feet—among the largest in the country at the time.[34] In addition to street and pedestrian traffic, the bridge also carried tracks for the city's trolley system.

Photographs of the bridge along with copies of the engineering plans for its construction appeared in *Engineering Record*.[35] *Scientific American* carried a full-page-width photo of the bridge, and *Concrete Age* published a photo and article describing how the "concrete highway bridge" brought about "a very material increase in the price of property in West Asheville and the vicinity of the bridge."[36]

The final cost of the bridge was $67,800, an exceptional value considering the $125,000 cost of the concrete Southern Railway bridge that crosses the river less than a half mile away.[37] The railroad bridge is 200 feet shorter, a bit narrower, and only one-third as high, though it was constructed to handle somewhat heavier loads. The cost discrepancy between the two structures is likely due primarily to the excessive use of steel reinforcement and concrete in structures not built with the Kahn System, a judgment buttressed by the fact that the bridge is still in use by the Norfolk Southern Railway.

On December 15, 1967, the Silver Bridge, a steel suspension bridge crossing the Ohio River near Gallipolis, Ohio, collapsed during rush hour, killing 46 people. The disaster shocked the public and prompted state highway commissions to evaluate their procedures for determining the safety of older bridges. Five days later the chief highway engineer for North Carolina ordered a special survey of all bridges in the state. The West Asheville Bridge was judged to be "in very poor condition" and an eight-ton load limit was imposed, effectively banning most bus and truck traffic. Oddly, given the heightened concern over safety, the state highway commission did not publicize the ban, but merely changed the load limit signs on the bridge. The supervisor of the city transit system only learned his buses could not use the bridge when an alert bus driver noticed the new limits and telephoned the office to report the change.[38]

In 1970 the North Carolina state highway commission approved construction of a new bridge "to replace the deteriorating West Asheville Bridge."[39] Demolition of the bridge, however, proved quite a challenge. Bob Terrell of the *Asheville Citizen-Times* reported, "The men tearing down the old West Asheville Bridge found the structure to be far stronger than anyone suspected." The bridge's strength was attributed to the "wing bar" reinforcing steel found within the concrete, a piece of which was featured in an accompanying photograph, which clearly showed a piece of Kahn Bar. Terrell opined that the bridge "might still be carrying [traffic] if its concrete hadn't begun to crumble. There was certainly no problem with the reinforcing steel. Any bridge builder in the country would like to have steel like that to work with today."[40] Indeed, it appears the bridge was prematurely condemned due to a bit of crumbling concrete and inspectors unfamiliar with its structural details.

One of the most picturesque bridges in the country is the Benson Bridge at Multnomah Falls near Portland, Oregon. Multnomah Creek drops 620 feet in two tiers, creating a dramatic scene, the most visited site in Oregon. The footbridge spans the narrow cleft in the rocky face through which water from the upper falls flows before descending the second tier of the falls. The elegantly arched bridge adds a sense of scale to the spectacular scene and permits one to behold the falls from a remarkable vantage point.

The original design for the bridge was a Melan arch having a steel framework embedded in concrete, an approach that would reduce the amount of formwork in the difficult-to-access location. When the design was priced out, however, it was found that the cost of the steel frame was unacceptably high, prompting a redesign of the structure as reinforced concrete construction.[41]

Though modest in size—just under six feet wide with a span of 45 feet—the bridge is over 100 feet above the base of the lower falls, which presented challenges during its construction. Material and equipment for the bridge were hoisted 135 feet from the staging area below using a pulley and cable system, but those working on the bridge had to climb on all fours to access the site. To facilitate building the forms for the concrete, a wooden truss bridge was constructed from which the formwork was suspended.[42]

Karl P. Billner, engineer for the Oregon State Highway Commission, designed the bridge and more than a dozen others during 1914–15 as part of the Columbia River Highway project in Multnomah County. Billner made liberal use of Kahn Bars in these structures, as well as other Truscon steel reinforcement products that by then had been added to the company's line of goods. In the Benson Bridge, the entire lower face of the arch was constructed with Truscon Hy-Rib, a lightweight steel reinforcement product that combined stiff ribs with expanded metal lath.[43] The columns that extend up from the arch to support the bridge deck were reinforced with Hy-Rib and Rib Studs, which combined vertical steel bars with attached cross members and looked much like a steel ladder. Smaller Rib Studs reinforce the handrails. The bridge deck is reinforced with Truscon Rib Metal, essentially a large sheet of rigidly connected reinforcement bars. The Benson footbridge, though a small structure, demonstrates the wide variety and flexible application of Truscon steel products in use at the time of its construction.

It might seem that the Benson Bridge had little to fear from Mother Nature, but its location close to a high waterfall carried unusual risk. On Labor Day in 1995 a rock the size of a Greyhound bus and weighing about 236 tons, fell 150 feet from the face of the falls. The massive boulder landed in the pool at the base of the upper falls, sending a shower of water and stones "hundreds of feet in the air." Sixty people on and near the bridge 95 feet above the pool were struck by the debris-laden water, sending 13 of them to the hospital with broken bones and bruises.[44] Then one evening in 2014, a boulder fell 400 feet from the cliff above, striking the bridge on its north side and taking out a three-by-four-foot section of the deck, several of the handrail supports, and one of the vertical deck support columns. After repairs, the bridge reopened five months later.

The potential advantages of concrete bridges in cost and durability over steel or timber construction were apparent early on. Bridges of solid concrete came into use first, followed by Melan and similar bridges that combined steel and concrete. But in the absence of a scientific understanding of reinforcement, Melan-type structures required an excessive quantity of steel, negating much of the potential cost savings. Nevertheless, the maintenance and longevity advantages gained by enclosing steel within concrete prompted an increasing preference for the type, particularly for smaller, light-duty bridges. Prior to around 1904, the number of concrete bridges built in the United States was quite small. Writing in 1911, civil engineer Henry Tyrrell stated that from 1894 to 1904 "about 100 concrete bridges were erected in the United States."[45]

With the introduction of the Kahn System, the construction of reinforced concrete bridges rapidly accelerated. This was due in part to Truscon's promoting the Kahn Bar for bridge construction in its earliest catalogs—the spring 1904 catalog provided detailed instructions for making the engineering calculations required for parabolic arches—and because Truscon would provide specific plans for any customer who desired to construct a bridge using the system. The Ferry Street Bridge, Richmond and Chesapeake viaduct, and West Asheville Bridge were all designed by Truscon.[46] According to Julius Kahn, more than 5,000 reinforced concrete bridges were constructed in the United States in 1907.[47] Though most of these bridges were not constructed using the Kahn System, the highly publicized successes of the system for reinforced concrete bridges constructed at significant cost savings over alternatives encouraged much wider interest in, and rapid acceptance of, the new construction technology for bridges.

11

Tested by
Conflagration

In the late 19th century the term *fireproof* came into use as a description of metal frame buildings that had been fireproofed by enclosing the cast iron or steel structural members within brick or, more commonly, hollow terra cotta tile. The brick or tile insulated the frame members from the heat of a fire, thereby preventing them from becoming weakened and deformed, which would likely result in structural failure. Concrete construction was, from its beginning, referred to as fireproof, as concrete is fairly immune to the effects of fire and the reinforcing steel within is insulated from heat by the concrete.[1]

Due to the lack of experimental data, countless debates among academics and engineers on the relative advantages of the various fireproof construction methods filled many pages of trade and scientific journals. These debates were often motivated by the vested interests of those promoting one material over another.

In 1904 the Manhattan Bureau of Buildings sponsored a test of Kahn System beams and floors at the fire-testing station of Columbia University. The experiment involved building a concrete floor supported by two concrete beams over a brick structure 19 by 14 feet in size (the floor, in effect, was the roof of the building). The floor and beams were constructed by Truscon using Kahn System reinforcement and overseen by

Moritz Kahn. Once the concrete had cured, the floor was loaded to 150 pounds per square foot. The test was conducted by maintaining a fire of 1,700 degrees Fahrenheit within the brick structure for four hours and then subjecting the underside of the floor "while still red hot" to the stream of a fire hose for five minutes. Once the floor cooled, it was loaded to 600 pounds per square foot for 16 hours. At the conclusion of the test, the floor was found to be "in excellent condition" and there was "no exposure of the reinforce[ment] metal."[2] Tests of this type established basic characteristics of concrete behavior when exposed to fire but fell short of demonstrating how well a reinforced concrete building would withstand fire under real world conditions and, in particular, how well mill construction, concrete, and fireproofed steel frame compared with each other at protecting a building and its contents.

On February 7, 1904, fire broke out in a Baltimore dry-goods store and rapidly consumed the building. Fueled by explosions and carried by high winds, the fire quickly spread to nearby structures. The conflagration raged for two days, by which time it had wiped out the city's banking, business, and wholesale districts and consumed nearly all of the 2,000 buildings in its path. To no one's surprise, non-fireproof buildings "suffered total destruction"; the only evidence of their having existed being "heaps of bricks and jagged spires of wall."[3]

Within the burned area were seven fireproof metal frame buildings, all of which were still standing, though their contents were totally destroyed, all windows were gone, and every bit of woodwork was turned to ash. Much effort was expended in evaluating how effectively the fireproofing had protected the structural metal frameworks of these buildings from the heat of the fire. Where hollow terra cotta tiles had been used to protect steel columns, "in nearly every case, [the tiles] had saved the column from damage," wrote Captain John Sewell, but "were a total loss themselves; . . . all were so badly damaged that they ought to be entirely removed." As for beams supporting the floors, some of the terra cotta tiles that protected them were lost, causing the beams to warp from the heat.[4] In describing damage to the 10-story Equitable Building, one report stated, "From top to bottom every floor panel for about half the area of the building had collapsed and the basement was littered with safes precipitated from the offices above."[5] It was common practice for businesses during this era to have large safes on-site to store cash, business records, and valuables. Beams deformed by the heat of the fire weakened the floor, allowing the heavy safes to break through.

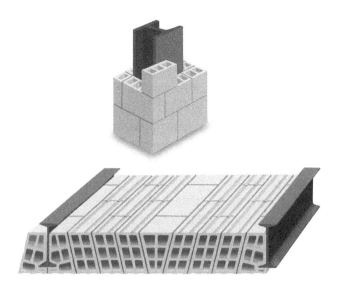

The columns and beams of a steel frame building were protected from fire by terra cotta blocks. These blocks also formed the floors of the structure.

Once they began falling, they traveled nonstop to the basement, taking out the intervening floors in the process.

The terra cotta tile used for fireproofing, for cost-saving reasons, was manufactured as thin as possible, "rarely more than 5/8 of an inch in thickness." When exposed to the fire, according to Sewell, the exterior of the tile would become red hot, while the interior remained cool, causing a fracture at the junction of the two.[6] It was this circumstance that caused so much of the fireproofing to be wrecked.

Based on his examination of the fireproof buildings, Sewell figured the cost of "fully restoring them will not be less than 60% of their original value." He estimated that only 10 percent of the steel frame would require repair, but 50 percent of the floor systems and 100 percent of the column fireproofing tile would require replacement. Considered in the best light, the fireproof buildings survived and, with appropriate repairs, could be returned to service. But the extent of damage and cost of repairs was greater than expected. In its report on the fire, the National Fire Protection Association stated in reference to the steel frame buildings with terra cotta fireproofing: "This conflagration strongly emphasizes the fact that many features and practices in the construction of fire-resistive buildings are faulty."[7]

One smaller building at 111 East German Street (now known as Redwood Street) was the subject of much interest and debate. This structure, the four-story annex of the United States Fidelity and Guaranty Building had an interesting history. The building was originally constructed as a brick-and-timber structure; in the year prior to the fire, the entire interior, composed of wooden floors and beams, was removed, leaving the freestanding exterior brick and mortar walls. A new interior was constructed of reinforced concrete using the Hennebique system. There was ample evidence that the building had been subjected to intense heat during the conflagration: the surrounding structures were entirely destroyed, and within the building itself all "combustible materials were consumed and produced a fire sufficient to melt brass, fuse typewriter machines and produce other evidences of high temperature."[8] Nevertheless, the building survived the fire with its concrete structure in generally good condition with negligible, but repairable, damage.[9] The exterior brick walls on one side of the building at the third and fourth floors had been stripped away when the adjacent building collapsed.[10]

A loading test was conducted on one of the building's floors. The floors, designed to sustain a live load of 150 pounds per square foot, were tested to 300 pounds, which caused a deflection of 1/8 of an inch. The load was left in place for 24 hours and, when removed, the floors showed no permanent deflection or other damage.[11]

Comprehensive reports on the condition of fireproof buildings in the Baltimore fire soon appeared in journals, and all featured some positive mention of the concrete in the US Fidelity annex building. *Fireproof Magazine*, a journal generally aligned with the terra cotta tile industry, immediately hired testing engineer A. N. Johnson from the US Geological Survey to examine the building. His report claimed that the first and second floors "experienced but a comparatively small degree of heat" as evidenced by the "large amount of half-burned papers." The third story suffered greater destruction, though "in places, the woodwork has not entirely burned."[12] These observations directly contradicted those of other reporters, including Captain Sewell and investigators from the National Fire Protection Association who stated, "The interior combustible material and furnishings were destroyed."[13]

Johnson claimed in his report, "Wherever the concrete in this building has been subjected to the direct actions of the fire it is disintegrated and irreparably injured." "The effect of the heat on the exposed concrete has been to render it non-elastic," he continued, "which caused the concrete to become detached from the embedded steel rods, thus destroying its structural strength and value." In spite of his claim that the concrete had lost its strength, Johnson was not discouraged from climbing to the roof of the building to secure core samples of the concrete. He tested the breaking strength of samples taken from the first floor, fourth floor, and ceiling of the fourth floor and reported that only the ceiling sample was noticeably weakened.[14]

The same issue of *Fireproof* in which Johnson's eight-paragraph report appeared featured an editorial attempting to discredit other reports. It quoted the National Fire Protection Association report as stating that temperatures in the US Fidelity building "were not extreme," implying the fire did not reach high temperatures in the building.[15] What the report actually said was, "While the heat was severe in this building, particularly in the front parts of the third and fourth floors, the temperatures were not extreme."[16] The *Fireproof* editorial claimed that load tests conducted on the building's floors were conducted only upon the lower floors, "because the concrete upon the upper floor is so badly disintegrated as to be without sufficient strength to withstand superimposed weights, live and dead loads." The load test carried out on the building was accomplished by piling roughly 80,000 pounds of bricks (taken from the nearby rubble) onto the floor. The *Engineering Record* article on the test explained that they would have tested the upper floors, "but the building was devoid of elevators or stairways and it would have been difficult to raise the bricks so high."[17] *Fireproof* claimed, "The entire building is now being dismantled as untenable," when in fact, the original contractor, Baltimore Ferro Concrete Company, offered to restore the building for $650.[18] The building was razed when US Fidelity elected to construct in its place a larger building (occupying much of the block between South Calvert, Mercer, and East German Streets).[19]

Just over two years after the Baltimore conflagration, San Francisco was struck by an intense earthquake that caused widespread damage. The earthquake set off a number of fires throughout the city that firefighters were helpless to quell, as the quake ruptured many of the water mains and reservoir supply conduits. Over the following three days, fire destroyed nearly 500 city blocks—80 percent of the city—including the central business district.

Two comprehensive reports on the fire were prepared, one by

the Geological Survey of the United States Department of the Interior, authored chiefly by Captain John Sewell, and the second by the National Board of Fire Underwriters, authored by consulting engineer S. Albert Reed.[20] These two investigators reported nearly identical findings, that steel frame, fireproof buildings in San Francisco suffered extensive damage from the fire. Sewell stated, "The collapse of protected steel frames, due to the destruction of the fireproof covering at a comparatively early stage in the fire was a common occurrence."[21] "Commercial methods of fireproofing," he continued, "are inadequate to stand any severe test."[22] According to Reed, "The behavior of the buildings of modern 'fireproof' type was closely the same as that of corresponding structures in Baltimore. The most marked difference was in the relatively greater number of column failures at San Francisco, all of which took the typical form of a mashed or bulged telescoping failure." Every column that failed "caused a sinking of the corresponding point in the building for all floors above," and the ensuing warping of the building's frame resulted in the destruction of adjacent floor panels.[23] The Geological Survey's report concluded that effective fireproofing of buildings "was the exception and not the rule," due largely to "cost restrictions insisted on by owners." Further contributing to the disappointing performance was the "poor workmanship" of the installation.[24]

Concrete was little used in San Francisco prior to the fire, a dearth that Sewell and others attributed primarily to the bricklayers' union, which "prevented the use of reinforced concrete in San Francisco for all parts of buildings."[25] The sole reinforced concrete building in the path of the fire was the Bekins Van and Storage Company warehouse at 190 West Mission Street. The building was under construction using the Kahn System, and just two of the planned four stories had been completed when the earthquake struck. According to the building's architect, Ralph W. Hart, "Because of outside influence, the city authorities refused us permit for this building until we conceded brick outside walls."[26] The earthquake severely damaged the building's brick walls, but the reinforced concrete columns, beams, and floors were "absolutely uninjured." Permanent fire doors had not yet been installed, so the fire was able to enter and cause some damage, but otherwise, the building's contents were unharmed.[27]

There were a small number of steel frame buildings where cinder concrete was used in place of terra cotta tiles to cover and insulate the frame members from fire. Sewell noted, "None of the columns covered with cinder concrete suffered any serious damage."[28] Reed pointed out that "the best results were shown by solid concrete column covering without air space. . . . The bracing effect of the solid concrete encasing the steel column is doubtless an important factor." Reinforced concrete floors (supported by steel joists) also performed well, and Reed championed "the excellent behavior of this type of floor" in over 30 buildings of significant height.[29]

Once the debris was cleared and reconstruction begun, it wasn't long before the bricklayers' union resumed its efforts to thwart the use of concrete. In the spring of 1907, the union barred its members from laying brick on reinforced concrete buildings, bringing a number of substantial projects to a halt. One of its targets was the rapidly growing local organization of the Cement Workers Union of the American Brotherhood of Cement Workers, which had acquired jurisdiction over all cement work. According to the bricklayers, "cement work originally belonged to the masons' trade," so if concrete buildings were to be built, bricklayers should be the ones carrying it out. The cement workers rebutted this by asserting that "their industry is a product of the evolution and progress of building construction."[30] The Structural Iron and Bridge Workers union also sought to curb the use of concrete, claiming that concrete "is not safe in tall buildings" and asking the San Francisco city government to "include a structural iron clause in the new building code."[31]

Nevertheless, after the earthquake and fire, the battle to stymie the use of concrete in San Francisco was a lost cause. There were 79 reinforced concrete buildings completed or under construction in the city by July 1907, including the Pacific Building, claimed to be the largest reinforced concrete building in the world, and the reconstructed tower of the Ferry Building. There were nearly as many steel frame buildings going up that contained some form of concrete in their construction.[32]

The increased use of concrete was not due solely to its strong performance in the fire but its seeming invincibility to earthquakes, as demonstrated by a handful of concrete buildings in the surrounding area. On the Palo Alto campus of Stanford University, Ransome's reinforced concrete buildings suffered negligible damage from the quake, while structures of traditional construction were heavily damaged.[33] Another consideration favoring concrete was its availability. Supplies of both concrete and reinforcement bars were readily available on short notice, whereas steel frame construction required a lengthy wait for the structural steel to be manufactured and shipped from the mill.[34]

Truscon secured a fair amount of business as San Francisco was rebuilt, including a three-story factory for Bemis Brothers Bag Company, the six-story Latham Building on Mission Street, a five-story store for Wellman, Peck and Company, the six-story Scatena Building, and the eight-story First National Bank Building in Oakland.[35] Prior to the fire, Truscon products were handled in San Francisco through an agent, civil engineer Maurice Couchot, but the increase in business following the fire prompted Truscon to have Julius's brother Felix open an office there in the fall of 1907.[36]

In cities where earthquake resistance was not a consideration, debate over the use of concrete continued. Bricklayers and iron workers lobbied city governments to revise building codes and curb the increased use of concrete, while concrete interests attempted to persuade recalcitrant city engineers and council members to permit greater use of concrete construction (or forego enacting limitations). In 1907 Truscon prepared plans for a 16-story reinforced concrete hotel to be built in Cleveland, Ohio. The city's recently revised building code specifically permitted trussed concrete construction but prohibited concrete buildings taller than six stories, effectively ending the project.[37]

The most protracted building code fight took place in New York City, where a revision to the code was initiated in 1906 by city aldermen. Conflicts over New York City's building code were foreshadowed during construction in 1906 of the city's first concrete apartment buildings at 616 and 622 West 137th Street. Construction costs for both brick and steel had risen dramatically, while concrete construction was less expensive, due to its being performed by lower paid, unskilled, non-union workers. The owner and developer of the 137th Street apartments, Cathedral Parkway Realty Company, chose reinforced concrete for the two six-story buildings because of its lower cost. Concrete also offered other advantages that Cathedral trumpeted in ads for the buildings. "These are the first houses in New York constructed completely of concrete," stated an ad, and "walls of concrete have four times the strength of brick and constitute the best fire proof material known." When construction began on the buildings, the bricklayers' union demanded that the concrete work be performed by bricklayers. Bricklayers were paid 70 cents an hour, while the hourly rate for concrete workers was 30 cents. Cathedral disregarded the bricklayers' demand, but as the buildings reached the fifth floor, the city halted construction. Despite the city's building department having approved the plans, the Tenement House Department cited an ordinance that apartment houses over three stories must be of brick with a staircase enclosure of brick. In order to proceed, Cathedral agreed to construct an eight-inch-thick brick wall around the staircase, a redundant accessory for a concrete building.[38]

J. William Buzzell, a civil engineer for one of the local contractors, wrote a *New York Times* article in which he hailed the advantages of concrete and bluntly stated reasons why certain unions so strongly opposed its use. The steel frame building, Buzzell wrote, "requires in its construction the services of skilled mechanics who receive the highest rates of wages, including stone masons, bricklayers, plasterers, steel erectors, terra cotta setters, and carpenters." When constructing a reinforced concrete building, "with the exception of carpenters, practically all of the labor is of the unskilled type, drawing low rates of wages." But cost wasn't the only consideration. Buzzell pointed out that, with far fewer unionized workers on the job, "the possibility of labor difficulties is greatly reduced."[39]

In September 1906 the "labor difficulties" experienced by Cathedral emerged as the declared policy of the New York City bricklayers' union. The union announced that henceforth "all concrete work in building construction must be done by union bricklayers." Among the tasks the highly paid bricklayers laid claim to was "the right to pour concrete," work that entailed pushing a wheelbarrow loaded with concrete and tipping it out into a form, a task commonly performed by day laborers. The reason for the bricklayers' sudden interest in performing concrete work was clearly stated: "We realize that concrete has come to stay, and we intend to take the bull by the horns. It is useless to try to stop the use of concrete." Their demand was backed up with the threat that "strikes will be ordered against all contractors, owners or architects who employ others than bricklayers where concrete is used in building construction."[40] The threat failed to alarm builders, one of whom responded that a strike by bricklayers "would likely lead the contractors to abandon the use of brick altogether."[41]

Thus was the climate in which New York City endeavored to update its building code. The city appointed a committee to write and submit to the Board of Aldermen a new draft code. The committee's first effort was made public in December 1907 and immediately drew criticism for its severe restrictions on the use of concrete. The new code would have limited the height of concrete buildings to 85 feet and, oddly, prohibit concrete construction for most industrial, warehouse, and commercial buildings, the very structures for which it was best suited. Embedded in the fine print of the draft code were numerous conditions and requirements that further inhibited concrete use. For example, one of concrete's advantages over steel beams is its ability to inexpensively span large areas, yet the code limited beams of any type in industrial buildings to five feet in length.[42] In fact, many of the city's existing concrete buildings would have been prohibited under the proposed code. In 1907 alone, $4 million worth of concrete buildings were constructed in New York City.[43]

Mindful that implementation of the draft code's restrictions by the country's largest city would lead many other cities to follow suit, the restrictions were aggressively fought by national concrete industry associations. In February 1908 New York's building code committee heard testimony from several concrete and insurance industry engineers and received from them a 132-page book detailing the advantages of concrete construction, including its commendable performance in recent fires. The disappointing performance of terra cotta tiles in the Baltimore and San Francisco fires was extensively documented with numerous photographs.[44]

In his presentation to the committee, civil engineer Robert Lesley, representing the Association of American Portland Cement Manufacturers, cited the example of a fire in the reinforced concrete building of the Thompson and Norris Company of Brooklyn, constructed using the Kahn System. The fire broke out among sacks of cork stored on the seventh floor of the eight-story building. Fed by cork dust, the fire burned with great intensity, causing exposed surfaces to become so hot that "the steam generated from the contact of the streams of water almost obscured the building." Yet employees on the floor above and those below "unconcernedly watched the firemen . . . from their excellent point of vantage." The employees, according to one report, "had great confidence in the structure, apparently, for they declined to be panic-stricken." The fire did not spread beyond the floor on which it began, and a representative of Thompson and Norris claimed that "no time was lost in the regular work of the factory except during the worst of the fire." The damage sustained by the concrete structure was minor and repaired at a cost of $50.[45]

In contrast to the Thompson and Norris fire, Lesley cited the example of a fire from the previous month in New York's Parker Building. Constructed in 1900 at the corner of Fourth Avenue (now Park Avenue South) and Nineteenth Street, the building was of typical fireproof design with cast iron columns and steel floor beams, all fireproofed with terra cotta tile. On the evening of January 10, 1908, a blaze began on the fifth floor of the 12-story structure. Sections of both the fifth and sixth floors were on fire at around 8:15 p.m. when firefighters arrived, and more than 50 of them entered the building hoping to quell the flames. By nine o'clock, fire was observed on the eighth floor and soon after, had spread to all the floors above. Suddenly, just before ten o'clock, one of the cast iron columns on the sixth floor failed, causing a section of the building, 40 by 24 feet in size, to collapse. This section of every floor, including the roof, fell and was carried into the basement.[46]

Firefighters working within the building had no warning of the collapse, as it was not preceded by less significant failures. As a consequence, many of those battling the flames were struck by falling debris or buried beneath it. Tragically, three firemen were killed, and 14 others were seriously injured. George O'Connor had been fighting the fire on the fifth floor and was knocked unconscious by falling debris at the time of the collapse. Captain Davin of his engine company grabbed him by the hand and was pulling him toward an exit when he too was struck, nearly knocking him out and badly injuring his hand. Having lost sight of O'Connor and, in any case, too weak to stand, Davin was carried out by others. John Fallon was on the second floor, which was not on fire when the collapse occurred, but when his team escaped the building, he was not among them. Six days later, O'Connor's body was extricated from beneath several tons of wreckage on the ground floor. Fallon's badly burned remains were found on the same floor amid a pile of charred debris.[47]

By the time the fire was brought under control, many smaller sections of floor had collapsed. Safes and machinery, as well as terra cotta floor arches, continued to crash down for days after the fire.[48] The walls of the building remained standing as did most of the cast iron and steel frame, but everything within was destroyed.

The nearly complete destruction of a fireproof building—from an internal fire, not a conflagration—shocked many in the construction and insurance industries. A thorough investigation of the fire was conducted by W. C. Robinson, chief engineer of the National Board of Fire

Underwriters; his findings were published in a lengthy report several months after the fire. Robinson described the Parker Building as "fairly representative of fire-proof buildings occupied for mercantile and light manufacturing purposes in New York City." "That the destruction of such a building is not only possible," he wrote, "but quite probable" made it clear that the city's standards for buildings of this type were insufficient.[49]

The cast iron columns supporting the building were fireproofed with one-inch-thick terra cotta tiles. Robinson found that at least one-quarter of them were badly damaged by the fire and, as a result, failed to protect the columns.[50] "The collapse of the various portions of the building," he concluded, "was primarily due to the inadequacy of the fire proofing on the columns." In Robinson's opinion, the fire did not discredit fireproof building construction but rather demonstrated the need for better design and more effective use of fireproofing materials, reinforcing lessons learned in the Baltimore and San Francisco fires. To be effective, terra cotta fireproofing had to be thick enough to insulate a structure's metal frame, and the installation had to be such that the tiles could withstand a hot fire without significant damage. Robinson calculated the cost to repair the building as $369,000, or about 66 percent of the building's pre-fire value.[51] The fireproofing protected none of the building's contents and preserved only about a third of the value of the building—a disappointing outcome.

The burned-out shell of the Parker Building stood for two years as a reminder of the deadly fire. Late in 1909, 40 of the of the 120 feet of the building fronting on Park Avenue South was demolished, and the interior of the remainder of the structure was rebuilt with the frame enclosed in three inches of hard-burned terra cotta tile set in Portland cement. Renamed the Pocono Building, the transformed structure was almost fully leased by the time it was completed in the fall of 1910; its tenants were mostly clothing manufacturers.[52] Now known as 233 Park Avenue South, the building is primarily residential.

Six weeks after the Parker Building burned, a fire occurred at the factory of the Dayton Motor Car Company in Dayton, Ohio. This blaze received a great deal of attention in engineering, construction, and insurance journals due to its unusual circumstances. Dayton Motor's six-story reinforced concrete factory was constructed by the Keppele Hall Company using the Kahn System during the summer of 1907. Just 63 days were required to erect the new structure adjacent to Dayton

Motor Car's existing five-story, mill construction factory and office building. In the early hours of February 21, 1908, a fire broke out on the fourth floor of the new building and, fueled by upholstering materials, quickly spread across the entire floor. The fire was so hot that "the iron pipes of the sprinkler system [which was not yet functional or charged with water] were bent completely out of shape, in some instances having sagged clear down to the floor." A passageway between the new and old buildings—not yet protected by a fire door—allowed the flames unhindered access to the older structure, which soon began to burn. Arriving firefighters saw little reason for concern that the fire would spread beyond the fourth floor of the concrete building, so they focused their efforts on saving the brick-and-timber structure. The fire in the new building remained confined to the fourth floor and eventually burned itself out. The flames on the fourth floor of the old building, however, spread to the fifth floor and roof, eventually causing them to collapse in a charred mess onto the third floor. The building's second, first, and basement levels were heavily damaged by water.[53]

Reports that the factory "was destroyed by fire"—as would normally be the case—appeared in hundreds of newspapers across the country, but Dayton Motor immediately sent out telegrams stating, "Report of fire grossly exaggerated, will be running full force Monday morning." Indeed, according to subsequent newspaper reports, the company's full workforce was back on the job Monday.[54]

The morning of the fire, a photographer for the *Dayton Herald* snapped a photo of the scene. Taken from an ideal vantage point across the street, it showed the two buildings side by side, the gutted shell of the old building and the new building, generally undamaged, save for the burned-out fourth floor.[55] This and other photos of the blaze were reproduced in many journal articles that described the disparate effects of the fire on structures under real-world conditions. In *Engineering Record* J. B. Gilbert wrote, "From [the photo] it is evident what happened. The two top floors of the brick building are entirely wiped out, and the damage to the concrete building is confined to the window frames and sash." An article in *Insurance Engineering* stated, "To substantiate the well-won reputation of reinforced concrete as a fire-proof material reference need only be made to the Dayton Motor Car Works." In the judgment of *Engineering News*, "the concrete itself stood the test very well indeed, especially in view of the fact that the ordinary building adjoining was much more seriously damaged by the same

The Dayton Motor Car Company factory after the fire of February 21, 1908. One floor of the reinforced concrete building on the right was gutted, but the remainder of the building was unharmed. The older mill construction building on the left was badly damaged. The upper three floors were completely destroyed, while the lower floors suffered heavy water damage. (*Dayton Herald*, February 29, 1908)

fire and under the same fire department protection." The *Quarterly of the National Fire Protection Association* reported that, on the concrete building, the fire burned out the windows, which were of "ordinary, light, wood sash and thin glass," and it spoiled "the concrete covering on one pier and numerous girders." But "integrity of structure [was] not impaired for sustaining weight." The adjoining brick building of ordinary construction, however, "was practically destroyed except for the walls." In a letter to Truscon reprinted in *Concrete Review*, Frank B. Ramby, chief of the Dayton Fire Department, stated, "This being the first fire we have had in a building of concrete construction, I am highly pleased with the results of this fire." The entire contents of the fourth floor were destroyed; "the building, however, escaped with slight damage." The concrete building, he said, "aided us greatly in preventing the fire from wiping out the entire plant, as we were able to concentrate practically our entire force on the old building."[56]

If any skepticism remained on the part of owners, builders, and insurers as to the superiority of concrete for industrial and commercial buildings, the Dayton Motor fire largely eliminated it. At the same time, the insurance industry was increasingly discouraging the use of mill construction for manufacturing, warehousing, and retailing; the essential characteristics of mill construction that provided some protection against the rapid spread of fire were often compromised when the method was employed for large buildings in an urban environment.[57] Mill construction buildings, properly constructed, were generally no higher than four stories so that the entire structure was within the reach of streams from a fire hose, but in cities this limit was often exceeded due to the lack of available land. As factories grew, structures became crowded together, making it difficult for firefighters to place water on all sections of the structure and increasing the likelihood that flames would spread to adjacent buildings. The placement of stairways and elevators in external brick towers, to deter transmission of fire from floor to floor, was another feature that often went by the wayside in urban locations. So while the fire-resisting quality of concrete construction was being decisively demonstrated, confidence in mill construction was rapidly ebbing.

Owners, builders, and insurers had largely come to view reinforced concrete as the preferred fireproof option, yet those charged with writing New York City's building code remained mired in discord. In 1909 the Building Code Revision Commission was so riven by conflicts of interest that it split into majority and minority factions, with each producing a draft code. On the majority side were the terra cotta tile interests, led by the National Fireproofing Company, the largest manufacturer of hollow tile in the United States. The minority interests included Roebling Construction Company, the country's largest cinder concrete fireproofing company. The draft code written by the majority essentially banned the use of cinder concrete in favor of tile.[58] Both draft codes limited reinforced concrete buildings to seven stories (even though there were already 12-story reinforced concrete buildings in the city).[59] The city aldermen voted 40 to 38 to enact the code in July, but New York's mayor quickly vetoed the measure. Among the reasons offered for his veto was the limitation on the height of reinforced concrete buildings.[60]

As this haggling took place, a tragic fire occurred that had a dramatic effect on fire safety. The Triangle Shirtwaist factory occupied the eighth through tenth floors of New York City's Asch Building (now the Brown Building). Constructed in 1901, the building has a steel and cast iron skeleton, fireproofed with terra cotta blocks. The floors are composed of hollow terra cotta blocks enclosing and supported by steel I-beams, and covered with a layer of cinder concrete. The shirtwaist company employed primarily women between the ages of 14 and 23. Just before 5:00 p.m. on March 25, 1911, fire broke out in one of the bins of scrap cloth and grew rapidly, spread by floating pieces of flaming ash. The heat and pressure of the fire caused the building's windows to shatter, allowing the fire to spread upward to the ninth and tenth floors. Employees on the eighth floor managed to escape the fire by way of stairways and elevators; those on the tenth floor ascended stairs to the roof, from which they were rescued. The nearly 300 workers on the ninth floor attempted to escape by way of the two stairwells, but the door to one was found to be locked and, unlike on the eighth floor, it could not be pried open. The second stairwell was soon blocked by flames at the eighth floor. Many crowded onto the fire escape, but its top flight collapsed, rendering it unusable. The elevators, which had transported workers from the eighth floor to safety, became stuck due to the heat of the fire warping the tracks. When it was all over, 146 people had lost their lives in the deadliest workplace fire in American history.[61]

The loss of life was shocking, particularly as it occurred in a fireproof building. As one editorial put it, "New York's latest holocaust has demonstrated that too much confidence has been placed in 'fireproof buildings.' It seems the mere fact that a structure has been adjudged 'fireproof' has been excuse of omission to provide adequate fire escapes."[62] Indeed, in spite of the high death toll, damage to the building was minimal.

In the aftermath, attention focused on the myriad factors that resulted in so many deaths in a building that was largely unharmed by the fire. The chief shortcoming was a lack of automatic sprinklers that likely would have doused the flames before they could spread. The fire escape did not reach to ground level and was located in the rear of the building within a court from which there was no exit. The interior stairways and fire escape, being inadequately isolated from the floors, became engulfed in flames and impassable for occupants attempting to descend from above. The fire department's efforts to douse the flames were largely ineffective; their streams of water could reach to the 10th floor, but were nearly vertical and unable, therefore, to penetrate more than a few feet in from the windows.

The state of New York established the State Factory Investigating Commission to inspect workplaces and make specific safety recommendations. Private organizations, such as the Committee on Safety of the City of New York, were established as watchdogs to assure that the government would follow through with effective legislation and enforcement. Responsibility for fire prevention and safety had been under the purview of multiple agencies. Legislation was passed in November 1911 that consolidated authority in a Bureau of Fire Prevention for New York City and a similar organization to oversee fire safety for the balance of the state. State labor laws were also changed as a result of the fire: every factory was required to register with the State Labor Department; limits were placed on the number of hours per week worked by those under age 18; and restrictions were placed on the hours of the day that minors and women could work. Other legislation prohibited smoking in factories (the likely cause of the Triangle blaze) and required fireproof receptacles for waste and flammable material. By 1913 the state had in place effective and detailed laws that prohibited most of the shortcomings that led to the Triangle disaster.[63]

Incredibly, and in spite of the Triangle fire, New York City's Building Code Revision Commission staggered along, having by 1914 proposed 13 different drafts, all of which failed to pass into law. In April 1914 city aldermen appointed Manhattan's highly regarded superintendent of buildings Rudolph P. Miller to revise the building code. Miller, a Vladimir Lenin lookalike, managed to get a new code passed by breaking it up into pieces, getting public input on each, and then enacting them individually. By the end of 1915, the new code was finally implemented and included recognition of reinforced concrete as a standard form of construction.[64]

12

Dominating the Market

Truscon's business saw a phenomenal increase in 1907, with total sales exceeding $1 million for the first time.[1] Kahn System buildings were under construction throughout the country, and by midyear, the company maintained that over 1,500 buildings had been erected with the system. Worldwide, in addition to the sales office in London, Truscon had established successful sales agents in Cuba, Jamaica, Chile, Bolivia, Peru, Uruguay, China, Australia, India, and Holland.

In Detroit, Truscon had outgrown its offices and sought larger quarters. During the summer of 1906, the company came to an agreement with the John Owen estate to rent at least two floors in a new, eight-story office building to be financed and owned by the estate. The building was designed by Albert Kahn's firm and constructed by the Concrete Steel and Tile Construction Company beginning in late 1906 and reaching completion in early summer 1907—it was the first reinforced concrete office building in Detroit. Known as the Trussed Concrete Building, it gave Truscon additional marketing leverage in that their address, which appeared in all advertising, was "Trussed Concrete Building, Detroit." By this time, Albert Kahn's firm was doing enough business that it frequently reused building designs in order to reduce the time required to plan and construct similar types of structures. The

Trussed Concrete Building was nearly identical to the original Stambaugh Building in Youngstown, Ohio, also designed by Kahn's firm and constructed by Concrete Steel and Tile in 1907.[2]

Sadly, two workers died during construction of the Trussed Concrete Building in two separate incidents. The first death resulted from carelessness on the part of a worker who leaned too far when looking down an elevator shaft and lost his balance. In the second incident, three workers were standing on scaffolding, installing the cornice that topped the eight-story building; though the men had tested the scaffolding earlier in the day, it suddenly gave way, plummeting to the street below. One of the men grabbed hold of the cornice, eventually making his way into the building through a window. The other two men fell with the scaffold, one having the good fortune to land on a pile of sand and suffering only cuts and bruises. The second was fatally injured. Adding to the casualties, three bricklayers working on another scaffold at the third floor heard the scaffold above give way and dove through open windows to safety, suffering considerable cuts and bruises as a result. As a consequence of the death, the city's building inspector required the use of safety platforms below scaffolds to catch falling workers.[3]

Truscon's factory and warehouse for Kahn Bars was in Detroit. This required the rolled steel from which the bars were manufactured to be shipped to Detroit from the steel mills in Ohio and Pennsylvania. By 1906, with bar sales rapidly increasing, the cost of shipping the steel to Detroit had become quite substantial. Moving the factory and warehouse close to the steel mill would nearly eliminate the additional shipping expense and reduce production delays as well. Truscon acquired a site in Youngstown, Ohio, and constructed a factory on the northwest corner of McGuffey Road and Albert Street; it began operating in May 1907 with 100 employees. Around the same time, the company also set up a small factory in Walkerville, Ontario, Canada. To eliminate the cost and delay of shipping bars to Europe, the London branch in 1908 established a relationship with the Round Oak Steelworks to produce Kahn Bars, and in 1913, built and operated its own factory. The Youngstown plant grew at a dramatic rate, expanding to over 25 acres and employing 5,000 by 1914, with each product line inhabiting its own building. United Steel Sash, having by then become the company's best-selling product, occupied several buildings. As the Youngstown factory evolved from a small, single-product operation to a vast and diverse manufacturing complex, managing from Detroit became increasingly inconvenient. Though reluctant to leave family and friends behind in Detroit, Julius bowed to the inevitable in 1914 and relocated the firm's offices to Youngstown.[4]

Though the offices and factory of Truscon departed Detroit, the company had a division that remained in the city: Truscon Laboratories. This division began in 1906 when Truscon hired a recent graduate of the University of Michigan's chemical engineering program, Roy Alfred Plumb (1883–1954), to test cement, a service required by Concrete Steel and Tile. Within a short time Plumb sold Julius on the idea of establishing a complete chemical testing laboratory, and the Michigan Technical Laboratory was created with Plumb as its head. The laboratory advertised that it provided superintendents and inspectors for reinforced concrete construction and specialized in "sampling, testing and analyzing cement and concrete."[5]

Plumb perceived a weakness in concrete construction: a lack of effective means to protect structures from the destructive effects of contact with water. By 1909 Truscon was marketing waterproofing products developed by Plumb, and in May 1913 the firm—now known as Truscon Laboratories—opened a three-story plant in Detroit to research and manufacture products. This division was a major innovator in the field of chemical coatings, developing widely used compounds for damp proofing and waterproofing industrial, commercial, and residential structures. Plumb remained with Truscon Laboratories as its chief executive until his retirement in 1952, making him Truscon's longest-serving employee.[6]

Truscon expanded its reach domestically by opening offices in secondary cities and quickly met with success. An April 1907 article in an Omaha, Nebraska, paper stated that the Truscon office "has been opened only a short time, but a number of large contracts have been secured by the firm. Among these [is] the new building of the Carpenter Paper Company, which was originally designed for seven stories, but on account of the cheapness of construction will be extended to eight." Three weeks later, the paper reported that the floors of the Carpenter building were being tested to 800 pounds per square foot "without the slightest indication of deflection."[7] The following month the paper announced that Truscon was to construct a telephone exchange for Independent Telephone and four powerhouse substations for Omaha's streetcar company.[8] Truscon also secured contracts within the year for Haarmann Vinegar and Pickle's eight-story warehouse, the eight-story

Henshaw Hotel, and floors for the flagship Brandeis department store in downtown Omaha.[9]

One of the less obvious advantages of concrete factories was the improved safety of food that was produced within them. Wallace R. Montague, owner of the La Crosse Cracker and Candy Company of La Crosse, Wisconsin, had contemplated for some time the idea of an automated factory where crackers could be produced "without any direct contact with human hands from the time the raw material enters the building until the finished product is loaded for shipment." In April 1907 the firm's existing facility was destroyed by fire. Montague planned a new, automated plant in a fireproof, reinforced concrete building. Aside from lowering the cost of production through automation, Montague's products would be cleaner and healthier. Food poisoning was a common and serious problem at the time. Upton Sinclair's book *The Jungle*, describing unsanitary practices in the meatpacking industry, was published in 1906 and focused the public's attention on food manufacturing concerns. The brick-and-timber factories of the time were often infested with rodents, birds, and insects which contaminated food. Concrete buildings, in contrast, were considered "germ proof" and less susceptible to invasion by animals; unlike wooden structures, concrete could be more easily cleaned using liquids, and even hosed down. By "producing food stuffs absolutely free from the unappetizing surroundings usual in food manufacturing plants," La Crosse Cracker and Candy could secure a decided marketing advantage.[10]

Montague's new factory would be challenging to design, as he envisioned it as "a huge piece of machinery in which the raw materials travel through a well defined path. . . . And, after being properly mixed and baked by automatic machinery, the resulting product again passes through a complicated series of machines and conveyors and is delivered to the shipping room." The building had to be designed around the production path and the equipment, some of which was quite large and heavy. Each of the four rotary ovens, for example, weighed more than three tons and had to be located on the top floor of the six-story building. To meet these challenges, the design of the building was placed in the hands of Truscon's engineers. Construction was begun in July 1907, and by July of the following year the factory was in operation. La Crosse Cracker and Candy became the largest independent firm of its type in the upper Midwest, producing over 3 million pounds of crackers and candy each year.[11]

A portrait of Julius Kahn. (Courtesy of The Jacob Rader Marcus Center of the American Jewish Archives, Cincinnati, Ohio, at americanjewisharchives.org)

Truscon's extraordinary growth placed great demands on Julius, yet he found time to develop and patent new products that were added to the company's product line. Inspiration for inventions often came to mind while he was occupied with other tasks. He would, for example, pause a business meeting to sketch an idea for a new product. One of Truscon's vice presidents attended a show with Julius in New York. "The curtain dropped on one of the most exciting scenes I ever witnessed in a theater," the VP stated, "Mr. Kahn turned to me and I expected some breathless comments about the show. Instead, he began showing me a diagram of a new invention he had scrawled over the program."[12]

Truscon manufactured its new products in the same manner as the Kahn Bar: rolled steel from the mill was cut and shaped using large steel presses and other metal-forming equipment. Products introduced between 1906 and 1908 included Rib Metal and Rib Lath. Rib Metal was a large sheet made up of nine steel ribs connected with cross pieces, all formed from a single piece of steel. In use, it functioned much like nine reinforcement bars, but being a single piece, required less labor to install. Rib Lath was a rough steel mesh, intended to provide a grip for plaster, supported at intervals by small ribs. The ribs provided strength to the sheet of mesh, allowing it to cover a larger expanse with fewer supporting studs.

Another new product was the Rib Bar (originally called Cup Bar). This was a six-sided reinforcement bar with ridges or ribs projecting from its upper and lower sides. These ridges helped prevent the bar from slipping within the concrete. The Rib Bar was used to supplement the Kahn Bar when additional reinforcement was necessary or when a simple straight bar without wings was adequate. The most innovative new product from Truscon was Hy-Rib, a steel lath sheet with deep, parallel V-shaped ribs running through it at intervals. The ribs gave the sheet exceptional strength, making it ideal for concrete floor, roof, and wall construction, often eliminating the need for much of the shoring and formwork. By combining lath with ribs in a single sheet, Hy-Rib reduced the number of pieces and the amount and skill level of labor required for construction. It became one of Truscon's most successful products.

Concrete construction had become commonplace by 1908, in large part due to the success in practice of the Kahn System and because Julius had provided a reliable theoretical basis for the technology. Such construction, previously seen as expensive and experimental, was now widely accepted by both the construction industry and its customers. As the quantity of structures built of reinforced concrete multiplied, the number of engineers, contractors, and laborers with knowledge and experience in the method increased, permeating the design and construction fields with expertise. Standards for concrete construction, including the minimum time shoring should be left in place, were generally agreed upon by the major construction firms.[13]

Truscon retained its position as the dominant supplier of reinforcement bars because of its widespread network of offices and agents, well-stocked warehouses in major cities, and engineering competence. Nevertheless, by the end of 1908, the Kahn Bar represented only half of the company's sales of steel products, while sales of the new Rib Bar already accounted for 31 percent and Rib Metal, Rib Lath, and Hy-Rib collectively accounted for 18 percent.[14] It was the new and innovative products that assured Truscon's continued growth and dominance of the market for steel reinforcement products.

In 1912 Truscon began marketing two related products, Floretyle and Floredome, that represented a significant improvement over the Kahn terra cotta floor by replacing the hollow tiles with lightweight steel products. Floretyle was an inverted, U-shaped section of pressed steel, 20 inches wide and available in three- or four-foot lengths. These metal sections performed the same function as the hollow terra cotta tiles in the Kahn floor: minimizing the need for wooden forms while creating a lighter floor without sacrificing strength. Floretyle, however, was much lighter than terra cotta, could be easily and inexpensively transported to and within the construction site, and could be stacked so as to occupy very little storage space. Floredome served the same purpose as Floretyle, but came as a square, domed panel 22 inches on each side, permitting Kahn Bars to be laid perpendicular to each other alongside the domes, increasing the strength of the floor. Both products could be placed on top of Hy-Rib mesh to facilitate finishing of the exposed ceiling of the floor below. Floretyle and Floredome were important products for Truscon, because they extended the life of the Kahn Bar as a product.

As for competitors, engineer Claude A. P. Turner (1869–1955) was perhaps the most important. He developed a "flat slab" system of floor construction around 1905 that did not require beams or joists for support. Turner accomplished this by enlarging the top part of supporting columns into a funnel shape. Above the column and within the floor was a cage of reinforcement bars that extended out through the floor, well beyond the broad top of the column within which they were anchored. These cages resisted shear and supported the floor like a cantilever. Also contained within the floor slab were bands of multiple, lightweight reinforcement bars extending from cage to cage, thereby supporting the area of the floor beyond the cage. This method of construction Turner called the "Mushroom System" because the steel reinforcement cage had the appearance of a mushroom cap. (These types of columns are sometimes referred to as "martini glass"-shaped due to the funnel shape of the column's top.) The flat slab system offered distinct advantages over other construction methods: lower cost and reduction in story height. The chief disadvantage of the Turner system is that it lacked a fully developed theoretical understanding of flat-slab behavior; Turner performed load tests to confirm the minimum capabilities of his system.[15]

Turner first used the system in 1906 to construct the Johnson-Bovey Building in Minneapolis, followed by an increasing number of structures in subsequent years. By 1910 use of the system had become common. Unfortunately for Turner, in 1911 he became embroiled in a patent fight over the system that lasted until 1916, at which point the courts rather surprisingly invalidated Turner's patent in favor of an earlier patent by Orlando Norcross. (A 1924 book by Hool and Kinne said of the Norcross patent that it "did not cover a practical type of construction, no buildings using the system described in the patent ever having been built."[16]) During the period of time the flat-slab patent was in litigation, other flat-slab designs were developed that varied from the Turner system but achieved the same end. Some of these systems added a square concrete "drop panel" beneath the floor slab and above the broadened funnel of the column top. This panel increased the thickness of the floor in the area above the column where shear stresses were greatest, helping to prevent the column from "punching through" the relatively thin floor slab.

The Floretyle and Floredome products permitted the Kahn floor system to remain competitive with the flat-slab systems coming into use, a point demonstrated in a thesis written by William S. Wolfe (1889–1944) for the College of Engineering at the University of Illinois in 1913. Wolfe was an exceptionally talented engineer who later became head of engineering for the Detroit architecture firm of Smith, Hinchman and Grylls. In that capacity he was responsible for devising innovative techniques to facilitate construction of Detroit's Greater Penobscot and Guardian buildings. For his thesis Wolfe compared 10 widely used concrete reinforcement systems and ranked them by cost per square foot of floor for a variety of applications, depending on span length and load supported. He concluded that the least expensive systems were the Kahn System (when used with Kahn Floretyle or Floredome) and the Turner flat-slab system. The Turner system was somewhat less costly than the Kahn System for heavy loads while the Kahn System had the advantage for lighter loads. The Turner system was similar to the other tested systems in the dead weight of the floor, while the Kahn System was the lightest. Wolfe predicted that the Turner and similar flat-slab systems, and systems based on hollow metal boxes, such as Floretyle and Floredome, would likely dominate the market in the future. He also made the significant assertion that, "wide commercial success will depend more on the type of company promoting the system and upon advertisement," a belief already fully incorporated into Truscon's marketing approach.[17]

Claude Turner's rough and, likely, unfair treatment by the court system justifies sympathy for the man's loss, but Turner was capable of dealing out rough treatment as well. In his book *Concrete Steel Construction*, published in 1909, before the patent squabbles began, Turner aggressively and deceptively criticized the Kahn System. In a chapter on load-testing of floors, he reproduced a photo of the Farwell, Ozmun and Kirk warehouse floor test with the caption "Illustrating a misleading test." In the text, Turner stated that "instead of the load being carried by the one beam it is carried in part by the three." Turner continued, "Were the beam cut away, a fair amount of reinforcement should be able to distribute this load to the adjacent beams." The clear implication being that the photo was misleading because it purported to show a single beam being tested when the load was actually being shared by several. The photo had originally appeared in the December 23, 1905, edition of *Engineering News*, accompanied by a letter from Truscon's Maurice Goldenberg. The gist of Goldenberg's letter was that the load in an actual building is not supported entirely by a single beam, but distributed to nearby structural members, and as a result beams in buildings could support greater weight than a single, isolated beam tested in a laboratory. The entire point of Goldenberg's letter was that loads were, in fact, distributed to adjacent beams, so Turner's claim that the photo was misleading was completely fabricated.[18]

In a chapter on the Kahn System, Turner brought up the Bixby Hotel collapse, going into great detail about the shortcomings of the plan of reinforcement for the building, but without mentioning that it was the building's architect who designed the reinforcement scheme, not Truscon, leading the reader to mistakenly assume that the litany of failings were inherent in the Kahn System. Turner went on to state, "A similar collapse with loss of life occurred with a design presenting the same defect at Rochester, N. Y., in a building for the Eastman Kodak Company. . . . The columns were constructed with four of these fin bars, the inwardly projecting fins tending to prevent a solid casting, resulted in weak columns as well as beams lacking in strength." This analysis of the Rochester accident falsely implied that the Kahn Bar, with its attached wings, was the cause of the collapse. Though Truscon was at fault for the accident, it was due to mistakes in construction, not the Kahn reinforcement system. Turner's comment concerning problems using Kahn

Bars in columns was likely based on the coroner's claim that Kahn Bars were not suitable for columns, an assertion later criticized by the British journal *Concrete and Constructional Engineering* as an improper "lay opinion."[19] Moreover, Turner was certainly aware that many thousands of columns had been constructed without incident using the bar. In short, Turner attempted to gain marketing advantage for his system by making a series of false and deceptive arguments intended to undermine confidence in the Kahn System.

One might imagine that Turner justified these fabrications on the basis that Truscon was the dominant firm in the reinforcement field and could take the heat, but he condemned smaller firms as well. In his chapter "Imitations of the Kahn System," Turner wrote, "As the Kahn or Trussed Concrete Steel Company, by exceptional push have succeeded in introducing their type of reinforcement in many buildings over a wide area, there have been quite a number of attempts to imitate the features of their design, namely the attached web member. Quite a few schemes have been gotten out which are even worse than the original." The firm on the receiving end of Turner's snarky comment was the Gabriel Concrete Reinforcement Company of Detroit. Gabriel's reinforcement bar was patented by Detroiter William Gabriel in 1905; it functioned essentially the same as the Kahn trussed bar, but instead of wings punched from a single piece of steel, it had loops of steel attached to a round main bar.[20] Gabriel also offered a floor that was identical to the Kahn floor with bars running between blocks of hollow terra cotta. The chief difference between the two systems was that Gabriel used high-carbon steel and Kahn used mild steel. In practice, high-carbon steel is the stronger of the two but stretches very little before its ultimate strength is reached and it breaks. Mild steel is more elastic and will stretch before reaching its ultimate strength, so failure is progressive rather than sudden. Though high-carbon steel is stronger, Julius preferred mild steel for reinforcement, because structures that become overloaded will sag and crack, thereby warning of imminent failure.[21]

The Gabriel Concrete Reinforcement Company was incorporated in the spring of 1906, and one of the notable investors was Detroit contractor Albert A. Albrecht. With Albrecht's backing, Gabriel was able to secure a number of substantial projects in the following years, mostly in Michigan, Indiana, and Ohio.[22] One of the firm's advertisements from 1908 stated, "Our designs are conservative, which accounts for the fact that we have had no failures."[23] The truth of this claim likely owed more to the small number of buildings constructed using Gabriel reinforcement rather than any characteristic of its design. In any case, the claim was invalidated on November 26, 1912, when a two-story building under construction in Detroit suffered a partial collapse, killing three workers and injuring several others. The cause of the accident was unusual. The building was planned to occupy the entire surface of a lot 70 by 120 feet in size. As the building went up and the rear of the lot was reached, it was discovered that the lot was actually six inches larger than 120 feet. To make up the difference, the last panel of the structure was extended six inches. This was done, however, without securing longer reinforcing rods for the six-inch-longer beams supporting the second floor. Consequently, the rods did not extend far enough into the adjoining columns to be properly anchored. When the concrete roof of the building above these beams was being poured, the shoring under one of the beams began to bend. A number of carpenters and laborers rushed to erect additional shoring beneath the beam, and while they were working beneath it, the beam gave way, bringing down the floor above as well as the partially completed concrete roof.[24]

The family of one of the deceased workers sued the contractor, building owner, and Gabriel, and the subsequent jury trial resulted in a verdict against all three. The building owner and Gabriel both appealed the verdict, and the case ultimately wound up in the Michigan Supreme Court. Two experts had testified that Gabriel's design for the structure was improper. Gabriel, however, trumped the lesser-known experts by calling on Julius Kahn to testify on the company's behalf. The Supreme Court justices described Julius as "an expert of large experience and conceded ability in his profession." Having examined the collapsed portion of the building and made the appropriate calculations, Julius testified, "While not in accordance with the building code, it was such a design as first-class engineers might submit, and . . . the design had nothing to do with the collapse." Significantly, Julius observed that a number of reinforcement bars that appeared on the plans had been omitted from the structure, which "materially decreased the efficiency of the beam" that failed. The bars that were placed were improperly located, "reducing the effectiveness of the beam at that place pretty near 50 percent."[25] It was clear from this testimony that the building had not been constructed according to the plans provided by Gabriel. As a consequence, the court found that neither Gabriel nor the building owner could be held responsible for the worker's death; the lower court should have dismissed the two defendants from the case on the grounds that the building was not constructed according to the plans and only the contractor should have been held accountable. The principle was an important one: the designer of a structure cannot be held responsible for an accident if the plans were not followed. Julius was likely motivated to participate in the case in order to uphold this important principle, which had obvious applicability to his own firm.

The steel reinforcing products of Truscon were largely manufactured using massive presses that shaped and cut the raw steel. Unlike the Kahn Bar, which was rolled at the mill to a specific shape before Truscon cut the wings, other Truscon steel products were formed from simple sheets of steel. In 1913 Julius and Truscon engineer Thomas Kane submitted a patent for an I-beam manufactured from three sheets of pressed steel. This item was notable, as it went beyond Truscon's focus on products to be used in conjunction with reinforced concrete. The firm's experience with construction brought about a realization that there was a need for fire-resistant structural materials for small to medium sized buildings that would normally be constructed of wood. Truscon's extensive expertise in pressed steel manufacturing methods aided the two inventors in devising a beam design that was both economical and overcame the shortcomings of existing pressed steel beams. In particular, the flanges connecting the pieces of steel together in other designs tended to pull apart under certain stresses, a problem eliminated in the Truscon beam by having a second set of flanges holding the first firmly in place. These beams were less costly and more consistent in size and shape than I-beams rolled at the mill, and only slightly more expensive than wood. Truscon soon added steel joists, studs, cap plates, and lintels to its product line, engineered so that they snapped together, requiring only a hammer to assemble. The framing system worked with Hy-Rib lath under and above the joists so the ceiling below could be readily plastered and a concrete floor could be easily poured on top, improving durability, fire-resistance, and noise suppression.[26]

After World War I broke out in Europe in 1914, a purchasing officer for the British government contacted Truscon with an unusual request: the British army needed a prefabricated building to be used as an army field hospital. The structure would have to be easily and quickly constructed by unskilled labor and capable of being taken down and reassembled at another location. Truscon was already producing many of the parts that would comprise such a building, including steel joists, doors, and windows. By adding steel trusses and pressed-steel wall and roof panels, the company developed a standard hospital building that was 20 by 64 feet in size. The British army was supplied with 100 of these building kits.[27] Realizing the enormous potential for easily assembled steel buildings that were durable and fireproof, the company developed the concept into a marketable product line. The Truscon Steel Building could be configured in a nearly infinite number of single-story shapes and sizes; all doors, windows, and hardware required to finish the structure were included. Buildings could be erected in as little as three days by unskilled labor using only a hammer. Far less costly than any other form of fire-resistant construction, a 260-by-28-foot building could be acquired for $3,600, including labor.[28] These structures were ideal for large industrial firms that experienced a sudden increase in business, requiring additional manufacturing or warehouse space. The structures were considered permanent—and indeed many are still in use—but the ease of construction also meant ease of disassembly, so they could be taken apart and moved to another location. Being modular, existing buildings could be reconfigured or enlarged as well. Available by 1916, these buildings permitted many firms to rapidly increase the output of products required by the Allies during World War I.

The Truscon Steel Building illustrates the application of a principle that Julius considered essential to successful manufacturing: "simplification." Using the steel buildings as an example, Julius stated, "By standardizing all the parts required for the construction of a complete building, we make a building of any size, shape, or type." Over time, he continued, "we are steadily standardizing and simplifying; for example, a year ago we had 86 different sizes of steel panels for walls. Today we use 28 sizes. . . . The cost of making the panels has dropped off." All the wall and roof panels were of a single type of 18-gauge steel. The building's windows, doors, and joists were standard off-the-shelf Truscon steel products. "By simplifying all the way through the line," Julius pointed out, "we are thus able to manufacture the parts for these buildings in quantity, and to carry the parts in warehouse stock."[29] That manufacturing in quantity lowers the cost per unit is a fairly well-understood principle; the point about warehousing is less obvious. In order to assure rapid delivery, Truscon stocked all the parts for these buildings in every one of its nearly 20 warehouses throughout the country. Consequently, each reduction in the number of parts reduced the storage space required in every warehouse.

From Monday to Wednesday to Erect This All-Steel Building

These substantial all-steel buildings solve the problem where quick expansion is necessary—they are great savers of time and money.

The illustrations show the various stages of erecting a building that was put up in three days, the only tool required being a hammer.

Not only are they quickly erected, but they are easy to take down and move from one location to another—more economical than wood—never wear out and can be used over and over again.

Monday Noon

Kahn Steel Buildings

are especially suitable for garages, storehouses, factories, offices, schools, hospitals, cottages, election booths, boat houses, etc. Widely used by manufacturers, railroads and contractors. Weather-tight, sanitary, rigid, fireproof. Kahn Steel Buildings are made from interchangeable pressed steel panels—strong, permanent. Provided with steel sash, steel doors and steel tile roof.

Tuesday Noon

"A hammer is the only tool required"

Send for This Free Book
and learn all about Kahn Steel Buildings and their many uses.

TRUSSED CONCRETE STEEL CO.
Dept. P-29, Youngstown, Ohio

KAHN Building Products

TRUSSED CONCRETE STEEL CO

Wednesday, Building ready for Occupancy

An ad for Kahn steel buildings from the September 1916 issue of *Factory* shows a building assembled in three days using only a hammer.

When the United States entered World War I in 1917, many manufacturing firms, including Truscon, converted at least some of their operations to production of war material. One characteristic feature of this war was the incredible number of artillery shells fired, the total numbering in the billions. Truscon's capacity for steel stamping was put to work manufacturing these shells and their components. At the war's conclusion, having engaged in the production of non-construction-related items, the firm realized there was great potential for profit in the manufacturing of pressed steel products. At the time, many steel products were manufactured of cast iron; they could be replaced with similar pressed steel products that were lighter in weight and less costly. Truscon began manufacturing a wide range of goods that included parts bins, vehicle radiators and oil pans, tractor seats, and loading platforms. The firm even developed a unique foundry flask that was as strong as cast iron but weighed 40 percent less and reduced the amount of sand required for casting.[30]

Due to the ever-expanding range of products turned out by the company, a decision was made in 1918 to change its name from Trussed Concrete Steel to Truscon Steel Company. The new name reflected the growing importance of the company's many steel products unrelated to concrete reinforcement. By the 20th anniversary of Truscon's founding, the Kahn Bar department occupied less than 5 percent of the Youngstown factory's space, while the steel window sash and structural steel departments each were six times as large as the Bar department.

One reason for the dramatic growth of Truscon's steel sash products was a change in the nature of factory construction. Architecturally, there were two options for manufacturing facilities: multi-story or single-story. Multi-story structures were generally preferred for light manufacturing and assembly work, while single-story buildings were preferred for machine shops, foundries, and where overhead cranes were required to move heavy materials. Multi-story buildings had an advantage in that they required less land, were less expensive to construct on a square-foot basis, and had lower heating costs. In the early 20th century, moving materials and finished goods within a factory relied primarily on manual laborers using carts. In multi-story buildings, elevators moved material between floors, thereby reducing labor costs by lessening the distance material had to travel by hand. In some plants, conveyers or overhead trolleys were used to bring parts to work stations. Slides or chutes also moved items down through the plant, propelled by gravity. Single-story buildings were better suited for machine shops due to the size and weight of the equipment and because more effective illumination throughout could be provided with a glass or sawtooth roof.

Prior to the 20th century, large factories tended to be multi-story, because the machinery within was powered by either waterwheel or steam engine. Power was carried from the source to the machines by shafts and belts from floor to floor and then to the individual machines by the same method. The distance that shafts could carry power horizontally was quite limited, so the only practical form for factories was a multi-story arrangement. In the early 20th century, steam power came to dominate, though the engine was no longer connected directly to the plant's machines but to dynamos that generated electricity, which powered large motors that ran the shafting in the plant. Electrifying the plant in this way eliminated the necessity for multi-story structures with work areas in close proximity to the power source.

When Henry Ford's Highland Park factory began production in 1910, its layout was fairly typical for the time, with both a multi-story and a single-story building. The two buildings were parallel and roughly 860 feet long. One was a four-story reinforced concrete structure 75 feet in width, housing vehicle assembly, a wood shop, radiator manufacturing, and painting. The adjacent, single-story machine shop was 135 feet wide, with a full sawtooth roof supported by steel columns and trusses, and a concrete floor.[31] By 1915 the Highland Park plant had been greatly enlarged; floor space in the machine shop had more than doubled in size and the space in multi-story buildings was nearly quadrupled.[32] Ford partially solved the problem of transporting material through the factory by establishing the moving assembly line. Raw materials and parts, though, still needed to be brought to stations along the line. At Highland Park, much of the incoming material arrived by railroad, the train cars pulling into a glass-covered court between two of the six-story assembly buildings. An overhead traveling crane was then used to move the material from the railroad siding up to the appropriate floors of the buildings, the sides of which were open to the court.[33] That the crane could deliver materials directly to the floor on which they would be used substantially reduced the amount of manual shuttling of material that would have been required had the plant been on a single floor.

In 1906 the Pennsylvania Railroad started experimenting with battery-powered baggage carts in an effort to reduce the number of laborers and the amount of time needed to transfer baggage. By 1909, successive improvements in the cart's design resulted in a highly effective "baggage truck" that was 12 feet long, had a capacity of 4,000 pounds, and could be operated from either end (eliminating the need for it to turn around). At the Jersey City Terminal, these trucks permitted the regular baggage handlers to accommodate the summer rush without the need for the 18 to 24 seasonal laborers normally brought on.[34] Soon these trucks began appearing in factories, put to use moving materials. In 1914 low lift fork trucks, predecessors to the forklift, appeared. With the onset of World War 1, the need to handle large volumes of materials while the labor force of young men was depleted accelerated the development of mechanized material handling. Between 1917 and 1919 several companies in Great Britain and the United States, including Elwell-Parker and Clark, developed powered lift trucks, which were rapidly adopted as a replacement for muscle power.[35]

With the development of powered material handling, the factory elevator was transformed from a mechanized assistant into a production bottleneck, and the advantage held by multi-story buildings declined in favor of the single-story layout. Aside from eliminating the elevator bottleneck, there were other important advantages to the one-story factory. Illumination in single-story structures could be provided by windows within the roof as well as the exterior walls. This not only improved workspace lighting, it eliminated restrictions on the width of the building—multi-story structures generally were not much wider than 60 feet, because illumination was considered inadequate if a work space was more than 26 feet from windows in the side of a building.[36] Multi-story buildings inhibited the expansion and reconfiguration of departments as a firm increased production and introduced new equipment over time. At Ford's Highland Park plant, for example, by 1915 nearly every department had been moved to a new location within the plant from the one originally occupied in 1910. Given that interior columns in a single-story building had to support only the roof, they could be placed further apart, reducing obstructions within the production area.

According to Albert Kahn, "It was [Henry] Ford who, after building hundreds of acres of floor space in multiple story buildings, concluded that raising materials to upper floors by elevators was a waste because of the time consumed and the cost of transporting materials." Having come to that realization, Ford "abandoned one [factory] after the other, replacing them with one-story structures."[37] Ford saw the advantages of single-story plants early on and realized that the one-story buildings within which his machine shops were located would better serve his entire manufacturing operation than the multi-story buildings he was using. Henry Ford began his shift to single-story operations in 1915 when he acquired 2,000 acres of land along the River Rouge in Dearborn, Michigan, with the intent that 600 acres would be used for the construction of a large, integrated manufacturing facility.[38]

The chief impediment to fully adopting single-story plants was that they required a far greater amount of land, particularly as future additions to buildings would require even more space. Large plots of land were available primarily in areas beyond the reach of a city's mass transit system, so the success of such a move hinged, to an extent, upon a high level of automobile ownership among the workforce.

Reinforced concrete was not ideally suited for construction of single-story factories, so most were constructed with a concrete floor, a structural steel frame, and an exterior of steel sash windows. While these buildings did not require Kahn Bars, the exterior walls were largely composed of Truscon steel window sash. Where solid exterior walls were needed, Hy-Rib covered with cement mortar was used; many of the steel framework pieces were provided by Truscon as well. The amount of Truscon steel in these buildings was greater than in a reinforced concrete structure.

An early example of the single-story, steel frame factory was the Industrial Works in Bay City, Michigan, designed by Albert Kahn's firm in 1910. The building was 530 feet long and 156 feet wide, broken up into three bays of various heights and widths. The building had four rows of steel columns supporting the walls and roof trusses. The exterior walls were composed of horizontal bands of Truscon steel window sash and bands of Hy-Rib plastered with cement. Each of the three bays had a roof of Hy-Rib with a band of steel sash windows running down the middle third.[39]

By 1917 the single-story plant with walls of glass was becoming common. With the United State's entry into World War I, the urgent need for war-related manufacturing spurred the construction of new plants. The largest US manufacturer of aircraft, the Curtiss Aeroplane and Motor Corporation, found its existing plants inadequate for the volume of production demanded, so in July 1917, Curtiss signed a contract for construction of a new plant. Within three months, the new North

Elmwood factory was turning out completed aircraft. Covering an area the size of 10 city blocks, it was the largest aircraft plant in the world. The building had a steel frame and roof trusses, and an exterior of steel Truscon windows.[40]

One factory constructed by Henry Ford at his new River Rouge complex was notable for its enormous size and the fact that it manufactured Navy boats. During World War I, German U-boats sank millions of tons of shipping headed for Great Britain, threatening that nation's capacity to feed its population and maintain its armed forces. Destroyers were desperately needed to protect merchant ships from submarines, but because destroyers were complex and time-consuming to build, a smaller and simpler boat was designed to chase submarines. American shipyards were backed up constructing other high-priority ships, so the Navy asked Ford if his company could manufacture the submarine chasers. In January 1918 Ford Motor, in conjunction with Albert Kahn's firm, began planning a factory to produce the Eagle-class patrol boats. Plans for the building were completed on February 11, 1918, and incredibly, the first completed boat was launched five months later on July 11. The building was 1,700 feet long and 250 feet wide with a structural steel frame; its exterior walls were enclosed in four acres of Truscon steel windows. Inside were three ship construction tracks, each with seven stations at which a particular series of steps were carried out until the completed hull emerged from the end of the building and was launched, ready to be fitted out.[41] The war ended before any of the boats entered service, though eight of them served in some capacity during World War II, one of which was sunk by a German submarine.[42]

After the war, new plants were constructed in both single-story and multi-story designs, the choice often based on the availability of land and the willingness of the company to relocate farther from the city. The Hinkley Motors Corporation, for example, was a manufacturer of truck engines that in 1921 constructed a new plant in Ecorse, Michigan, eight miles from downtown Detroit. The main section of the plant was a single story, roughly 300 by 250 feet in size, with a two-story office wing at one end. The exterior of the structure was steel sash windows, and each of the building's seven bays had a large roof monitor with windows on both sides to admit light. *Motor West* magazine said of the plant, "It conforms to modern practice by housing all activities on the ground floor," with "provision for daylight on all sides and above." As for the site, the article noted that it "comprises over seven acres, and will permit an almost indefinite further expansion." The plant's location so far from the city's labor pool may have raised concerns at Hinkley, but the *Motor West* write-up nevertheless asserted that it meant "freedom from the congested labor conditions of Detroit, and a position of local dominance."[43]

Packard Motor, Murray Corporation, and Fisher Body were among the large auto-industry firms that continued adding to their multi-storied plants during the 1920s. All three companies operated factories within the city of Detroit long after Ford and Chrysler began a shift to single-story plants in the suburbs.[44]

During the twenties and thirties, Albert Kahn's firm produced a series of exceptional and iconic factory designs, made possible by Truscon's steel construction products. Ford Motor Company's 1923 River Rouge Glass Plant was a stunning achievement in successfully meeting its intended purpose and in its dramatic appearance. The 760-foot-long building contained four glass-making furnaces capable of producing 12 million square feet of glass per year. The building itself was essentially a lightweight enclosure of glass sufficient to keep the weather out while allowing sunlight to enter and heat to circulate out. Nearly all the exterior walls were Truscon steel sash windows, most of which were operable to allow air circulation. The small areas which were not of glass were Hy-Rib with cement plaster.

Though many reinforced concrete factories were constructed during the late teens and twenties, the general trend was toward steel and glass. Among Julius's more than 75 patents were products that accelerated that trend, and resulted in new products that were ultimately as successful as the Kahn Bar. By the mid-twenties, Truscon steel sash was not only the firm's largest and most profitable division, Truscon was the largest supplier of steel sash in the world. Unlike the situation with the Kahn Bar, Truscon was not the first company to market steel sash. Detroit Steel Products was first with their Fenestra brand, which was quite successful. But Truscon developed a superior product that better met the needs of customers, an outcome likely due in part to Truscon applying its greater understanding of metal forming processes to eliminate the weaknesses in the Fenestra window's design. Moreover, Truscon's sales offices or agents in more than 30 cities nationally gave it an enormous advantage over Detroit Steel.

Truscon's new products continued to fuel its growth. By the 1920s, Truscon had domestic sales offices in 60 cities and warehouses in 20

The main plant of the Truscon Steel Company in its heyday. The factory was located west of Albert Street between McGuffey Road and Truscon Court in Youngstown, Ohio. The offices were across the street in the L-shaped building in the lower center of the photo. (Truscon sales brochure, courtesy the collection of the Archives Research Center of the Mahoning Valley Historical Society)

cities. Eight years later, Truscon had a plant in Los Angeles, which reduced shipping expenses for West Coast customers, and had acquired a pressed-steel business in Cleveland that manufactured vehicle parts. Plants in Canada, England, and Japan helped supply international customers. Total sales for the company in 1928 were $34 million, more than triple the total of 10 years earlier. Truscon, with more than 5,000 employees, was the largest steel fabricating company on the continent.[45]

Julius Kahn's strategy for growing the company included rapidly expanding the sales efforts throughout the United States and then into foreign markets, providing engineering and construction services, and continual development of problem-solving products. These were "outward facing" efforts that primarily involved the company's relationship with the marketplace. Julius also utilized inward-facing strategies to encourage inventiveness and commitment among employees, the most important of which was hiring excellent people. Among them was Maurice Goldenberg, an M.I.T.-educated engineer hired in 1903; he remained with Truscon until his retirement, serving as an officer and a director of the firm. In contrast to the highly educated Goldenberg, there was Thomas H. Kane, who left school at age 15 to work in a Detroit machinist shop. By 1908 he had 20 years experience in the steel industry and was hired by Truscon as manager of the Youngstown factory. Kane became a director of the company in 1920, replacing Joseph Boyer (who chose not to serve on account of his age). Most impressive, though, was Kane's skill at invention, securing on behalf of Truscon more than 25 patents between 1909 and 1925.[46]

The engineering department of the firm sought to hire inventors and encouraged them to develop new products and improve existing ones. The engineers, according to a company official, "are encouraged by the president to work on new devices which may reward them financially and also help Truscon to keep at the forefront of the industry."[47] This encouragement resulted in important new products for Truscon, among them a widely adopted aviation hangar door. Hangars were a natural extension of the Truscon steel building product line. The doors, first marketed in the late 1920s, were a steel version of a telescoping door system first developed by Albert Kahn's firm in 1918 for US Army Air Corps hangars at training fields.[48] By 1928 Truscon was building two hangars a day. Then Truscon engineer David H. Morgan developed a new type of power operated lift door that was far superior to the telescoping types. The door could be fully opened in 50 seconds across its entire length, would operate under any weather and wind conditions, and did not place undue stress on the roof truss from which it was suspended. These doors were widely adopted during the 1930s, when many airports were constructed. They also provided Truscon an important source of revenue during the Depression when other construction activity declined precipitously.[49]

A spirit of cooperation and friendly competition was fostered within the company by rewarding department managers with generous bonuses tied to the firm's profitability. For the sales department, monthly contests provided bonuses to sales representatives, while district sales managers received bonuses based on profitability. On the shop floor, machine operators received additional pay when their output exceeded 80 percent of the rated capacity of their machine.[50]

Truscon was one of the first companies to provide group accident and life insurance for all its employees. In addition to insurance coverage, the plan provided a visiting nurse service for employees homebound due to illness or accident. An attorney was available at no cost to employees who had—or wished to avoid—legal difficulties, a service that was said to have prevented numerous mortgage foreclosures and even divorces.[51]

Aside from monetary inducements and beneficial services, there was an intangible quality in the nature of Julius's leadership of Truscon. "He possessed an unusual faculty for inspiring men and getting the best out of them," wrote Maurice Goldenberg. "His organization was not merely faithful, but imbued with an intense desire to please him."[52] This loyalty was demonstrated in 1933 when, largely due to provisions of the National Industrial Recovery Act, union membership in the steel industry swelled from about 20 percent to over 80 percent, yet Truscon employees, as reported by the *Wall Street Journal*, "by a large majority [had] voted against formation of a company union."[53]

Conclusion

The stock market crash of 1929 and subsequent Great Depression brought about a dramatic reduction in the construction of buildings, particularly those types that would require Truscon steel products. The total amount spent on new, nonresidential private construction—industrial structures, warehouses, office buildings, and stores—in the United States during 1929 was just over $2 billion. By 1932 that amount had collapsed to $290 million, an 86 percent drop.[1]

The lack of construction activity is apparent from the paltry listings in the order book of Albert Kahn's architecture firm: fewer than 15 jobs were recorded in 1932, consisting of mostly minor repair work and inspections. The sole building design was a warehouse for Kellogg's in Battle Creek. In contrast, the company recorded over 70 jobs in 1929, with more than 30 of them being factories, factory complexes, or warehouses.[2]

Truscon had its best year in 1929, with sales exceeding $38 million and net income of $2.8 million; two years later, however, sales had fallen to $18.5 million, resulting in Truscon's first profitless year. Sales were even worse in 1932, dropping to $10 million and producing a loss of $1.7 million, followed by further losses in 1933. In January 1934 Truscon's Youngstown plant was operating at only 30 percent of capacity, a severe drop from the late 1920s when the company was often running at full capacity. At the same time, the country's two largest steel producers, US Steel and Bethlehem Steel, were expanding into the fabrication field, potentially posing a competitive threat to Truscon. The third-largest steel producer was Republic Steel, a major supplier to Truscon, and it, too, sought to enter the fabrication field. During the summer of 1934, Republic approached Truscon with the idea of merging the two companies. By the end of August, Julius had arranged with officials at Republic a merger that he described as very favorable to the stockholders of Truscon; it was executed in October 1935. At the time merger talks began, Truscon was sustaining financial losses that could only be reversed by a substantial improvement in the country's economic situation. Most of Truscon's senior managers and stockholders were in their sixties or older and likely felt that accepting the offer from Republic was a better option than waiting for the economy to improve.

Most of Truscon's employees remained with the company, though as one former manager put it, "Few of Mr. Kahn's associates were able to survive under the Republic ownership. The key men of a smaller organization are the ones who suffer whenever there is an amalgamation between a smaller institution and a much larger commercial concern."[3] Julius joined Republic as vice president of product development and was elected to Republic's board of directors. At Republic, Julius continued to invent, securing several construction-related patents. His employment change also entailed moving from Youngstown to Cleveland where Republic was headquartered.

In 1939 Julius, then 65 years old, resigned from Republic. He spent time working with Truscon Laboratories as chairman of the board (it was spun off from Truscon shortly after the merger) and as president of Kahn Realty, a Detroit real estate firm operated by Julius, Albert, and their wives. But Julius still craved the innovation and fast-paced environment of a small company. At the time Julius resigned from Republic, four other former Truscon managers left as well and formed a new company: United Steel Fabricators. The opportunity that prompted this seemingly high-risk leap of faith during a depression was the announcement by United Engineering and Foundry of Wooster, Ohio, that it was moving its plant to Japan. United Steel Fabricators purchased the empty plant, acquired steel fabricating equipment, and began operations. Julius took an active role as a founder and advisor to the new firm and provided a generous loan to get it up and running. The company was successful. It made important contributions to the war effort and remained in operation more than 50 years, closing its doors in 1991.[4]

The first member of the close-knit Kahn family to pass away was mother Rosalie, who died at the age of 66 in 1912 from complications due to atrial fibrillation, a condition she had lived with for 15 years. Joseph lived to the ripe old age of 90, passing away in 1935 at home in Detroit. In January 1939 Moritz died of a heart attack at age 59, the third of the eight Kahn siblings to pass away, Paula having died in 1924 at age 46 and Gustave in 1938 at 70. At the time of his death, Moritz was a vice president in Albert Kahn's architectural firm, a position he had taken in 1923 after leaving London. He had served as managing director of Truscon's English subsidiary from its founding until 1923, four years after the subsidiary was bought out by its British partners.

Mollie Kahn's Multi-Color Company continued on quite successfully and by the 1940s was the largest reproduction company in Michigan. Mollie married Walter Fuchs in 1906, and he subsequently gave up a promising career with Burroughs to help Mollie run Multi-Color. Shortly before the couple's first child was born, Mollie stepped aside from an active role in the business. In 1950 management of the company passed to the couple's son, Albert L. Fuchs, who ran it for nearly 40 years, selling it in the late 1980s. The business continued on under new owners until 2001. Mollie died in 1940 at the age of 63.

In late October 1942, Julius contracted pneumonia and within days succumbed to the illness, passing away on November 4 at age 68 in his home in Cleveland. One month later, his brother Albert was stricken by a heart attack and died at home on December 8. With Albert's death, leadership of Albert Kahn Associated Architects and Engineers Inc. passed to his youngest brother, Louis, who had been with the firm since 1909 and was its executive head. Louis died in September 1945 at the age of 60.

After Louis's death, Felix Kahn was the sole living sibling of the eight children of Joseph and Rosalie Kahn. His San Francisco–based construction firm of McDonald and Kahn was enormously successful, and among its achievements was the Union Square Garage, the first multistory, public, underground parking garage, constructed in 1941.[5] Felix was indirectly responsible for one of the most interesting tributes to his brother Albert, a concrete ship constructed in October 1944: the SS *Albert Kahn*. The concrete shipbuilding program of World War II was an outgrowth of a similar effort during the First World War with ships

Albert (*left*) and Julius Kahn in Detroit
sometime in the 1930s.
(Albert Kahn Associates Inc.)

designed by McDonald and Kahn. Felix succumbed to a heart attack at
age 76 in June 1950.

Five of the six Kahn brothers received patents for inventions. Julius
was far and away the stellar performer in this respect, with more than
75, many of them of great significance. Moritz was next, with around
a half dozen patents registered in the United States and Great Britain,
including, oddly enough, one for a concrete ship. Patents that improved
the Truscon steel sash window were among at least four secured by
Gustave. Felix received two patents on construction related inventions.
Albert had at least two as well, one of which was for his design of the
Packard Forge Building.[6]

Republic Steel was well rewarded for its purchase of Truscon, which
was profitable again by 1936 on sales of almost $21 million. When pro-
duction of war-related products began, Truscon was swamped with
work, much of it critical to frontline fighting. The Youngstown plant
produced kits for LSTs (landing ship tank) that were transported to the

Philadelphia Navy Yard for assembly. These 328-foot-long oceangoing ships were used to transport troops and their tanks or tracked vehicles (LVTs) across the ocean and right to the landing beach. Truscon manufactured steel mats used to quickly build airfields on remote islands, as well as fuselages for the aircraft based there. Tank treads, ammunition boxes, steel buildings, storage boxes for tanks, and over 400 parts for military vehicles were all produced by Truscon. In England, Truscon built the reinforced concrete Phoenix breakwaters used to construct the prefabricated Mulberry Harbours for the D-Day landings. Concrete anti-aircraft domes, used to train gunners, were manufactured by the company. These half-round structures, 40 feet in diameter, looked like igloos and simulated air attacks by projecting images on the building's interior. Jigs made of concrete were constructed by the firm and used to manufacture the long-range Short Sunderland submarine hunter and rescue aircraft. Parts for aircraft, engines, and tanks were manufactured, and so were Bailey Bridges, transportable bridges used by troops and vehicles to cross rivers where existing bridges had been destroyed.[7]

After the war, Truscon operated profitably, selling the products it had developed prior to 1934. In 1948 the company's sales reached $60 million, but Truscon was no longer innovating as it had under Julius's leadership. Only a handful of patents were granted to the firm—the last submitted in 1951—a circumstance that did not bode well for the company's future. Moreover, Republic had unionized Truscon by including its workers in the basic steel workers contract, thereby making it more difficult for the company to compete with independent fabricators that were not restricted by union work rules.[8] As each of Truscon's product lines became unprofitable, it was discontinued. By 1957 employment at the Youngstown plant had fallen from its pre-war high of 2,000 to around 1,400, and just three years later it was down to 500. In the mid-1960s Truscon's window division, at one time its largest and most profitable, was closed. By 1981 Truscon was a money-losing division for Republic. In an effort to reduce expenses, Republic attempted to negotiate with the union a cut in pay, but was unable to reach an agreement. In April 1982 Republic announced that the Truscon division would be closed permanently, putting its 450 remaining employees out of work.[9]

The effectiveness of reinforced concrete construction in reducing fatalities and property loss due to fire is difficult to measure, but there can be no question that the effect has been substantial. The overall death rate from fire in the United States was 5.5 per 100,000 in 1890. The rate

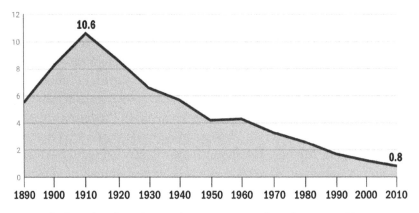

The death rate from fire in the United States per 100,000. (Data from Dept. of the Interior, Causes of Death, Burns and Scalds, 1896; Dept. of Commerce and Labor, Mortality Statistics, Table III, 1905, 1917; National Center for Health Statistics, Vital Statistics of the United States, tables 137–138; National Center for Health Statistics 2010–2019 Mortality Data Files)

climbed to a high of 10.6 in 1910 and then gradually declined to 1.1 in 2010. These rates are skewed by many factors, not the least being that most fire deaths in the United States occur in homes, not in large buildings. Reducing the threat of death and destruction from fire required the invention of fire resistant construction technology, but also the implementation of further safety measures, as the Triangle Shirtwaist factory fire demonstrated—"fireproof" construction was the first step, but adequate fire suppression and provision for occupant egress were necessary as well.

While reinforced concrete was rapidly adopted for much new commercial and industrial construction, the advantages of the technology accrued slowly, as older brick-and-timber buildings remained in use for many years. In spite of the advantages of concrete, mill construction continued to be popular for structures into the 1920s, in part due to promotional efforts mounted by brick manufacturers and bricklayers. An article conveying the contents of a report issued in 1924 by the Common Brick Manufacturers' Association claimed, "Two forms of construction using large quantities of brick, commonly used in the past but for a period displaced by more or less experimental forms, are coming again into strong favor." The two forms referred to were steel frame buildings with brick curtain walls and mill construction with timber framing and brick side walls. The steel frame building, it was stated, "has been displaced in some sections by other forms of fire resistive construction which were for a time believed to cost less." "In general factory and industrial building," it was claimed, "mill construction seems to be coming back strongly. This is unquestionably the most economical type of safe building possible to erect, and . . . it affords what is considered ample protection with sprinkler equipment." The chief concern of the Brick Manufacturers' Association is revealed late in the report: "The mill type building also is an outlet for vast quantities of bricks since the side walls are invariably solid brick load bearing." Contrary to the article's optimistic subhead—"Return of Two Forms of Construction Brings Increase in Demand"—the reader was informed that recent shipments of brick were about the same as in previous months while current orders showed a slight decrease.[10]

An effort by the National Lumber Manufacturer's Association to promote mill construction took a more constructive approach. "Any building material," the organization insisted, "is entitled to be judged on its results when used according to the best principles and practice." To this end, they noted that the common practice of topping wooden support columns with steel caps was a mistake; in case of fire, the heat would destroy the steel before the column failed. Instead, they suggested, a recently developed cap made of concrete would increase the fire resistance of the structure.[11] While this change improved the safety of mill construction, it begged the question: Why not construct the entire building of concrete?

Efforts to promote mill construction may have had some role in convincing Frederick E. Wadsworth to construct his six-story, 250,000-square-foot, auto body manufacturing plant using the method. Perhaps he was assured that, should a fire break out, it would be quickly doused by the 50,000 gallons of water in the tank that fed the building's sprinkler system. The Wadsworth Manufacturing plant was completed in 1916 on the north side of East Jefferson Avenue in Detroit. On the evening of Friday, August 1, 1919, flames were spotted pouring from the windows of the paint shop located in the northeast corner of the building's sixth floor. Within minutes, nearly all of the fire department's equipment was on the scene, but the blaze was so hot that firefighters made little headway. The intense fire boiled asphalt pavement and two fire engines had to be abandoned. Within a short time, the roof caved in, followed soon after by the exterior walls, one of which landed on the abandoned fire engines, destroying them. Burning timbers that had comprised the building's interior structure were sent flying by several explosions, spreading the fire to nearby buildings.

When it was over, all that remained of the big factory were small sections of the exterior walls up to the second floor. Unsurprisingly, the reinforced concrete towers enclosing the stairways were essentially undamaged. The utter failure of the sprinkler system to quell or even slow the fire was due to inadequate automatic fire doors. Protected by only a single fire door, the passageways through the building's interior firewalls should have had an automatic fire door on each side. Fed by highly flammable materials used for painting, upholstering, and varnishing, the expanding fire traversed the passageways before the single, heat-activated door closed, permitting it to spread rapidly throughout the entire building. The total loss came to $1.25 million, making it the worst fire in Detroit history. The plant was replaced the following year with a reinforced concrete building designed by Albert Kahn's firm.[12]

Ironically, as the Wadsworth factory burned, the city of Detroit was in the process of rewriting its building code with a particular emphasis on fire safety. Heeding the lessons of the Triangle Shirtwaist fire, those writing the code recognized that "the quickness of emptying the building of its occupants is the prime object." To that end, the code required multiple fireproof stairway enclosures located no more than 150 feet from any point in the building. The code also required greater safety measures for more densely occupied structures, and those where flammable materials were stored or in use. An article in *American Architect* noted that the code-writing committee's focus on stairways and rapid egress was an "important departure" from codes in place elsewhere, and that Detroit "will lead other cities in the adequacy of its regulation of this very important factor in a building code."[13]

The Wadsworth fire didn't reign long as Detroit's worst; it was surpassed in 1927 by a strikingly similar fire at Briggs Manufacturing. Like Wadsworth, Briggs was also a manufacturer of auto bodies, and its mill construction factory had been built just four years earlier. Once again, fire began in a paint shop, in this case caused by an explosion triggered by sparks from a broken light that ignited paint fumes. The paint shop was located on the fourth floor of the five-story building, and the force of the explosion caused the shop's floor to collapse onto the third floor, trapping some workers. Aside from those killed by the explosion and collapse, the building's roughly 200 occupants were able to quickly exit the structure ahead of the advancing flames. Between those who died in the building and those who died later of their injuries, 20 lives were lost. The blaze consumed the entire 750-foot-long building, and the loss was estimated to be $3 million.[14]

Unfortunately, lessons learned through experience are sometimes forgotten over time. In 1953 the most destructive industrial fire in American history struck the automobile industry and exposed how, after many years without major fire losses, factories were being constructed without adequate attention to the danger of fire.[15] General Motors Corporation invented the first automatic transmission and introduced it into production automobiles in 1939. Called the Hydra-Matic, the innovation was such a success that other automakers, including Ford, Hudson, Kaiser, and Nash, purchased Hydra-Matic transmissions for their own vehicles. In 1948 demand was such that GM made the decision to build an enormous new plant in suburban Detroit to manufacture the transmission. The plant was a single-story structure (except for the two-story office section) of over 1.5 million square feet—nearly 35 acres.

Around 4:00 p.m. on August 12, a contractor's welding crew was repairing a steam line near the ceiling. Nearby was a tank containing rust-inhibiting liquid into which transmission parts were dipped. As the parts left the tank, carried along by an overhead trolley, excess liquid would be caught in a 120-foot-long drip pan beneath. A spark from the welding torch fell into this pan, causing the flammable liquid to catch fire. The welding crew nearly succeeded in quelling the fire, but the two extinguishers they were using ran dry. The fire spread the length of the drip pan, which then collapsed, spilling burning liquid onto the floor. The steel roof trusses and panels over an adjacent heat treating area had acquired a layer of oily condensate, which now caught fire. The Hydra-Matic plant had a flat roof of steel panels covered with numerous layers of tar paper and asphalt. As heat from the fire reached the roof, the steel panels began to buckle and separate, exposing the three pounds per square foot of tar and asphalt above. The asphalt began to melt and drip through cracks between panels, igniting as it fell and setting fire to the oil-soaked wood floor, flammable oils used by the machinery, and dip tanks. Unlike many single-story, daylight factories built prior to World War II with sawtooth roofs and operable windows, this plant's flat roof had no vents or windows to allow the fire's heat to escape. Instead, the blaze was drawn toward those work areas equipped with exhaust fans to carry away fumes.[16]

When firefighting equipment arrived on the scene, the fire had already collapsed the central portion of the plant's roof, skewing the building's frame. This in turn caused the exterior walls to be pulled inward along the top, making it impossible for firefighters to enter the structure. Streams of water were sprayed on the building from its perimeter, but hose streams could reach no more than 75 feet and the building was nearly 900 feet wide. The blaze continued through the night and eventually burned itself out the next day.

Incredibly, only three lives were lost inside the building; more than 4,000 employees were able to safely evacuate through 83 exits, demonstrating one advantage of a single-story building. More than 3,300 machines, some of them custom built to manufacture GM's transmissions, were damaged, a thousand of them beyond repair. The building, of course, was entirely destroyed. The loss was estimated at between $50 and $70 million (more than a half billion in 2020 dollars) with insurance coverage of only $32 million. Worse, the company's inability to manufacture Hydra-Matic transmissions resulted in a loss of roughly 100,000 vehicle sales, which cost them an estimated $250 million.[17]

Much had been overlooked or ignored in the plant's design; the Hydra-Matic factory was less well-defended against complete loss by fire than the typical mill construction factory of the late 1800s. Serious failures in the design of the plant's fire defenses were legion. Sprinkler protection was grossly inadequate, with only about 15 percent of the building covered and no sprinklers in the manufacturing area. Nearly the entire plant was under one roof, with no firewalls to divide up the enormous space into smaller areas within which a fire might be contained (the two-story office structure at the front of the plant was saved by a firewall between it and the main building). The steel columns, trusses, and roof decking were unprotected, so structural collapse ensued not long after they were exposed to fire. The roof lacked any means of venting heat from a fire, causing flames and smoke to spread more rapidly within the structure. Only the obvious fire hazards were protected by automatic extinguishers—the dip tank, for example, but not its 120-foot-long drip pan containing the same flammable liquid. The heat treating area was inadequately ventilated, resulting in an accumulation of a flammable, oily condensate on the structural steel and underside of the roof. In spite of the building's size and more than 4,000 occupants, there apparently was no organized and well-equipped employee fire brigade capable of fighting the blaze before it gained headway.

The Hydra-Matic fire caused business leaders to reawaken to the possibility that fire could cripple their businesses. Nearly four months after the blaze, *Business Week* wrote, "Today the fire is still a major topic whenever businessmen get together." "Industry is shocked," the magazine continued, "by the fact that a relatively new plant like Livonia could go up in smoke in just a few hours. Staffs are working overtime to check fire-protection and insurance setups all across the country, and top management wants to see these reports personally."[18] Shock inspired action as numerous measures were put in place by manufacturers to analyze their risk and mitigate it, led, unsurprisingly, by General Motors. The firm hired a leading fire-protection expert to consult with the company on improving fire safety in its plants. One year after the Hydra-Matic fire, GM announced steps being taken to reduce the risk of fire loss. The most ambitious was to construct firewalls in all its plants so that no open area was larger than 250,000 square feet. Hazardous operations would be isolated by fire barriers or, with the highest-risk activities, moved to a different structure outside the main building. Sprinklers would cover the full extent of plants and would be fed by at least two sources of water. Finally, the company planned to revitalize its fire brigades with comprehensive training and adequate equipment, including mobile fire carts and fully equipped fire trucks.[19]

In a sense, the threat of fire in manufacturing buildings had come full circle. Mill construction factories, susceptible to destruction by fire, were replaced by safer and lower cost reinforced concrete buildings. Concrete factories made possible the mass production of affordable automobiles that, once acquired by the masses, facilitated the movement of factories to the suburbs and beyond. With an abundance of land available, single-story plants replaced multi-story structures, and the preferred method of construction became steel frame. World War II brought with it the need for plants to operate 24 hours a day using artificial illumination; the widespread use of economical fluorescent lights brought an end to the era of the daylight factory and its walls and ceilings of glass. Postwar factory engineers and architects lacked the experience with fire that had caused their predecessors to exercise so much caution in the design of buildings and fire suppression systems, so once again plants were susceptible to total destruction by fire.

The Packard Motor Company ran into financial difficulties after the war and shut down operations at its massive Detroit plant on East Grand Boulevard in 1956. Space in the Packard plant was leased to other businesses, including Jewel Waste and Materials and Detroit Mill Supply, each of which occupied a single floor of the seven-story, reinforced concrete Packard stock building (Building No. 5), constructed in 1910. Just before noon on February 9, 1959, a fire broke out in the rags stored by Jewel Waste on the fifth floor. By 3:30 that afternoon the fire was under control, but less than an hour later, it burst out again, this time among the rags of Detroit Mill Supply on the sixth floor. The fire department was called back to the scene and within 90 minutes, they had the blaze under control.[20] The owners claimed the fire caused $75,000 damage to their building, but this figure was likely motivated more by a desire for a plump insurance payout than actual harm to the structure. Another fire in 1966 caused around $500,000 worth of damage to businesses within the Packard complex but did little damage to the structure.[21] The old concrete buildings of the Packard plant, designed by Albert and Julius Kahn, simply could not be brought down by fire.

Though Kahn Bars are no longer used for reinforced concrete construction, the principles of concrete reinforcement set forth by Julius Kahn remain fundamental. Julius argued that shear stresses must be countered by reinforcement, and the shear reinforcement must be firmly attached to the main horizontal reinforcement bar. This was accomplished by the wings on his bar, and today by vertical stirrups firmly attached to the horizontal reinforcement bars. Julius correctly understood that the weight-bearing capacity of a beam could only be reliably calculated if failure always occurred due to the steel reinforcement bar snapping near the center of the beam. Once these essential principles were established and promoted by Julius, concrete construction was widely adopted.

Julius Kahn's impact on construction, architecture, and fire safety cannot be overstated. Captain John Sewell, writing about the rapid development of reinforced concrete construction, noted that the Kahn Bar had removed all previous "limitations as to [concrete's] possible uses." "This century," he continued, "is likely to be known as the Concrete Age."[22] If anything, this prediction proved an understatement. Sewell, Kahn, and others could hardly have imagined how essential and pervasive concrete would become. It is an essential part of our lives that we largely take for granted. This may explain, to some degree, why the story of Julius Kahn's breakthrough innovations, which made reinforced concrete so common and indispensable, have been taken for granted as well.

Acknowledgments

I would like to thank the following individuals, whose assistance with this book is greatly appreciated. William Brenner provided advice and vital assistance with my research for which I am tremendously grateful. Without the cheerful accommodation of my research needs by Caitlin Wunderlich, Heidi Pfannes, and Don Bauman of Albert Kahn Associates Inc., this book would not have been possible. The helpful staff at the Bentley Historical Library at the University of Michigan in Ann Arbor deserves credit for their acquisition of, and provision of access to, a phenomenal collection of material from the Kahn firm and Kahn family. A special thank you to Michael O. Smith for assisting me in locating an important set of building plans. Dale Carlson's indefatigable work on the web post "Albert Kahn: 400 Buildings in Metro Detroit" resulted in an essential reference. Previous research by Christopher Meister provided a foundation for important aspects of this project. My brother Dan Smith furnished an architect's input on technical matters. My friend Theodore D. Held was always available to help. Romie Minor and Carla Reczek at the Detroit Public Library helped me gain access to historical photographs in their collection. Requests for assistance locating important documents, plans, and photographs were answered by Bert Hartman and Sandi Gish at the Oregon Department of Transportation;

Amanda Wick at the Charles Babbage Institute Archives, University of Minnesota Libraries; Howard Rich of Rich Products Corporation, Buffalo; MaryAnn Bever, Wabash County Highway Department; Martha Bishop at the Youngstown Historical Center of Industry and Labor; Laura Gottlieb, curator of the Rabbi Leo Franklin Archives, Temple Beth El, Bloomfield Hills, Michigan; Sarah B. Wilschek of Congregation Rodef Sholom, Youngstown; and Tim Seman of the Public Library of Youngstown and Mahoning County. At the University of Michigan Press, I owe a debt of gratitude to Elizabeth Demers, Haley Winkle, Kevin Rennells, Shiraz Abdullahi Gallab, Danielle Coty-Fattal, Jamie Jones, and Matthew Somoroff.

Notes

CHAPTER 1

1. "Ten Men Jumped from Windows," *Detroit Free Press*, March 10, 1901, 1.

2. "Almost Fourteen Millions," *Hartford Courant*, March 6, 1901, 10; "Cork Factory Is Destroyed," *Omaha Daily Bee*, February 10, 1901, 5; "Tumbler Factory Destroyed," *Los Angeles Evening Express*, February 12, 1901, 1.

3. "Annual Fire Losses in the United States for Thirty-Six Years—1875–1910," in *The Insurance Year Book* (New York: Spectator Co., 1911), 39:516.

4. "Go Up," *Louisville Courier-Journal*, February 21, 1902, 1.

5. "Insurance Rates Up," *Buffalo Commercial*, February 27, 1902, 12.

6. A concise and detailed description of slow-burning or mill construction written by its foremost proponent, Edward Atkinson, may be found in *A Dictionary of Architecture and Building* by Russell Sturgis, vol. 3, 530–33. Originally published in 1901, it is available online at: https://hdl.handle.net/2027/uc2.ark:/13960/t2q52 w707?urlappend=%3Bseq=325

7. "Discussion on the Paper Presented at the Last Meeting," in Massachusetts Institute of Technology, Society of Arts, *Abstract of the Proceedings of the Society of Arts*, 1879–1880, Boston, 31–41.

8. "Slow-Burning Construction," *Century Magazine* 23, no. 2 (1881): 319.

9. Julius Kahn was born March 8, 1874, in Bad Münstereifel, Germany, according to his US passport application of June 16, 1922. He claimed US citizenship as the child of a naturalized citizen; his father was naturalized in 1889 in Jacksonville,

Florida. This passport application stated that Julius immigrated to the United States in 1880. Albert Kahn's passport application, dated November 10, 1890, gives the immigration date as July 21, 1881. Considering that Albert was older at the time of immigration and his passport application was completed just nine years after the event, Albert's version is most likely correct on the date. "United States Passport Applications, 1795–1925," database with images, *FamilySearch* (https://familysea rch.org/ark:/61903/3:1:3QSQ-G965-D8RP?cc=2185145&wc=3XZM-927%3A10 56306501%2C1056481801: September 4, 2015, accessed December 2023), United States Passport Applications, 1795–1925, National Archives and Records Administration, Washington, DC.

10. Jonathan Steinberg, *Bismarck: A Life* (Oxford: Oxford University Press, 2011), chap. 10, "Guest House of the Dead Jew."

11. Steinberg, *Bismarck*, chap. 10.

12. Steinberg, *Bismarck*, chap. 10.

13. Steinberg, *Bismarck*, chap. 10; "The Anti-Jewish Crusade," *New York Times*, January 4, 1981, 1.

14. Albert Kahn passport application August 20, 1920, "United States Passport Applications, 1795–1925," database with images, *FamilySearch* (https://familysear ch.org/ark:/61903/3:1:3QS7-89XM-XQHP?cc=2185145&wc=3XZQ-W3J%3A10 56306501%2C1056549601:22, accessed December 2016), (M1490) Passport Applications, January 2, 1906–March 31, 1925 > Roll 1331, 1920 Aug., certificate no. 80376–80749 > image 491 of 835; citing NARA microfilm publications M1490 and M1372 (Washington, DC: National Archives and Records Administration, n.d.).

15. In many Reform Jewish congregations at this time, including Beth El, services were conducted in German. *A History of Congregation Beth El, Detroit, Michigan: From Its Organization to Its Semi-Centennial, 1850–1900* (Detroit: Winn and Hammond, 1900), 37.

16. O. W. Irwin, "Memoir of Julius Kahn," *Transactions of the American Society of Civil Engineers*, vol. 110 (New York, 1945), 1742; Albert Kahn 1890 handwritten application for passport "United States Passport Applications, 1795–1925," database with images, *FamilySearch* (https://familysearch.org/ark:/61903/3:1:3QS7 -99DD-KP8G?cc=2185145&wc=3XCY-4WY%3A1056306401%2C1056398101, accessed October 4, 2016), (M1372) Passport Applications, 1795–1905 > Roll 361, vol. 706–707, 1890 Nov.–Dec. > image 169 of 1051; citing NARA microfilm publications M1490 and M1372 (Washington, DC: National Archives and Records Administration, n.d.).

17. "Sayings and Doings," *Detroit Free Press*, May 7, 1882, 18; Mollie Kahn Fuchs, "Memoirs," (unpublished), a copy is in the collection of the Bentley Historical Library, Ann Arbor, Michigan, Albert Kahn Family papers: 1869–1989, box 1; original is archived at the Archives of American Art, Smithsonian Institution, Washington, DC, Albert Kahn Papers, 1875–1970, container 4.48.

18. "The Honsedale Rabbi Resigns," *Carbondale Daily News*, September 2, 1887, 4.

19. That Albert Kahn remained in Detroit during this period is certain, as he had left school and was employed first by the architecture firm of John Scott and then by George D. Mason. That the next two children, Gustave and Julius, remained in Detroit is inferred from the various biographies that indicate they were educated in Detroit public schools, and there is no mention of either man having lived outside of Detroit between 1881 and 1889. Nevertheless, evidence may someday come to light that one or both boys remained with their parents during this time.

20. "Gates of Prayer," *New Orleans Times-Democrat*, October 1, 1892, 3.

21. Mollie Kahn Fuchs, sister of Julius Kahn, in her unpublished "Memoirs" recounts some of her father's out-of-state positions, but the dates in many cases are incorrect. The dates here were acquired from contemporary newspaper articles, including the following: "Honesdale Rabbi Resigns," *Carbondale Daily News*, September 2, 1887, 4; "Jacksonville, Florida," *American Israelite* (Cincinnati), June 6, 1889, P2; "Rabbi J. Kahn," *American Israelite*, November 21, 1889, P2; "Gates of Prayer," *New Orleans Times-Democrat*, October 1, 1892, 3; "Personal," February 23, 1893, 1, and "Temple Notes," *Davenport Morning Democrat*, February 25, 1893, 4; "Cohen-Wolf," *Pensacola News*, August 1, 1894, 1; "Pensacola, Fla," *American Israelite*, October 18, 1894, P5; "Rabbi Called," *Marshall (TX) Evening Messenger*, August 12, 1900, 8; "City Briefs," *Leavenworth Chronicle-Tribune*, November 29, 1901, 8; "A Leavenworth Rabbi Leaves the Pulpit," *Kansas City Star*, July 16, 1904, 7.

22. Biographical sketch of Gustave Kahn in the collection of the Mahoning Valley Historical Society, Youngstown, OH.

23. Some sources claim that Julius completed high school in three years and college in three as well. The source for this is a January 1, 1933, article "Julius Kahn" by Jack Orr in the *Youngstown Telegram*. Julius graduated from the University of Michigan in 1896 at the age of 22 (rather than in 1894 at age 20), which casts doubt on the claim.

24. Mollie Kahn Fuchs, "Memoirs."

25. Letters from Julius to Albert Kahn from New York, July 13, 1897, and March 20, 1898, Albert Kahn Papers, 1875–1970, Archives of American Art, Smithsonian Institution, box 3, folders 22–26.

26. Julius Kahn, "The Coal Hoists of the Calumet and Hecla Mining Company," *Proceedings of the American Society of Civil Engineers* 24, no. 10 (1898): 835–58.

27. "Report of Committee to Recommend Award of Prizes," *Proceedings of the American Society of Civil Engineers* 26, no. 2 (1900): 27.

28. Letter from Julius to Albert Kahn from New York, August 25, 1898, Albert Kahn Papers, 1875–1970, Archives of American Art, Smithsonian Institution, box 3, folders 22–26.

29. "Personal," *Engineering News*, supplement 43, no. 13 (1900): 105; O. W. Irwin, "Memoir of Julius Kahn," *Transactions of the American Society of Civil Engineers*, vol. 110 (New York, 1945), 1742–47.

30. Letter from Julius to Albert Kahn from Yokohama, March 10, 1901, Albert

Kahn Papers, 1875–1970, Archives of American Art, Smithsonian Institution, box 3, folders 22–26.

31. Letter from Julius to Albert Kahn from Yokohama, September 26, 1901, Albert Kahn Papers, 1875–1970, Archives of American Art, Smithsonian Institution, box 3, folders 22–26.

32. Letter from Julius to Albert Kahn from Yokohama, May 16, 1901, Albert Kahn Papers, 1875–1970, Archives of American Art, Smithsonian Institution, box 3, folders 22–26.

33. Letter from Julius to Albert Kahn from Yokohama, June 15, 1901, Albert Kahn Papers, 1875–1970, Archives of American Art, Smithsonian Institution, box 3, folders 22–26.

34. Julius was not at the time of this letter to Albert committed to joining him as a partner as he states, "I return to the U.S. once more to look for a job." Letter from Julius to Albert Kahn from Yokohama, September 26, 1901, Albert Kahn Papers, 1875–1970, Archives of American Art, Smithsonian Institution, box 3, folders 22–26.

CHAPTER 2

1. "College of Architecture," *Rochester Democrat and Chronicle*, April 29, 1897, 1; "Society," *Brooklyn Life*, August 21, 1897, 8.

2. The former Bethany Presbyterian Church is located at 7835 E. Lafayette in Detroit, Michigan. The Grace Hospital Nurses' Home (later, Helen Newberry Nurses Home, and currently, Newberry Hall apartments) is located at 100 East Willis Ave. in Detroit. Bethany Memorial Church: "Illustrations," *American Architect and Building News* 58, no. 1147 (1897): 98; "Grace Hospital Nurses' Home," *Detroit Free Press*, September 25, 1898, 9; Sigma Phi: "News of the Architects," *Detroit Free Press*, June 18, 1899, 11; "Pierson Apartments," *Detroit Free Press*, September 3, 1899, 11.

3. "Died," *Detroit Free Press*, December 17, 1900, 5; "Hard Work and Confidence Won Fame for Albert Kahn," *Detroit Times*, May 5, 1921, 8.

4. "Personal," *Detroit Free Press*, February 23, 1902, 7, and "Personal," March 23, 1902, 18. The Union Trust Building (demolished) was located on the northeast corner of Griswold and Congress Streets and was not the same as the 1929 Guardian Building that was formerly known as the Union Trust Building.

5. The Palms Apartments are located at 1001 E. Jefferson Ave. in Detroit. The Belle Isle Aquarium and the adjacent Anna Scripps Whitcomb Conservatory are located on Inselruhe Ave. on Detroit's Belle Isle. The commission for these buildings was originally awarded to Nettleton and Kahn, but passed on to Mason and Kahn. The University of Michigan Engineering Building (now West Hall) is located at 1085 S. University Ave. in Ann Arbor, Michigan. The Century Club is now a part of the Gem Theater and located at 333 Madison Ave. in Detroit.

The Palms Apartments: "Detroit, Mich." *Engineering News* supplement, June

6, 1901, 199; Aquarium and Horticultural buildings: "Miscellaneous Buildings," *Detroit Free Press*, January 1, 1902, 14; Psychopathic Hospital and Engineering Building: "News of the Architects," *Detroit Free Press*, May 18, 1902, 14; Century Association Club: "News of the Architects," *Detroit Free Press*, April 27, 1902, 11.

6. "6 Per Cent of Cost is Architects' Least Fee," *Detroit Free Press*, January 10, 1909, 32.

7. "Real Estate Field," *Detroit Free Press*, November 11, 1900, 30.

8. "Real Estate Field," *Detroit Free Press*, March 24, 1901, 11.

9. "Real Estate Field," *Detroit Free Press*, March 24, 1901, 11.

10. "Real Estate Field," *Detroit Free Press*, April 7, 1901, 21.

11. Letter from Julius to Albert Kahn from Yokohama, Japan, June 15, 1901, referring to Albert's previous letter dated May 14, 1901, Albert Kahn Papers, 1875–1970, Archives of American Art, Smithsonian Institution, box 3, folders 22–26.

12. "Business Cards," *Detroit Advertiser and Tribune*, December 11, 1875, 2; "Notice to Builders," *Detroit Advertiser and Tribune*, July 3, 1875, 4; "Notice," *Detroit Free Press*, June 23, 1877, 2; "Beginning of the Boom," *Detroit Free Press*, March 12, 1885, 5; "It Now Looks Hopeful," *Detroit Free Press*, September 22, 1888, 5; "Windsor," *Detroit Free Press*, July 1, 1889, 4; "Last of Old Family Dies," *Detroit Free Press*, July 30, 1931, 8; Albert N. Marquis, ed., *The Book of Detroiters* (Chicago: A. N. Marquis, 1914), 433; entries for John Scott and Arthur Hillman Scott in *Biographical Dictionary of Architects in Canada 1800–1950*, online at dictionaryofarchitectsincanada.org, accessed July 30, 2020.

13. "The Roof Was Shaky," *Detroit Free Press*, November 22, 1898, 1.

14. "Scott & Co." *Detroit Free Press*, December 10, 1898, 1.

15. "The East Wall Goes Down With a Crash," *Detroit Free Press*, November 6, 1898, 2.

16. "Positive Denial!," *Detroit Free Press*, December 2, 1898, 2.

17. "Bad Errors!," *Detroit Free Press*, December 1, 1898, 10.

18. "Bad Errors!"

19. "Positive Denial!"

20. "News of the Architects," *Detroit Free Press*, March 16, 1902, 7.

21. "Personal," *Detroit Free Press*, March 23, 1902, 18.

22. Henry Leland was one of the founders of the Leland, Faulconer and Norton Company (Leland and Faulconer after 1895) and later the Cadillac and Lincoln automobile companies. John Greusel, "Joseph Boyer, Inventor," *Detroit Free Press*, January 14, 1906, C3; Jim Donnelly, "Henry M. Leland, The Founding Genius of Cadillac and Lincoln," *Hemmings*, June 2016, online at https://www.hemmings.com/stories/article/henry-m-leland#, accessed March 3, 2022.

23. "Important Manufacturing Plant," *Detroit Free Press*, June 3, 1900, 28.

24. "The New Detroit Shops of the Boyer Machine Company," *American Machinist* 24, no. 10 (1901): 248–54; "Boyer Machine Company's Plant at Detroit," *Railway Age* 31, no. 10 (1901): 182–85.

25. "Permanent Officers," *Detroit Free Press*, January 15, 1901, 9.

26. Albert Kahn Inc. job list (unpublished), job number 102. Boyer purchased a home on December 31, 1902, at 637 Woodward Avenue (renumbered to 3565 in 1920), built around 1892, on which Kahn also did renovations.

27. "Detroit Man is Treasurer," *Detroit Free Press*, January 3, 1902, 1.

28. "Improvements for Detroit Tool Co. Plant," *Detroit Free Press*, January 18, 1902, 9; "News of the Architects," *Detroit Free Press*, March 9, 1902, 23; "Other Manufacturing Buildings," *Detroit Free Press*, May 4, 1902, 18; "Building Permits," *Detroit Free Press*, May 11, 1902, 18; Albert Kahn Inc. job list (unpublished), job number 131; *Insurance Maps of Detroit Michigan*, vol. 6, no. 34 (New York: Sanborn Map Co., 1910); architectural drawings for "Chicago Pneumatic Tool Co., Detroit Mich., Plan of extension," job no. 131, unnumbered and undated, on file at Albert Kahn Associates Inc., archived with job number 177 (as of 2020).

29. "News of the Architects," *Detroit Free Press*, March 30, 1902, 18; "Miscellaneous Buildings," *Detroit Free Press*, May 18, 1902, 15; "Building Permits," *Detroit Free Press*, June 1, 1902, 14.

30. "Coal Co. Sells Woodward Yard," *Detroit Free Press*, August 10, 1910, 6.

31. "News of the Architects," *Detroit Free Press*, May 4, 1902, 19; *Insurance Maps of Detroit Michigan*, vol. 4, no. 114 (New York: Sanborn Map Co., 1922).

32. Architectural drawings for "Addition to Machine Shop, Chicago Pneumatic Tool Co., at Detroit Mich.," Job No. 177, job number 177, dated November 3, 1902, on file at Albert Kahn Associates Inc. (as of 2020).

33. GB Historical GIS, University of Portsmouth, Vision of Britain through Time, "Documentation for individual data value," Fraserburgh ScoP at http://www .visionofbritain.org.uk/datavalue/38182059, accessed August 20, 2020.

34. "Factory for the Consolidated Pneumatic Tool Co., Scotland," Albert Kahn, Architect, job number 181, November 12, 1902, original drawings. In the collection of the Bentley Historical Library, Ann Arbor, Michigan (not yet cataloged as of this writing); "On and Off 'The Ways,'" *Syren and Shipping*, December 10, 1902, 53–54.

35. As of this writing, the office section still stands; the factory sections were demolished sometime after 2015. The location is on the southeast corner of Maconochie Road and Kessock Road in Fraserburgh.

36. A small addition to the building used by American Can Company as a factory, job number 138, was secured while Albert was with Mason and Kahn. It was completed during the summer of 1902: a three-story addition of 36 by 50 feet and a single-story foundry, 50 by 50 feet, located at 659 E. Lafayette (demolished). "News of the Architects," *Detroit Free Press*, May 11, 1902, 18; *Insurance Maps of Detroit Michigan*, vol. 4, no. 23 (1922), and vol. 4, no. 17 (1897) (New York: Sanborn Map Co., 1922 and 1897).

37. "Miscellaneous Buildings," *Detroit Free Press*, October 12, 1902, 23; "Large Foundry for Three Rivers," *Detroit Free Press*, November 30, 1902, 15.

38. "The Book Apartments," *Detroit Free Press*, July 7, 1901, A3; "Sayings and

Doings," *Detroit Free Press*, August 29, 1901, 5; Revised Floor Plans, Dr. J. B. Book Apartments Building, job number 95, construction drawings by George D. Mason and Albert Kahn, on file at the Bentley Historical Library, Ann Arbor, Michigan, drawer 18, folders 7 and 8.

39. Cinder concrete is lighter in weight and less strong than stone concrete.

40. "Mammoth 100-Suite Apartment Building is Nearing Completion," *Detroit Free Press*, December 3, 1905, 30.

41. Architectural drawings for "Dr. J. B. Book Apartment Building ('The Palms'), Job Nos. 93 and 105, Detroit, Michigan 1901–1902" on file at the Bentley Historical Library, Ann Arbor, Michigan, drawer 18, folders 7 and 8. Though the Bentley labels the Palms as jobs number 93 and 105, it appears from the card index of jobs at Albert Kahn Inc. that the Palms was either job number 95 or numbers 93 and 95. The confusion may be due to the fact that the Palms was a Mason and Kahn job, and the job numbers may have been assigned after the fact by Albert Kahn in order to include all previous jobs in his own firm's numbering system.

42. "Expanded Metal-Concrete," *Insurance Engineering* 2, no. 6 (1901): 568–69.

43. "Those Floors in the 'The Palms,'" *Detroit News*, April 20, 1902. The article appears on page 23, but the section is unknown due to a large number of missing pages in the microfilm. The full text of the article recounting the incident is as follows: "Architect A. Kahn has provided floors of cement and steel for 'The Palms,' the apartment house being erected at the corner of Jefferson and Rivard. The steel is inside the cement, and someone who couldn't see through the latter got into communication with the building inspector last week. The latter proceeded to make severe tests of the floors. After placing six tons in the weakest place he could find, where one ton is all that will ever be placed on it, in all likelihood, and noting the lack of serious result, he concluded that the floors would do. As a matter of fact, if anything solider than those floors can be found, Architect Kahn would doubtless like to know about it."

44. Albert Kahn, "Industrial Architecture," *Weekly Bulletin of the Michigan Society of Architects*, December 27, 1939, 5–10.

45. "Cleveland Silex Stone Co.," *Detroit Free Press*, July 23, 1903, 31.

46. There is some dispute over the nature of the concrete work in the New Engineering Building (West Hall). The plans clearly show that the floors were of concrete with expanded metal used as reinforcement and supported by steel beams, just as with the Palms Apartments.

47. "Will Do Extra Work," *Detroit Free Press*, March 15, 1902, 3; "Will Begin Work at Once," *Detroit Free Press*, June 25, 1902, 7; "Independent Water Supply," *Detroit Free Press*, 2; "Will Have to Keep Contract," *Ann Arbor Daily Argus*, January 10, 1903, 1; "Regents Insist," *Detroit Free Press*, January 10, 1983, 2; "University of Michigan," *Saginaw News*, March 14, 1903, 6; "Sixty-Eighth," *Adrian (Michigan) Telegram*, September 27, 1904, 1; Julius Kahn, "Using Simplification to Increase Our Sales," *System* 48, no. 2 (1925): 151–56, 220–24; Architectural drawings for

"Engineering Building, University of Michigan, Job No. 145, Ann Arbor, Michigan 1902–1903," on file at the Bentley Historical Library, Ann Arbor, Michigan, drawer 3, folders 10 and 11.

48. The Otsego Hotel is now known as the Otsego Apartments and is located at 102 Francis Street. The three Detroit architects who examined the plans for the building were E. O. Fullis, John McMichael, and William G. Malcomson. "Fell With a Great Crash," *Detroit Free Press*, October 12, 1902, 3; "Accident Blamed on Heavy Rains," *Detroit Free Press*, October 18, 1902, 12; "Present Plans Inadequate," *Detroit Free Press*, December 3, 1902, 2; "Notes From Jackson," *Livingston County Daily Press and Argus*, December 3, 1902, 2; "Latest Concrete Collapses," *Fireproof* 1, no. 5 (1902): 11–15.

49. "Failure of a Concrete Floor at Chicago," *Engineering News* 48, no. 23 (1902): 23.

50. Edgar A. Kahn (Albert's son), "Albert Kahn—Architect," 5, unpublished manuscript on file at the Bentley Historical Library, Ann Arbor, Michigan, box 157, Dr. Edgar Kahn, 1985–1988.

51. William Kendrick Hatt, "Theory of the Strength of Beams of Concrete," *Engineering Record* 45, no. 19 (1902): 433–35.

52. William Kendrick Hatt, "Tests of Reinforced Concrete Beams," *Engineering Record* 45, no. 26 (1902): 601–5.

CHAPTER 3

1. Henri Kampmann, *The Hennebique Ferro-Concrete System* (Paris: Hennebique Construction Company, 1902), 3.

2. Albert Kahn, "Industrial Architecture," *Weekly Bulletin of the Michigan Society of Architects*, December 27, 1939, 5–10.

3. William E. Ward, "Beton in Combination with Iron as a Building Material," *Transactions of the American Society of Mechanical Engineers* 4 (November 1882/ June 1883), 105–17.

4. Ward, "Beton."

5. Ward, "Beton."

6. "The City on the Matanzas," *New York Times*, February 17, 1892, 9.

7. "City on the Matanzas."

8. Ernest L. Ransome, *Reinforced Concrete Buildings*, chap. 1, "Personal Reminiscence" (New York: McGraw-Hill, 1912), 2–3.

9. Ransome, *Reinforced Concrete Buildings*, 3.

10. "Industrial Topics," *San Francisco Chronicle*, May 13, 1884, 8; "All of Concrete," *Buffalo Enquirer*, June 13, 1894, 1; Ransome, *Reinforced Concrete Buildings*, frontispiece; Stephen Mikesell, Ernest Leslie Ransome, "A Vital California Engineer and Builder," *California History* 96, no. 3 (2019): 77–96.

11. "An Oil Warehouse," *San Francisco Examiner*, August 22, 1884, 1; *Insurance Maps of San Francisco, California*, vol. 5, no. 542 (New York: Sanborn Map Co., 1900).

12. It could be argued that the Arctic Oil Works processing building was the first reinforced concrete factory, though only its walls were of reinforced concrete. Distinctions are difficult to make, as both buildings are gone and no record exists of the exact construction of either one. Moreover, the definition of *factory* is not entirely specific. Regardless of which building deserves the title, it's certain that Ransome deserves credit for the design.

13. Ransome, *Reinforced Concrete Buildings*, 6; C. W. Whitney, "Ransome Construction in California," *Architect and Engineer of California* 12, no. 3 (1908): 48A–48H.

14. George W. Percy, "Concrete Construction," *Engineering Record* 29, no. 17 (1884): 272–73. A similar floor had been constructed by Ransome in 1888 for the Bourn & Wise wine cellar in St. Helena, California. The first floor of the three-story building was of reinforced concrete.

15. The building was located at 833 Market Street in San Francisco. "In the Land Market," *San Francisco Examiner*, February 8, 1889, 5; "The Academy of Sciences," *San Francisco Examiner*, January 6, 1891, 3.

16. "Harbor Fortification," *San Francisco Examiner*, July 10, 1890, 6; "The Harbor's Fortifications," *San Francisco Call*, January 8, 1891, 3.

17. "Finishing Concrete and Artificial Stone Surfaces," US patent number 405,800, June 25, 1889.

18. Percy, "Concrete Construction;" "A Free Use of Concrete," *San Francisco Chronicle*, October, 2, 1891, 7; *Stanford University and the 1906 Earthquake*, "Opportunity and Rebirth," online at: https://quake06.stanford.edu/centennial/tour/stop1.html, accessed Sept. 24, 2020.

19. "Trade Publications," *Engineering Record*, July 14, 1894, 113. Ransome's partner, Francis M. Smith, was the head of Pacific Coast Borax.

20. Ransome, *Reinforced Concrete Buildings*, 7.

21. "Testing a House," *Buffalo Enquirer*, September 26, 1894, 7.

22. "Testing a House."

23. "Alabama Flats," *Buffalo Evening News*, March 2, 1897, 9; "The Berkeley" advertisement, *Buffalo Commercial*, October 8, 1897, 7.

24. "The Graystone," *Buffalo Commercial*, January 14, 1911, 10.

25. "Worker Hurt as Roof Collapses in Buffalo Building," *Elmira Star-Gazette*, September 10, 2003, 4C.

26. "The Plans of Borax King," *Oakland Tribune*, August 5, 1897, 2; "Borax Factory in Bayonne," *Yonkers Statesman*, December 10, 1897, 3; "A Large Monolithic Factory Building," *Engineering Record* 38, no. 9 (1898): 188–90; "Constructing a Large Monolithic Concrete Building," *Engineering Record* 38, no. 12 (1898): 254–56; "Borax Factory Closed Down," *Los Angeles Herald*, August 26, 1898, 11.

27. *Reinforced Concrete Factory Construction* (New York: Atlas Portland Cement Company, 1907), 51; "Large Monolithic Factory Building."

28. "Large Monolithic Factory Building."

29. "A Successful Fire Test of Concrete-Steel Factory Construction," *Engineering Record* 45, no. 15 (1902): 341–42; "A Successful Fire Test of Concrete Factory Construction," *Iron Age* 69 (May 8, 1902): 17–20.

30. "Fireproof Until Kindled," *Boston Globe*, April 8, 1902, 5.

31. *Reinforced Concrete Factory Construction*, 55; "Successful Fire Test of Concrete Factory Construction."

32. Ransome, *Reinforced Concrete Buildings*, 12–13.

33. "Discussion on Steel-Concrete Construction," *Transactions of the American Society of Civil Engineers* no. 46 (December 1901): 102–10.

34. "Industrial Notes," *Engineering News* 35, no. 21 (1896): 166.

35. "New Suits," *Cincinnati Enquirer*, April 8, 1902, 8; "Too Much Business," *Cincinnati Enquirer*, April 29, 1902, 5; "Ransome Company's Claim," *Indianapolis News*, April 20, 1903, 13; "Efforts to Settle Out of Court," *Indianapolis Journal*, April 21, 1903, 7. It appears the Ransome Concrete Fire Proofing Company of Cincinnati and the Paige Concrete Fire-Proofing Company were the same organization, as they were both under the direction of Jerry P. Bliss: "Must Pay," *Cincinnati Post*, August 13, 1903, 1; "New Grand Stand," *Cincinnati Enquirer*, March 20, 1901, 4; "Inspected, Palace of the Fans," *Cincinnati Enquirer*, November 1, 1901, 4.

36. Halbert Gillette, "Ernest L. Ransome," *Engineering and Contracting* 47, no. 13 (1917): 291–92.

37. Ransome, *Reinforced Concrete Buildings*, 1–17.

CHAPTER 4

1. Kampmann, *The Hennebique Ferro-Concrete System*, 7–10.

2. Leopold Mensch, "The Hennebique System of Armored Concrete Construction," *Journal of the Association of Engineering Societies* 29, no. 3 (1902), 103–4; "Hennebique Fireproof Construction in New York and Cleveland," *Engineering Record* 47, no. 5 (1903): 126–28; Hennebique Construction Company, *The Hennebique Ferro-Concrete System* (Paris?, 1900), 5–10; David P. Billington, *The Tower and the Bridge* (Princeton: Princeton University Press, 1985), 149, 151, 176.

3. Julius Kahn, *Kahn System of Reinforced Concrete*, General Catalogue D (Detroit: Trussed Concrete Steel Co., 1904), 7–8; Moritz Kahn (Julius's brother), "A Reinforced Concrete System with Rigid Shear Members," *Concrete and Constructional Engineering* 1, no. 1 (1906): 67–69. Julius's beliefs were later confirmed by tests; see *Proceedings of the National Association of Cement Users*, Seventh Convention, vol. 7, 1911, 255.

4. J. Kahn, *Kahn System of Reinforced Concrete*, 11.

5. Mollie Kahn Fuchs, "Memoirs," (unpublished), a copy is in the collection of the Bentley Historical Library, Ann Arbor, Michigan, Albert Kahn Family papers: 1869–1989, box 1; original is archived at the Archives of American Art, Smithsonian Institution, Washington, DC, Albert Kahn Papers, 1875–1970, container 4.48.

6. Mollie Kahn Fuchs, "Memoirs"; Julius Kahn, *Kahn System of Reinforced Concrete*, 7–14; Julius Kahn, "Concrete Reinforcement," *Engineering Record* 48, no. 16 (1903), 465–67; Julius Kahn, "Some of the Causes of Recent Failures of Reinforced Concrete," *Engineering News* 51, no. 3 (1904): 66–68.

7. J. Kahn, "Some of the Causes of Recent Failures," 66–68.

8. J. Kahn, "Some of the Causes of Recent Failures," 66–68; Julius Kahn, US Patent 736,602, Concrete and Metal Construction, filed December 11, 1902, granted August 18, 1903.

9. Michigan Bolt and Nut Works was at 6426 Wight Street, between Iron Street and Meldrum Avenue where Mt. Elliott Park is now located. Entry for December 18, 1903, "Kahn," Diary of George D. Mason, 1903 (unpublished), in the Burton Historical Collection, Detroit Public Library.

10. J. Kahn, *Kahn System of Reinforced Concrete*, 20.

11. Kahn, "Concrete Reinforcement"; Julius Kahn, "A New System of Concrete Reinforcement," *Engineering News* 50, no. 17 (1903): 349–52.

12. Mollie Kahn Fuchs, "Memoirs."

13. Mollie Kahn Fuchs, "Memoirs"; "Architectural Club," *Detroit Free Press*, December 1, 1901, 11; "Court Brevities," *Detroit Free Press*, December 6, 1902, 7; "Cut Rate Spectacle Store—Felix Kahn," *Detroit Free Press*, July 18, 1899, 8; "Ladies Taylor Wanted," *Detroit Free Press*, September 13, 1899, 5; "For Sale—Residence Property" column three, "I Will Sell," *Detroit Free Press*, April 17, 1898, 28.

14. 26 Miami is now known as 1310 Broadway, just north of its intersection with Gratiot Avenue.

15. Mollie Kahn Fuchs, "Memoirs."

16. "Miss Whittemore's Escape," *Detroit Free Press*, March 5, 1901, 10.

17. "Concrete and Metal Construction," US Patent number 736,602, patented August 18, 1903.

18. "Ingalls Buys the Taft Property," *Cincinnati Enquirer*, December 25, 1901, 7.

19. Larz Anderson (husband of Catherine Longworth) and his son shared the same name and do not appear to have employed the designations *Sr.* and *Jr.* To avoid confusion, those designations have been used here. The same was true of William P. Anderson (son of Larz and Catherine) and his son of the same name. The designations have been added to their names as well.

20. "Noted Architect is Dead," *Cincinnati Enquirer*, November 27, 1933, 1; "George M. Anderson Dies," *Cincinnati Enquirer*, October 5, 1916, 8; Architectural Foundation of Cincinnati, "Elzner, A. O." and "Anderson, George M.," online at https://www.designlearnandbuild.org/azarchitect-a, accessed December 15, 2023.

21. "A Large Party Left Last Evening," *Cincinnati Enquirer*, July 4, 1886, 14; *History of Cincinnati and Hamilton County* (Cincinnati: S. B. Nelson, 1904), 293; "Facts and Fancies," *Cincinnati Enquirer*, April 3, 1900, 5.

22. "Solid, As One of the Pyramids," *Cincinnati Enquirer*, June 3, 1902, 5.

23. "Permit," *Cincinnati Enquirer*, November 25, 1902, 12; Fritz Von Emperger, "A Melan Concrete Arch in Eden Park, Cincinnati, O.," *Engineering News* 34, no. 14 (1895): 214.

24. *Proceedings of the 36th Annual Convention of the American Institute of Architects*, December 1902 (Washington, DC: Gibson Brothers, 1903), 24.

25. "Inspected Palace of the Fans," *Cincinnati Enquirer*, November 1, 1901, 4; "Too Much Business," *Cincinnati Enquirer*, April 29, 1902, 5.

26. Originally known as the Cincinnati Fire Proofing Company, the firm changed its name to Cincinnati Ferro-Concrete Construction Company in October 1902. "Traders' Gossip," *Pittsburgh Press*, September 6, 1902, 6.

27. Hooper's father and son all shared the same name: Henry Northey Hooper.

28. "Ingalls Building," *Lexington Morning Herald*, June 15, 1902, 3; "A Concrete Skyscraper," *New York Tribune*, July 26, 1903, 26; "Concrete Buildings," *Lancaster New Era*, August 3, 1903, 4.

29. "Permit, for Concrete Skyscraper," *Cincinnati Enquirer*, August 27, 1902, 12.

30. "Among Real Estate Men," *Cincinnati Enquirer*, October 15, 1902, 5.

31. "Talk of the Town," *Cincinnati Enquirer*, October 30, 1902, 5.

32. "The Ingalls Building," *Scientific American*, May 12, 1906, 394–95.

33. "Refuses To Issue a Permit," *Cincinnati Enquirer*, November 20, 1902, 12.

34. "Hitch As To Reference Board," *Cincinnati Enquirer*, November 21, 1902, 12.

35. The Algonquin Hotel addition on Ludlow Street at Third was successfully completed in 1904 and years later was demolished, leaving only the original 1899 structure in place. "The Victim of Serious Accident," *Dayton Herald*, October 1, 1902, 2; "J Elliott Pierce Protests," *Cincinnati Enquirer*, November 30, 1902, 3; "The New Algonquin Hotel at Dayton, Ohio," *National Builder* 35, no. 6 (1902): 32; "Concrete Building," *Cincinnati Post*, November 25, 1902, 2; "Algonquin Construction," *Dayton Herald*, December 1, 1902, 5.

36. "Permit Will Soon Be Issued," *Cincinnati Enquirer*, November 25, 1902, 12.

37. "Experts Will Report Favorably," *Cincinnati Enquirer*, December 10, 1902, 12.

38. "Fluid Concrete Will Be Used," *Cincinnati Enquirer*, December 12, 1902, 12.

39. Fred Baird, "New Salvation Army Building, Cleveland, Ohio," *Cement and Engineering News*, January 1903, 10.

40. "Issued," *Cincinnati Enquirer*, December 24, 1902, 5.

41. "Concrete Tests," *Cincinnati Enquirer*, January 26, 1903, 6.

CHAPTER 5

1. John Stephen Sewell, "A Neglected Point in the Theory of Concrete-Steel," *Engineering News* 49, no. 5 (January 29, 1903): 112–23.

2. John Stephen Sewell, "A Neglected Point in the Theory of Concrete-Steel."

3. "Superior Match Co. Has Filed Articles," *Detroit Free Press*, December 17, 1902, 9; "Match-Boxing Machine," US patent number 687,936, December 3, 1901.

4. "Two Important Factory Sites," *Detroit Free Press*, March 15, 1903, 22; "A Large Match Factory," *Detroit Free Press*, February 22, 1903, 11; James Cooke Mills, "Perpetual Inventory Forms," *Business Man's Magazine* 20, no. 4 (1907): 35–40.

5. "Real Estate Budget," *Detroit Free Press*, April 5, 1903, 23; "Building Permits," *Detroit Free Press*, May 24, 1903, 19; *Insurance Maps of Detroit Michigan*, vol. 2, no. 80 (New York: Sanborn Map Co, 1921).

6. Hoskins remained in the building until at least 1976, when the firm decamped after it was acquired by Armada Corporation. United Foundry then occupied the building until they were forced into bankruptcy in 1991. "Detroit Gets New Factory," *Detroit Free Press*, September 29, 1908, 2; "Offer to Purchase for Cash," tender offer announcement, *Detroit Free Press*, Jun 5, 1973, 20; "Bankruptcy," *Detroit Free Press*, October 7, 1991, 58; *Fiscal Year 1997 Funding Proposal*, Michigan Department of Environmental Quality, Environmental Response Division, Underground Storage Tank Division (Lansing, MI: D.E.Q., 1997), 118.

7. "Packard Will Move," *Motor World*, October 16, 1902, 1; letter from Henry B. Joy to J. W. Packard, January 9, 1903, MS 501, Miscellaneous Archive Collection, box 1, col. 1 ff1, National Automotive History Collection, Detroit Public Library, quoted in Chris Meister, "Albert Kahn's Partners in Industrial Architecture," *Journal of the Society of Architectural Historians* 72, no. 1 (2013): 78–95; "Minor Mention," *Horseless Age*, July 15, 1903, 81.

8. "Factory for the Packard Motor Car Co.," *Detroit Free Press*, June 14, 1903, part 3, 11–12. The actual text of the article is: "Albert and Louis Kahn . . . ," the name "Louis" instead of "Julius" is clearly an error; several paragraphs previously the article states that "Albert and Julius Kahn are the architects and engineers of the undertaking."

9. "Building Permits," *Detroit Free Press*, July 12, 1903, 27.

10. Albert Kahn, "The Architect in Industrial Building," *Architect and Engineer of California* 54, no. 3 (1918): 101–9.

11. "Building for the Packard Motor Co.," *Detroit Free Press*, August 2, 1903, 9.

12. "Building for the Packard Motor Co." A 90 percent decrease sounds high; the quoted article offers no description of the type of structure with which the Packard factory's insurance costs were being compared. The plant had an automatic sprinkler system, and the comparison may have been made with buildings lacking such a feature. Other features included automatic fire doors, concrete floors in the stair hall and some work areas, and corbelled brick walls to serve as a fire stop. The lightweight and inexpensive construction of the buildings would also have reduced their insurance costs.

13. "Building for the Packard Motor Co."

14. Architectural drawing, "Factory for the Packard Motor Car Co.," Albert Kahn, Architect, Julius Kahn, Engineer, Job Number 201, May 30, 1903, sheet number 8, in the archives of Albert Kahn Associates Inc., Detroit, Michigan.

15. The finishing building containing the concrete reservoir was referred to by Packard as Building Number 6. This building was demolished around 1916.

16. "The New Packard Works," *Automobile*, December 13, 1903, 612–14; "Century and Half's Work," *Detroit Free Press*, January 31, 1904, 4.

17. *Packard* 63, "Factory Number" (Packard Motor Car Company magazine), 11.

18. Architectural drawing "Factory for the Packard Motor Car Co.," Job number 201, sheet number 2, dated May 30, 1903, Albert Kahn Associates Inc. archives, Detroit, Michigan.

19. "Personal Notes," *Detroit Free Press*, March 22, 1903, 10. Henry G. Field, Theodore H. Hinchman Jr., and Ralph Collamore, all graduates of the University of Michigan's College of Engineering, along with architect Fred Smith were the original incorporators of Field, Hinchman and Smith. In 1906, architect H. J. Maxwell Grylls replaced Field in the firm and it reorganized under the name Smith, Hinchman and Grylls.

20. "Construction News; Buildings," *Engineering News* (*Supplement* section) 49, no. 1 (1903): 6; "Fire Consumed the Odeon," *Cincinnati Enquirer*, September 5, 1902, 7; "Plans for New College Classrooms Building are Approved," *Cincinnati Enquirer*, January 18, 1903, 12.

21. Leopold Mensch moved first to London, then Cleveland, Ohio, around 1900. He provided engineering services in both Cleveland and Cincinnati. In 1903 he settled permanently in Chicago, but maintained an active engineering practice in Cincinnati. The College of Music merged with the Cincinnati Conservatory of Music in 1955 and the building was demolished sometime in the early 1960s. "Tested With 100,000 Pounds," *Cincinnati Enquirer*, August 21, 1903, 12; "An Armored Concrete Building for the College of Music, Cincinnati," *Engineering Record* 48, no. 22 (1903): 666; "In Music's Domain," *Cincinnati Enquirer*, October 25, 1903, 35.

22. "New Storage Warehouse," *Cincinnati Enquirer*, March 10, 1903, 5; "Theater," *Cincinnati Enquirer*, March 29, 1905, 5; "Men and Matters," *Cincinnati Enquirer*, September 28, 1906, 5.

23. The building was designed by the architecture firm of Joseph Steinkamp & Brother and constructed by the Ferro Concrete Construction Company between August and December 1903. Shoe manufacturing began January 11, 1904, and the factory by 1908 was turning out 600 pairs a day. A later addition somewhat enlarged the building. Ransome's Kelly and Jones factory was completed in early 1904. The National Cash Register Company of Dayton, Ohio, completed a daylight factory of steel and brick sometime around 1898. "Will Move to Reading Road," *Cincinnati Post*, July 23, 1903, 8; "Real Estate and Building," *Cincinnati Enquirer*, August 23, 1903, 10; "High Lighting Prices Cause Private Plant," *Cincinnati Post*, January 8, 1904, 3; "Trade Notes from Cincinnati," *Shoe Retailer* 48, no. 13 (1904), 66; Leopold J. Mensch, *Architects' and Engineers' Hand-Book of Re-inforced Concrete Construc-*

tions (Chicago: Cement and Engineering News, 1904), 99; "'Billy' Kiley and His Associates," *Shoe Retailer* 69, no. 1 (1908): 95.

24. Achilles H. Pugh, founder and head of the company, was in the business of printing maps, tickets, and timetables for railroads. As an early adopter, he decided the building should be of fireproof concrete construction. When bids on construction for the Pugh Building were received, they varied by over 100 percent. Mensch offered the lowest bid and was hired for the project. The reinforcement he used consisted of round steel rods of varying diameter with hooks on the ends. Due to the slope of the land on which it stood, the building had seven stories in front on Pike Street and nine in the rear. But even before the building was completed, an additional story was added. "Real Estate and Building," *Cincinnati Enquirer*, March 20, 1903, 10; "Corners Doomed to Disappear," *Cincinnati Enquirer*, March 7, 1904, 5; "Real Estate and Building," *Cincinnati Enquirer*, April 19, 1904, 9; "The Largest Reinforced Concrete Building in the U.S.," *Cement and Engineering News*, July 1904, 2; "Leases," *Cincinnati Enquirer*, November 16, 1904, 8; "The Reinforced Concrete Pugh Power Building, Cincinnati," *Engineering Record* 51, no. 15 (1905): 438–39; "Real Estate and Building," *Cincinnati Enquirer*, June 19, 1905, 6.

25. "Flames Fed with Greedy Appetite," *Cincinnati Enquirer*, February 27, 1903, 3; "Cincinnati Had a Three Million Dollar Fire This Morning," *Chillicothe Gazette*, February 26, 1903, 1.

26. The building permit was issued on July 28, 1903, and the building was occupied by the end of November 1904. "Real Estate and Building," *Cincinnati Enquirer*, May 1, 1903, 8; "Plans Changed," *Cincinnati Enquirer*, May 4, 1903, 6; "Real Estate and Building," *Cincinnati Enquirer*, January 7, 1904, 5; "Activity in Building," *Cincinnati Post*, November 20, 1903, 16.

27. The building did not have a long life. The city decided in 1932 to widen Fifth Street and demolished the building to make way. It did not go quietly; the noise created by wrecking the concrete prompted the organizers of a religious conference to insist the city suspend demolition during the days of their meeting. "Landmark at Fifth and Broadway," *Cincinnati Enquirer*, April 13, 1903, 12; "Real Estate and Building," *Cincinnati Enquirer*, April 18, 1903, 10; "Special Reports," *Fireproof* 1, no. 5 (1902): 44; "Noise of Wrecking," *Cincinnati Enquirer*, August 18, 1932, 10.

28. The building, located on the northwest corner of Seventh and Main streets, was called the Hauck Building for its owner, but was initially referred to as the Brookfield Rye Building for its first occupants. "Real Estate and Building," *Cincinnati Enquirer*, October 16, 1903, 4; "Real Estate and Building," *Cincinnati Enquirer*, November 5, 1903, 8; William P. Anderson, "The Hauck Building of Reinforced Concrete, Cincinnati," *Engineering Record* 52, no. 1 (1905): 17–18.

29. "Scaffold for Use in Finishing Exterior Building Walls," *Engineering News* 50, no. 8 (1903): 169.

30. "Real Estate and Building," *Cincinnati Enquirer*, April 30, 1903, 8.

31. "Tenants for Ingalls Block," *Cincinnati Enquirer*, May 8, 1903, 5.

32. "Ingalls Building," *Fireproof* 2, no. 5 (1903): 36.

33. "A Tall Concrete-Steel Office Building," *Engineering Record* 47, no. 21 (1903): 540–43.

34. "The Erection of a Tall Concrete Office Building," *Engineering Record* 48, no. 3 (1903): 64–67.

35. "Sixteen-Story Concrete-Steel Office Building at Cincinnati, O," *Engineering News* 50, no. 5 (1903): 90–97.

36. "A Tall Concrete-Steel Office Building—Ein Wolkenschaber aus Eisenbeton," *Beton und Eisen*, July 1903, 161–65.

37. "A Concrete Skyscraper," *New York Tribune*, July 26, 1903, 26.

38. "Huge Flag," *Cincinnati Enquirer*, August 29, 1903, 5.

39. "Plank Stretched Across Alley," *Cincinnati Enquirer*, December 31, 1903, 12; "First Tenants Will Move Into Ingalls Skyscraper To-day," *Cincinnati Enquirer*, December 31, 1903, 9.

40. Gasoline lamps using wicks were prohibited in Ohio at the time, though lamps that vaporized gasoline and burned the vapor were legal. "Gasoline Lamp," *Cincinnati Enquirer*, March 2, 1904, 12.

41. "Sixteen-Story Concrete-Steel Office Building at Cincinnati, O," *Engineering News* 50, no. 5 (1903): 90–97; "The Kelly & Jones Company's Concrete-Steel Factory Building," *Engineering Record* 49, no. 6 (1904): 153–54.

42. Alfred O. Elzner, "The First Concrete Skyscraper," *Architectural Record* 15, no. 6 (1904): 531–44.

43. Mensch, *Architects' and Engineers' Hand-book*, 111–12.

CHAPTER 6

1. Letters from Julius Kahn to Albert Kahn, June 27, 1903, and July 1, 1903, Archives of American Art, Smithsonian Institution, Albert Kahn papers, 1875–1970, box 3, containers 22–26, Julius Kahn, 1897–1920.

2. Julius Kahn to Albert Kahn, June 27, 1903, and July 1, 1903.

3. Julius Kahn to Albert Kahn, June 27, 1903, and July 1, 1903.

4. Julius Kahn to Albert Kahn, June 27, 1903, and July 1, 1903.

5. Letter from Julius Kahn to Albert Kahn, July 1, 1903.

6. Julius Kahn to Albert Kahn, July 1, 1903.

7. Julius Kahn to Albert Kahn, July 1, 1903.

8. Julius Kahn, US Patent 736,602, Concrete and Metal Construction, filed December 11, 1902, granted August 18, 1903.

9. Julius Kahn, US Patent 743,086, Composite Structural Member, filed May 4, 1903, granted November 3, 1903.

10. Julius Kahn, US Patent 751,921, Composite Building Construction, filed August 14, 1903, granted February 9, 1904.

11. Some may quibble with the Great Northern building being the "first" as it

may not have been fully completed. Recent photos of the structure attest to its ability to remain standing for over a century without being maintained, but it is not clear if the missing sections of roof were never installed or if they fell in. The apparent lack of debris on the ground suggests they were never installed and construction of the building was halted prior to completion, likely due to the company's financial difficulties.

12. The cement shed is located at 43.86034, -85.84048. "The Era of Cement," *Detroit Free Press*, September 20, 1903, 11; "The Greatest," *Detroit Free Press*, January 1, 1902, 13; "Begins Work on June 10," *Detroit Free Press*, June 8, 1903, 7; "Shut Down for Want of Coal," *Detroit Free Press*, April 6, 1906, 3; "Foreclosure Suit Begun," *Detroit Free Press*, November 23, 1906, 1–2.

13. *Kahn System of Reinforced Concrete*, General Catalogue D (Detroit: Trussed Concrete Steel Co., 1904), 14–16, 25; "Short Talks and Encores," compiled by Oscar W. Loew, remarks of Milton T. Clark at the Silver Anniversary Banquet in honor of Mr. Julius Kahn, held in Youngstown, Ohio, December 12, 1928, (unpublished), in the collection of the Archives Research Center of the Mahoning Valley Historical Society, 13.

14. "Contracts for Government Buildings," *Detroit Free Press*, October 4, 1903, 15; *Modern School Construction* (Detroit: Trussed Concrete Steel Co., 1914), 21; *System the Magazine of Business*, June 1906, advertising section 121.

15. "The Use of Burned Clay Products in the Fire-Proofing of Buildings—II," *American Architect and Building News* 90, no. 1602 (1906): 75–78.

16. Captain John Sewell, "Reinforced Concrete in the United States," *Concrete and Constructional Engineering* 1, no. 2 (1906): 79–87; John S. Sewell, "The Economical Design of Reinforced Concrete Floor Systems for Fire-Resisting Structures," presented February 21, 1906, American Society of Civil Engineers, *Papers and Discussions* 31, no. 10 (1905): 625–59.

17. Sewell, "Reinforced Concrete in the United States."

18. Sewell, "Reinforced Concrete in the United States." John Sewell resigned from the Army with the rank of major in 1908 to accept a position as vice president and general manager of the Alabama Marble Company. In 1917, he rejoined the Army as a colonel, heading the 17th Engineers, a railway construction regiment in France during the war. In 1919, he became president of Alabama Marble. Sewell died in 1940.

19. "The Trussed Concrete Steel Co. Organized," *Detroit Free Press*, October 8, 1903, 9.

20. Press reports from the time list the stockholders of the company and the number of shares received. However, an entry in the 1903 diary of George D. Mason in the "Memoranda" section under the headline "Trussed Concrete Steel Co." lists the dollar amounts invested by each stockholder. This list is identical to that published in news reports with the exception that Joseph Boyer rather than Henry M. Butzel is listed as having invested $5,000, a difference which makes sense in light of

the fact that Boyer became vice president of the company and Butzel is not mentioned in connection with the firm until a decade later. The investment amounts here are from the Mason diary. Diary of George D. Mason, 1903 (unpublished), in the Burton Historical Collection, Detroit Public Library.

George W. Patterson Jr. went missing in 1925 under highly mysterious circumstances. He was last seen on the deck of the ocean liner President Monroe departing from New York Harbor. He had served with the French foreign legion during World War I and suffered shell shock, which may have resulted in chronic depression. "'Enoch Arden' Law is Cited," *Detroit Free Press*, July 17, 1930, 1.

21. "Memoranda" section, Diary of George D. Mason, 1903 (unpublished), in the Burton Historical Collection, Detroit Public Library.

22. "Short Talks and Encores," compiled by Oscar W. Loew, remarks of Milton T. Clark at the Silver Anniversary Banquet in Honor of Mr. Julius Kahn, held in Youngstown, Ohio, December 12, 1928, (unpublished), in the collection of the Archives Research Center of the Mahoning Valley Historical Society, 11–14.

23. Julius Kahn, "A New System of Concrete Re-Enforcement Designed to Resist Vertical Sheer," *Engineering News* 50, no. 17 (1903): 349–52; Julius Kahn, "Concrete Reinforcement," *Engineering Record* 48, no. 16 (1903): 465–67; Julius Kahn, "Concrete Reinforcement," *Railway Age* 36, no. 16 (1903): 527–29; Julius Kahn, "Concrete Reinforcement," *Railroad Gazette* 35, no. 42 (1903): 734–36.

24. *Kahn System of Reinforced Concrete*, General Catalogue D, 20.

25. *Kahn System of Reinforced Concrete*, 15–20, 25.

26. "Trade Publications," *Iron Trade Review* 36, no. 47 (1903): 50d.

27. "Roof Fell, Crushing One Man to Death," *Detroit Free Press*, February 7, 1903, 1; "Concrete-Steel for Building Construction," *Municipal Engineering* 27, no. 1 (1903): 28–30.

28. "Building Caves In," *Milwaukee Journal*, March 30, 1903, 3; "Of Public Interest," *Milwaukee Journal*, April 11, 1903, 2; "And it Came to Pass," *Fireproof* 2, no. 4 (1903): 13–16; "Failure of a Concrete Floor in a Milwaukee Building," *Engineering News* 49, no. 15 (1903): 328.

29. "Historic Designation Study Report," Preliminary Report, November 16, 1998, Johnson Service Company Building, 3.

30. "Johnson Controls Closing Downtown Milwaukee Offices," *Milwaukee Journal Sentinel*, January 21, 2021, online at https://www.jsonline.com/story/money /real-estate/commercial/2021/01/21/johnson-controls-relocating-downtown-mi lwaukee-operations-glendale/4235015001/, accessed February 9, 2021.

31. Bellefield Apartments is now known as Bellefield Dwellings and is located at 4400 Centre Avenue in Pittsburgh. "Concrete-Steel for Building Construction," *Municipal Engineering* 27, no. 1 (1903): 28–30; William Clendenin, "Concrete Disasters of 1903," *Fireproof* 4, no. 1 (1904): 30–32; Conreid Bronston, "Pittsburg Concrete Collapse," *Fireproof* 4, no. 1 (1904): 24–26; "The Concrete Floor Accident," *Engineering News* 50, no. 26 (1903): 578.

32. "Failure of a Reinforced Concrete Floor Under a Test at Trenton, NJ," *Engineering News* 50, no. 25 (1903): 553–54; "Coroner's Jury Blames the Test at the Mott Plant," *Trenton Evening Times*, December 21, 1903, 1; James B. Crissey, "Concrete Floor Collapse, Trenton, NJ," *Fireproof* 4, no. 1 (1904): 15–20.

33. "Failure of a Reinforced Concrete Floor Under a Test at Trenton, NJ."

34. The building is located at 325 Jersey Street in Trenton. At some point in time, the building received an addition to its northern end that extended its length by about 45 percent.

35. The Wing and Bostwick department store was located on the southwest corner of Pulteney and Bridge Streets in Corning. It was successfully completed and has since been demolished. "A Collapsed Concrete-Steel Building," *Engineering News* 51, no. 1 (1904): 21; C. T. Betty, "Concrete Collapse at Corning, NY," *Fireproof* 4, no. 1 (1904): 26–28.

36. The Norman Street School was demolished in the 1960s. Charles O. Breckenridge, "Boston Concrete Collapse," *Fireproof* 4, no. 1 (1904): 21–23; "Improper Mixing of Concrete," *Fireproof* 4, no. 2 (1904): 23–24; "School a Hoodoo From its Start," *Boston Journal*, March 8, 1904, 1–2; "Commission Has Not Refused Building," *Boston Journal*, March 12, 1904, 9.

37. Under the title: "Some of the Causes of Recent Failures of Re-Enforced Concrete," *Engineering News*, January 21, 1904; "A Plea for Re-Enforced Concrete," *Engineering Record*, January 23, 1904; *American Architect*, January 30, 1904; "A Study of Failures of Re-enforced Concrete," *Railroad Gazette*, January 22, 1904.

38. Julius Kahn, "Some of the Causes of Recent Failures of Re-Enforced Concrete," *Engineering News* 51, no. 3 (1904): 66–68.

39. Kahn, "Some of the Causes of Recent Failures of Re-Enforced Concrete."

40. Kahn, "Some of the Causes of Recent Failures of Re-Enforced Concrete."

41. Kahn, "Some of the Causes of Recent Failures of Re-Enforced Concrete."

42. "Concerning the Failures of Reinforced Concrete," letter from J. W. Schaub, *Engineering News* 51, no. 7 (1904): 156.

43. Letter from A. L. Johnson, *Engineering News* 51, no. 7 (1904): 157.

44. Letter from Julius Kahn, *Engineering News* 51, no. 7 (1904): 158–60.

45. Letter from Julius Kahn, *Engineering News* 51, no. 15 (1904): 356–58.

CHAPTER 7

1. Moritz's Trussed Concrete Steel office in New York was located in the building at 160 Fifth Avenue. *The Trow Copartnership and Corporation Directory of the Boroughs of Manhattan and the Bronx*, vol. 52 (New York, 1904), 609; *Polk's Detroit City Directory*, vol. 42 (Detroit: R. L. Polk and Co., 1904), 1442; "Moritz Kahn," *Detroit Free Press*, January 17, 1939, 19; *Truscon: The First Fifty Years, 1907–1957* (London: Bay Tree Press, 1957), 18.

2. "Officers of the Canadian Cement and Concrete Association," *Construction* 2, no. 5 (1909): 70; "Truscon Steel," *Wall Street Journal*, February 12, 1929, 13.

3. "Exhibits and the Maintenance of Way Convention," *Railway Age* 37, no. 12 (March 18, 1904): 642; "Copartnerships," *San Francisco Recorder*, January 28, 1913, 5; "Felix Kahn, Noted Contractor, Dies," *Oakland Tribune*, June 6, 1958, 13; "Concrete Ships to Win the War," *Concrete* 12, no. 4 (1918): 114, 143.

4. The exact construction of the building (which has since been demolished) is unclear from readily available documents. The building most likely had a full concrete frame, clad in brick, as it is unlikely that Truscon would have constructed a building with brick walls providing support. The *Sanborn Fire Insurance Map, Cleveland, Cuyahoga County, Ohio, 1912–1913*, vol. 2, sheet 11, shows the building as "Fire Proof Construction, Reinforced Concrete—Brick Walls." The *Cleveland Leader* article "News of the Builders," described the building as "press brick, with concrete trimmings, and the construction will be concrete fireproofing." An announcement in *Ohio Architect and Builder* 3, no. 3 (1904), 44, described it as "press brick and concrete construction." "News of the Builders," *Cleveland Leader*, March 6, 1904, 23; "Will Build $85,000 Residence," *Cleveland Plain Dealer*, March 24, 1904, 12.

5. "Amendments Printed," *Cleveland Plain Dealer*, May 10, 1904, 3; "Title X—Concrete Construction," *Cleveland Leader*, June 30, 1904, 15, and "Sec 3—Heights of VI Class Buildings," 13.

6. The building occupied 2172–2190 Ninth Street and 829–833 Bolivar and was demolished.

7. The Iowa School for the Deaf buildings were completed in 1905. "Industrial Notes," *Engineering News*, Supplement 52, no. 4 (1904): 45; "Bids for I. S. D. Building," *Council Bluffs Daily Nonpareil*, May 23, 1904, 3; *Council Bluffs Daily Nonpareil*, "Visit the School," May 19, 1905, 3.

8. The Sterling Public Library is located at 102 West Third Street and the Werner Brothers Storage building at 7613 North Paulina Street. "Industrial Notes," *Engineering News*, Supplement 52, no. 1 (1904): 251; "Work on Library Building," *Sterling Standard*, July 22, 1904, 1; "Werner Bros.," *Chicago Daily News*, November 26, 1904, 11.

9. The building, since demolished, was located on the southwest corner of Pine Street and Fourth Avenue. "Judge Palmer Builds to Accommodate Laundry," *Seattle Daily Times*, July 23, 1904, 3.

10. The library building is now a part of the Cedar Rapids Museum of Art and is located on the corner of Third Avenue SE and Fifth Street SE. "New Library Plans Adopted," *Cedar Rapids Gazette*, January 9, 1904, 66, and "Public Library Trustees Hold Monthly Meeting," March 30, 1904, 5; "The Library Building and the Kahn Concrete-Steel Truss," *Cedar Rapids Republican*, May 22, 1904, 10.

11. "Engineering Notes," *Scientific American* 90, no. 8 (1904): 155.

12. "The Kahn Trussed Bar in Reinforced Concrete," *Canadian Engineer* 11, no. 5 (1904): 125.

13. "Test of Reinforced Girder," *Concrete* 1, no. 4 (1904): 19–20.

14. "Franklin [*sic*] Arsenal, Building 211," Historic American Engineering Record No. PA-74E, prepared by John Milner Associates, Inc., Philadelphia, PA, 1988.

15. "The Latest News and Real Estate," *Philadelphia Inquirer*, June 21, 1904, 6, and June 28, 1904, 9.

16. "Test of Reinforced Concrete Floor Slabs, Beams and Girders at Frankford, Pa." *Municipal Engineering* 28, no. 5 (1905): 401–3; "Test of a Reinforced Concrete Floor," *Railroad Gazette* 38, no. 6 (1905): 42; "A Load Test of a Reinforced Concrete Floor," *Engineering News* 52, no. 24 (1904): 548.

17. The building was demolished around 1988. Presumably the lead used for the tests was on hand for the manufacturing of bullets and was later employed for that purpose. "Test of Reinforced Concrete Floor Slabs, Beams and Girders at Frankford, Pa."

18. "Adding Machine Men Dine," *St. Louis Republic*, December 28, 1902, 5; "Factory Building For Rent," *St. Louis Republic*, October 2, 1904, 45; architectural drawings, Factory for the American Arithmometer Co., Detroit, Michigan, Albert Kahn Architect, Job No. 232, April 30, 1904, Albert Kahn Associates Inc.

19. "The Factory of the American Arithmometer Co.," *Engineering Record* 51, no. 13 (1905): 382–83.

20. Architectural drawings, Factory for the American Arithmometer Co., Detroit, Michigan, Albert Kahn Architect, Job No. 232, April 30, 1904, archived at Albert Kahn Associates Inc., Detroit, Michigan.

21. The building permit for the factory was issued the week prior to June 12, 1904: "Building Permits," *Detroit Free Press*, June 12, 1904, 38. "Illustrations; Factory of the American Arithmometer Co., Detroit, Mich.," *American Architect* 87, no. 1527 (1905): 107–8 and two plates; "The Factory of the American Arithmometer Co.," *Engineering Record* 51, no. 13 (1905): 382–83.

22. "Heartily Welcomed," *Detroit Free Press*, October 9, 1904, 1, 3; "The Machinery Started," *Detroit Free Press*, October 28, 1904, 8.

23. "The Cement Exhibits and the St. Louis Exhibition," *Engineering News* 52, no. 19 (1904): 407–8.

24. "Reinforced Concrete Construction," *Railway and Engineering Review, Special Issue, Railroad Transportation at the Universal Exposition*, 1904 World's Fair Number, December 31, 1904, 79–80.

25. The gold medal award is mentioned in a number of Truscon ads, but no further verification was located.

26. Transcript of Record, Court of Appeals, District of Columbia, October Term, 1909, No. 2057, Fidelity Storage Corporation et al vs. Trussed Concrete Steel Company, 136, 152, 257.

27. *Kahn System of Reinforced Concrete*, General Catalogue D (Detroit: Trussed Concrete Steel Co., 1904), 45, 75; *Kahn System Standards, A Hand Book of Practical Calculation* (Detroit: Trussed Concrete Steel Co., 1907), 15; Transcript of Record,

Court of Appeals, District of Columbia, October Term, 1909, No. 2057, Fidelity Storage Corporation et al vs. Trussed Concrete Steel Company, 138, 174–75.

28. "New Business Enterprises," *Detroit Free Press*, October 30, 1904, 23; "Supply Trade Notes," *Railway Age* 38, no. 19 (1904): 673.

29. "Construction of the Steel-Concrete Shops at Beverly, Mass.," *Engineering Record* 51, no. 9 (1905): 257–61.

30. The Kelly and Jones factory was demolished. The former United Shoe Machinery complex is located at 181 Elliott Street in Beverly, MA. The former Robert Gair Building is located on the southeast corner of Washington and Water Streets in Brooklyn, NY. "Robert Gair Reinforced-Concrete Factory and Warehouse," *Engineering Record* 51, no. 9 (1905): 279–80; "Insurance Men Watch Fireproof Building," *Brooklyn Citizen*, July 16, 1905, 7.

31. "Insurance Men Watch Fireproof Building."

32. "Turner Construction Company History," (online at fundinguniverse.com /company-histories/turner-construction-company-history/) quoting from *International Directory of Company Histories*, vol. 66, St. James Press, 2004.

33. The engineering of the concrete work on the Ingalls Building would seem to contradict the assertion that only Ransome and a small number of his former engineers could design a Ransome building. The building's engineer, Henry Hooper, was the chief engineer of the Ferro-Concrete Construction Company, which was licensed to employ the Ransome system. Hooper was not a former Ransome employee. The most plausible explanation is that Ernest Ransome carried out the engineering on the Ingalls Building on behalf of his licensee, Ferro-Concrete. Given the potential damage to Ransome's reputation should a problem arise in constructing the building, he would have been compelled to be closely involved in the project even if his name was not publicly associated with it.

34. "Most significant" is, of course, a subjective judgment. The Marlboro-Blenheim Hotel received an enormous amount of coverage in journals. The Farwell, Ozmun, Kirk and Company building received generous coverage in journals, though a certain amount of it was written by employees of Truscon.

35. The Blenheim may well have been the largest reinforced concrete building in the world upon its completion in December 1905, but was soon eclipsed by a number of other structures within the next few years.

36. "Did Incendiaries Fire Atlantic City," *Paterson (NJ) Morning Call*, April 4, 1902, 1, 10; "Marlborough House" advertisement, *New York Tribune*, September 25, 1905, 13; "September Days in Atlantic City," *Philadelphia Inquirer*, September 10, 1905, 33.

37. J. Fletcher Street, "The Hotel Blenheim," *Brickbuilder* 15, no. 4 (1906): 78–84. J. Fletcher Street was an architect in William Price's firm of Price and McLanahan from 1903 to 1914.

38. "Reinforced Concrete and Tile Construction in an Atlantic City Hotel," part 1, *Engineering Record* 52, no. 26 (1905): 719–22, and part 2, no. 27 (1905): 743–45.

39. Street, "Hotel Blenheim."

40. Early photos of the building show brackets beneath the balconies, but later photos show them removed, indicating that they were merely decorative. "Reinforced Concrete and Tile Construction in an Atlantic City Hotel."

41. "Atlantic City Has Big Winter Colony," *Philadelphia Inquirer*, March 18, 1906, 11.

42. William L. Price, "Architectural Form and Finish in Concrete Construction," *Engineering News* 55, no. 21 (1906): 576–77.

43. A majority of the building, exclusive of the section containing the dome, was imploded in 1978. After efforts to preserve the domed section failed, it too was imploded in January 1979.

44. W. H. Dillon, "The Farwell, Ozmun & Kirk Co. Warehouse at St. Paul," *Engineering Record* 53, no. 16 (1906): 517–18.

45. Dillon, "Farwell, Ozmun & Kirk Co. Warehouse."

46. The building, located at 215 S. Fourth Street, is less than a third the size of the Farwell building. "Building Waits on Steel Mills' Whim," *Minneapolis Journal*, June 17, 1905, 8; "Safety, Comfort, Convenience, and Elegance All Provided," *Minneapolis Journal*, July 8, 1906, 20.

47. Maurice Goldenberg, "Letters to the Editor," *Engineering Record*, December 23, 1905, 725.

48. "Rats Start Fire," *Minneapolis Journal*, April 1, 1906, 7.

49. "A Reinforced Concrete Shoe Factory in Brooklyn," *Engineering Record* 53, no. 3 (1906): 78–80.

50. "Reinforced Concrete Roundhouse, Toronto," *Engineering Record* 52, no. 4 (1905): 96; "News of Railroads," *Montreal Gazette*, March 14, 1905, 9.

51. "Tests of Special Reinforced Concrete Construction in a Roundhouse," *Engineering Record* 52, no. 14 (1905): 381.

52. "Tests of Special Reinforced Concrete Construction in a Roundhouse."

53. F. F. Weld, "Reinforced Concrete Roundhouses," *Railway and Engineering Review* 46, no. 11 (1906): 178.

54. Alfred Church's mother was the second wife of Gail Borden. "Quits Elgin Because of Tax," *Chicago Inter Ocean*, January 4, 1903, 3; "Watch Case Factory Burns," *Streator (IL) Times*, January 9, 1904, 7; "Scissorinctums," *Palatine Enterprise*, August 11, 1905, 5.

55. It appears the Star Watch Case building was largely completed by September 29, 1905, as a photograph of it was published on that date. A newspaper report from April 19, 1905, stated that the construction contract "had just been let." The fully concrete addition to the Burroughs plant in Detroit was completed prior to November 16, 1905, as a photograph of it appeared on that date. The construction contract for the addition was reported on June 25 to have been awarded. A *Detroit Free Press* article from November 6, 1905, stated that construction on the Burroughs addition began "around August 1" and the new building had been in use "for per-

haps thirty days." The granting of a building permit for the addition was reported on August 13. However, Concrete Steel and Tile placed a help-wanted ad for carpenters' helpers at Second Avenue and Vienna Street (location of the Burroughs plant) on July 9, and an article in *Manufacturers' Record* from November 16, 1905, states that "construction was begun in June . . . and in less than two months the entire skeleton construction was complete. Later the brick curtain walls were built and the windows set in place." Taken together, it is most likely that the Star building was completed prior to the Burroughs addition.

"Ludington Has Boom," *Grand Rapids Press*, April 19, 1905, 5; "Watch Factory for Ludington," *Detroit Free Press*, May 21, 1905, 36; "Seeing Western Michigan by Proxy," *Grand Rapids Press*, September 29, 1906, 4.

56. "What Industry Means to This Community," *Ludington Daily News*, September 25, 1963, 4; "Watch Plant Closes," *Battle Creek Enquirer*, May 4, 1982, 21; "Remembering the Star Watch Case Company," *Ludington Daily News*, April 16, 1994, 1–2.

57. *Second Annual Report of the Youngstown Chamber of Commerce*, Youngstown, Ohio, 1907, Youngstown Printing Company, 9–10.

58. Margaret Kohut Kahn, "Our Baby," *Young Israel* 1, no. 9 (1908): 268–71.

59. Elaine Woo, "Gisela Gresser; Chess Pioneer Won National Title 9 Times," *Los Angeles Times*, December 16, 2000, B15.

60. George D. Mason designed the Hotel Tuller (demolished), Pontchartrain Hotel (demolished), and the Cadillac Motor Car Company factory in Detroit (see next chapter). John Scott & Co. designed the A. Booth and Co. cold storage warehouse (demolished). In fairness to Albert Kahn, he was hired to design the Scripps Power Building, job number 260, a reinforced concrete, six-story-and-basement building for light manufacturing. The plans for the building are dated June 12, 1905, but the project was shelved when James E. Scripps fell ill around that time, and the building was never constructed. "Bright Outlook in Building for Incoming 1906," *Detroit Free Press*, December 31, 1905, 15.

CHAPTER 8

1. *Statistical Abstract of the United States; 1934*, Motor Vehicles, "No. 381.—Production and Registration of Motor Vehicles," sources cited: National Automobile Chamber of Commerce and Bureau of Public Roads, Government Printing Office, 339.

2. "Automobile Industry and Trade in Detroit," *Automobile* 9, no. 24 (1903): 609–12.

3. "Cold Weather Fires," *Detroit Free Press*, January 19, 1904, 10.

4. "$200,000 Damage," *Detroit Free Press*, April 14, 1904, 1.

5. "Court Brevities," *Detroit Free Press*, February 18, 1905, 12.

6. "Cold Weather Fires," *Detroit Free Press*, January 19, 1904, 10.

7. "Make Them Fire Proof," *Detroit Free Press*, May 8, 1904, 35; "A Significant Case," *Fireproof Magazine* 4, no. 6 (1904): 13.

8. "Start Big Building," *Kenosha News*, June 19, 1903, 1; "The New Rambler Factory," *Automobile* 9, no. 9 (1903): 221. Photographs of the interior and exterior of the factory buildings are available from the Kenosha County Historical Society Inc. through the University of Wisconsin Digital Collections.

9. "Flour Vault Falls," *Kenosha News*, July 17, 1908, 1; "C. A. Dickhaut Dead," *Kenosha News*, July 18, 1908, 1; "Accidental Death," *Kenosha News*, July 20, 1908, 1.

10. "Detroit's Loss Is Lansing's Gain," *Detroit Free Press*, August 14, 1901, 9; "Going to Lansing," July 2, 1905, 10. Many sources maintain that Olds moved to Lansing immediately following the fire, but this was not the case. The company continued to invest in and expand the Detroit factory complex through 1905, when it began a migration of operations to Lansing. See "Largest in the World," *Detroit Free Press*, May 8, 1904, 35: "Of the great factories in Detroit, the Olds motor works has, during the last few weeks, expended $100,000 for machinery and new equipment to keep pace with the demands of the growing business." The article notes that Olds employed 700 men and had more than 550,000 feet of floor space in Detroit. In "Real Estate Budget," *Detroit Free Press*, July 31, 1904, 8, it was reported that the Detroit United Railway sold its car barns adjacent to the Olds factory to the Olds Motor Works, which would use the building to "enlarge its already big present plant."

11. "Contracts Let," *Detroit Free Press*, July 17, 1904, 10; "News of the Architects," *Detroit Free Press*, August 21, 1904, 8.

12. "Conservative Boston Club to Enlarge Its Garage Premises," *Automobile* 9, no. 19 (1903): 495.

13. "New Home for Autoists," *New York Tribune*, May 21, 1905, 7; Perry, Harry W., "The New Home of the Automobile Club of America," *Scientific American* 96, no. 17 (1907): 349–50. The building was designed by architect Ernest Flagg, completed in 1907, and has since been demolished. The *Scientific American* article mentioned that vehicles were fueled from tanks on wheeled carts equipped with pumps, "thereby avoiding the carrying of gasoline about in open buckets."

14. Woodruff moved to the West Coast to seek his fortune in construction after the 1906 San Francisco earthquake and fire. The "Hollywood" sign at the time it was constructed said "Hollywoodland."

15. "Immense Expansion of a Local Packing Plant," *Buffalo Courier*, May 17, 1905, 11; "Concrete Plant for Dold Com'y," *Buffalo Courier*, May 17, 1905, 10; "New Plants to be Built for Two Local Concerns," *Buffalo Courier*, June 5, 1905, 11.

16. Original architectural drawings of the E. R. Thomas plant, kindly provided by the Rich Products Corporation, which now owns the buildings.

17. "News and Trade Miscellany," *Automobile* 13, no. 11 (October 5, 1905), 392; "Automobile Topics," *Buffalo Commercial*, December 4, 1905, 4.

18. For more on the E. R. Thomas factory, see Michael G. Smith, "The First

Concrete Auto Factory: An Error in the Historical Record," *Journal of the Society of Architectural Historians* 78, no. 4 (2019): 442–53.

19. Dates and other details are from George D. Mason's personal diary for 1905 in the Burton Historical Collection of the Detroit Public Library.

20. "Wanted—Help—Male," *Detroit Free Press*, September 7, 1905, 6.

21. "Addition to Cadillac Auto Plant," *Detroit Free Press*, September 10, 1905, 8. Later reports estimated the cost at $80,000.

22. "Fine New Building for the Cadillac Automobile Co.," *Detroit Free Press*, October 16, 1905, 7.

23. Construction of the Cadillac Automobile Company, November 4, 1905, Burton Historical Collection of the Detroit Public Library, resource ID: MR0351.

24. Marsh, Charles Fleming and William Dunn, *Reinforced Concrete* (New York: D. Van Nostrand, 1906), 21.

25. For more on the Cadillac factory as the nation's first concrete automobile plant, see Smith, "First Concrete Auto Factory." The completion time of 67 days is reported in "The Cadillac and Packard Automobile Shops of Reinforced Concrete," *Engineering Record* 54, no. 20 (1906): 544–46, and is confirmed by dated photographs in the Burton Historical Collection and published in Marsh and Dunn. Square footage was reported in "Cadillac and Packard Automobile Shops of Reinforced Concrete" and confirmed using the Sanborn Map Company *Insurance Maps of Detroit* for 1910.

26. The square footage for Packard No. 10 was calculated from the original building plans, which are in the collection of the Bentley Historical Library in Ann Arbor, Michigan. The original building was later modified by the addition of two stories.

27. The architectural drawings for Packard No. 10 (Albert Kahn—Architect; Ernest Wilby—Associate; Job No 277; in the collection of the Bentley Historical Library, Ann Arbor, Michigan) are dated October 25, 1905. The start date of construction is based on the date of the building permit, reported in "Ten Millions," *Detroit Free Press*, December 3, 1905, 1, as having been issued "last week;" a help-wanted classified ad that appeared in the *Detroit Free Press*, November 12, 1905, 21, by the "Concrete, Steel and Power [*sic*] Construction Co." stating "Laborers Wanted At rear of Packard Motor Works;" and a single-paragraph announcement in *Motor Way* 13, no. 22 (1905): 20, under the headline "Increase in Space of 100,000 Square Feet": "When the additional two-story fireproof building is completed, the Packard Motor Car Company, of Detroit, will have 21,000 feet of additional floor space." That the building was completed in January 1906 is an estimate based on the time construction began and the amount of time it likely took to complete such a building. There does not appear to have been any media coverage of the building having been completed or placed in service.

28. For a full discussion of Packard No. 10 and the erroneous claims about its influence see Smith, "First Concrete Auto Factory."

29. As of 1904, Truscon listed offices in 13 U.S. cities and one in Toronto, Canada, in an ad in *Municipal Engineering* 27, no. 6 (1904): 65.

30. "Pierce Company Buys Land for New Factory," *Buffalo Evening News*, January 2, 1906, 17.

31. "Great New Plant for Pierce Co.," *Buffalo Times*, January 24, 1906, 7.

32. It is incorrect to assume that Albert was the one attempting to convince Lockwood Greene of the advantages of concrete merely because he is the one relating the story. It was most likely Julius or another representative of Truscon who was attempting to make the sale to Lockwood Greene and Pierce. As a part owner of Truscon, Albert would certainly have been aware of these efforts at the time or shortly afterward. "Industrial Architecture; A Talk by Albert Kahn," *Weekly Bulletin of the Michigan Society of Architects* 12, no. 52 (1939): 5–10.

33. "Big Blaze in Bubble Plant," *Buffalo Morning Express*, February 26, 1906, 1; "Auto Plant Fire," *Buffalo Commercial*, February 26, 1906, 8; "E. G. Bull, local sales manager," *Buffalo Enquirer*, March 8, 1906, 7.

34. "Industrial Architecture; A Talk by Albert Kahn"; "Structural Materials" (advertisement for Concrete Steel and Tile Construction Co.), *Engineering Magazine* 31, no. 5 (1906): 121; Correspondence, Pierce Building Committee to Lockwood, Greene & Co., April 16, 1906, microfilm roll 1111, frame 501, Albert Kahn Papers, American Archives of Art, Washington, DC, as quoted in Chris Meister, "Albert Kahn's Partners in Industrial Architecture," *Journal of the Society of Architectural Historians* 72, no. 1 (2013): 78–95.

35. "Pierce Plant is Under Way," *Motor Way* 14, no. 19 (1906): 17; "New Record Made by Buffalo in Building," *Buffalo Times*, January 13, 1907, 40; "The Typical Factory," *Concrete Engineering* 1, no. 10 (1907): 240.

36. "Pierce Plant is Under Way" and "Turning the First Spadeful," *Buffalo Morning Express*, May 6, 1906, 4; "Recent Trade Removals," *Automobile* 16, no. 3 (1907): 173; Howard S. Knowlton, "The Manufacturing Plant of the George N. Pierce Co., Buffalo, N. Y.," *Engineering Record* 56, no. 10 (1907): 263–67.

37. "The Producers," *Motor Way* 14, no. 21 (1906): 26; "The Cadillac and Packard Automobile Shops of Reinforced Concrete," *Engineering Record* 54, no. 20 (1906): 544–46; "Demand for Permits," *Detroit Free Press*, April 8, 1906, part II, 14. Square footage of the building was derived from the original architectural plans: Plot Plan of Buildings 10-11-12 Showing Columns & Conductors, Packard Motor Company Factory Addition, Job number 289, Construction Drawings by Albert Kahn, Architect, Ernest Wilby, Associate (undated), Drawer 1, Folder 5, Bentley Historical Library, Ann Arbor, Michigan.

38. "Garford Co. Succeeds Federal Mfg. Company," *Elyria Reporter*, May 17, 1905, 1; "Garford Automobile Works May Move to Cleveland," *Elyria Reporter*, February 3, 1906, 1, 6; "Houses are Assured; Site Fund is Wanted," *Elyria Republican*, March 1, 1906, 1.

39. "An Interesting Letter Received from L. A. Pratt," *Elyria Reporter*, October

24, 1906, 1–2; "New Garford Factory is Occupied," *Elyria Republican*, March 14, 1907, 2. The factory was no doubt completed well before early 1907 but was only placed in service after all the equipment was installed and ready to operate.

40. "Automobile Plant," *Buffalo Commercial*, June 2, 1906, 13; "The Producers," *Motor Way* 15, no. 9 (1906): 26–27; Albert Kahn Inc. job list (unpublished), job number 304, dated June 12, 1906.

41. The assumption that Truscon brought the work to Albert Kahn rather than the other way around is inescapable. Truscon had sales offices in Buffalo and Cleveland and would have sought to secure the business from Pierce immediately after the fire and from Garford as soon as its intent to build a plant combining its Cleveland and Elyria operations became public. It is likely that Truscon salespeople were calling on these companies even earlier, based on the reasonable expectation that as manufacturing firms in the rapidly growing automobile industry they would soon require larger factories. Architecture firms, however, did not solicit work, and Albert's firm did not have the wherewithal to pursue commissions in other states.

42. The square footage numbers provided here are based on statements made in numerous journals, newspapers, and books from the period: Pierce Arrow, 325,000; Packard, 90,000; Garford, 100,000; and E. R. Thomas, 60,000.

43. The list of commissions ("job list") is maintained by Albert Kahn Associates Inc. and is unpublished. While not error free, the list includes nearly every job number assigned, client name, year, and location. The commissions referred to here have been independently confirmed through contemporary newspaper and journal sources and, where necessary, corrected. The year associated with each job number on the list may refer to the date the job number was assigned, the date appearing on the architectural drawings, or the date the job was completed. For example, Packard No. 10 is correctly listed as job no. 277, but labeled 1906, the year the building was completed. For the purposes of this text, 1905, the year in which Kahn's firm began work on the job, was used.

44. "New Ford Factory," *Los Angeles Daily Herald*, July 12, 1908, 10.

45. Though the building was completed during the summer of 1909, the plant was put into service on January 1, 1910, after the adjacent single-story machine shop was constructed.

46. "Fireproof Buildings at Low Cost" (ad), *Construction* 1, no. 2 (1908): 5; "Contracts," *Engineering News*, supplement 60, no. 7 (1908): 61.

47. Ernest Wilby was associated with Albert Kahn's firm from around 1905 until 1916, when he retired from the active practice of architecture for medical reasons. Wilby lived in Windsor, Ontario, Canada, and was a British citizen, which may be why he was familiar with the Fenestra windows being marketed in England. "Trade Catalogues," *Builder* 93, no. 3385 (1907): 681; "Closes Good Contract," *Detroit Free Press*, March 11, 1908, 9; "Detroit-Fenestra Window Sash" advertisement, *Architectural Record* 24, no. 4 (1908): 10; "Ford Factory Building is One Sixth of a Mile Long," *Detroit Free Press*, July 4, 1909, 7; Ernest Wilby, American Institute of

Architects, Nomination for Fellowship by Chapter, February 24, 1938, "Nominee's Achievement in Science of Construction," 4, contained in the membership file for the architect maintained by the American Institute of Architects, Washington DC, and available online at: https://aiahistoricaldirectory.atlassian.net/wiki/spaces /AHDAA/pages/38020083/ahd1048448, accessed December 2023; Fiske Kimball, *American Architecture* (Indianapolis: Bobbs-Merrill, 1928), 197–98.

48. "Window-Frame," US patent number 491,375, September 14, 1909; "Window-Glass Fastener," US patent number 531,147, August 15, 1911; "Window-Frame," US patent number 636,512, August 22, 1911.

49. "Standard Steel Sash," *American Architect* 97, no. 1783 (1910): 4; "A New Metal Sash," *Southwest Contractor and Manufacturer* 2, no. 20 (1909): 7, 18; "Extensive Fireproof Factory for Dodge Bros.," *Detroit Free Press*, June 29, 1910, 3; "Detroit Company Gets Order," *Michigan Manufacturer and Financial Record* 5, no. 20 (1910): 21; *United Steel Sash Catalog*, 5th ed. (Detroit: Trussed Concrete Steel Company, 1912), 90.

50. "Short Talks and Encores," compiled by Oscar W. Loew, Remarks of Milton T. Clark at the Silver Anniversary Banquet in Honor of Mr. Julius Kahn, held in Youngstown, Ohio, December 12, 1928 (unpublished), in the collection of the Archives Research Center of the Mahoning Valley Historical Society.

51. "Pierce Plant is Underway" and "The Producers," *Motor Way* 14, no. 21 (1906): 26; "Latest Addition to Factory of Packard Motor Car Company" illustration with caption, *Automobile* 14, no. 21 (1906): 847; "The Producers," *Motor Way* 15, no. 9 (1906): 26–27; "New Addition to Thomas Plant," *Automobile* 15, no. 9 (1906): 288.

52. "The Cadillac and Packard Automobile Shops of Reinforced Concrete," *Engineering Record* 54, no. 20 (1906): 544–46.

53. *Everybody's Magazine* 16, no. 1 (January 1907), 103; *The World Today* 12, no. 1 (January 1907), advertising section; *Concrete* 7, no. 1 (January 1907), 18; *Sunset Magazine* 18, no. 4 (February 1907), 432; *Pacific Monthly* 17, nos. 1 and 2 (January and February 1906): 143 and 248s.

54. "Anderson Factory Swept by Fire," *Detroit Free Press*, September 10, 1906, 1–2; "Fire Destroys Detroit Body Factory," *Motor World* 13, no. 15 (1906): 675.

55. "Fire Destroys Detroit Body Factory"; "Peculiar Sprinkler Loss," *Western Underwriter* 10, no. 38 (1906): 6.

56. George J. Seymour, "Another Reinforced Concrete Speed Record," *Cement Age* 4, no. 3 (March 1907), 175–80 (reprinted in *Cement Era*, March 1907, 124–35). Seymour was an advocate for reinforced concrete construction but not necessarily a cheerleader for Concrete Steel and Tile. In a January 1907 article in *Cement Era* (5, no. 1, 62), he criticized the firm's "ignorance and inexperience" that led to the collapse of a building under construction at Eastman Kodak (covered in the next chapter).

57. Seymour's article stated that the contract was signed on October 4, 1906,

while the Truscon advertisement gave the contract date as October 3. The dates for the 40 and 80 working days were calculated based on a six-day work week. It is possible that some work was done on Sundays and even holidays, as George D. Mason's diary entry for Thanksgiving Day, November 30, 1905, stated, "Many men didn't show up today [at the Cadillac plant construction site.]"

58. Burton Historical Collection of the Detroit Public Library, photographs numbered MR0264, MR0266-MR0272, created by George D. Mason & Co.

59. "The Typical Factory—Trussed Concrete," *Manufacturers' Record* 51, no. 14 (1907): 429; "Reinforced Concrete Factory Building," *Railroad Gazette* 42, no. 17 (1907): 594; "The Typical Factory," *Concrete Engineering* 1, no. 10 (1907): 240; "The Typical Factory," *Cement Era* 5, no. 5 (1907): 190; "Trade Publications," *Cement Age* 4, no. 6 (1907): 444; "Trade Literature Received," *Motor* 3, no. 2 (1907): 72H.

60. *Cement Era* 5, no. 5 (May 1907), 190.

61. "Reinforced Concrete Construction," *Canadian Cement and Concrete Review* 2, no. 8 (1908): 179–80; "Notes on a New Factory," *Industrial Magazine* 8, no. 8 (1908): 498; "Advantages of Reinforced Concrete Construction," *Concrete Age* 7, no. 4 (1908): 19; "Concrete in a Manufacturing Building," *Cement Age* 8, no. 1 (1909): 77.

62. "Reinforced Concrete Construction," *Canadian Cement and Concrete Review* 2, no. 8 (1908).

CHAPTER 9

1. "Steel and Reinforced Concrete Construction," *Engineering Record* 63, no. 4 (1911): 121.

2. "Concrete Collapses Killing Two at Garford Factory," *Elyria Reporter*, September 6, 1906, 1.

3. "Are Here on Business," *Elyria Reporter*, September 7, 1906, 1.

4. "Concrete Pillars Unable to Bear Weight of Floor," *Elyria Chronicle-Telegram*, September 6, 1906, 1; Albert Kahn company, list of jobs, job number 295 (unpublished).

5. "Inquest Dropped," *Elyria Chronicle-Telegram*, November 5, 1906, 4.

6. "Says Concrete Was Not Properly Set," *Elyria Chronicle-Telegram*, September 13, 1906, 1 & 4.

7. "Suit for $25,000 to Be Dismissed," *Elyria Reporter*, October 22, 1906 1.

8. "Inquest Dropped," *Washington Post*, December 9, 1906, R8.

9. "Supposed Corpses Go Up to Rescue," *Los Angeles Times*, November 11, 1906, 6; "Eleventh Victim of Bixby," *Long Beach Tribune*, January 5, 1907, 1. The building was located on the southwest corner of Ocean Blvd. and Chestnut Ave.

10. "Nine Workers Killed in Hotel Bixby Disaster," *Los Angeles Herald*, November 10, 1906, 1–2.

11. "Nine Workers Killed in Hotel Bixby Disaster."

12. "Nine Workers Killed in Hotel Bixby Disaster."

13. "Nine Meet Death in Ruins of Hotel," *San Francisco Chronicle*, November 10, 1906, 3; "Death in the Ruins of Falling Building," *San Bernardino County Sun*, November 10, 1906, 1–2.

14. "Green Cement, Weak Supports," *Los Angeles Times*, November 10, 1906, sect. 2, 1 and 9.

15. "Kahn Company's Representatives Make Pertinent Statement," *Los Angeles Herald*, November 10, 1906, 2.

16. H. Hawgood, "Collapse of the Bixby Hotel at Long Beach, Cal., on Nov. 9," *Engineering News* 56, no. 22 (1906): 557–58.

17. Hawgood, "Collapse."

18. Hawgood, "Collapse."

19. Hawgood, "Collapse." Hawgood states, "The beams and floors are of the Kahn system of reinforced concrete in combination with hollow tile and are built for the following floor loads: 1st floor, 150 lbs. per sq. ft. plus dead load. All other floors, 60 lbs. per sq. ft. plus dead load." John B. Leonard, "The Failure of the Bixby Hotel," *Architect and Engineer of California* 7, no. 1 (1906), [seven unnumbered pages appearing between pages 48 and 49]. Leonard states, "The building was designed to carry a live load of forty pounds per square foot." Trussed Concrete Steel Company advertisement, *Los Angeles Times*, November 25, 1906, 106. The ad copy states, "This load is six times the load for which these floors were designed."

20. Hawgood, "Collapse."

21. Thomas E. Keough, "Failure of the Bixby Hotel," *Architect and Engineer of California* 7, no. 2 (December 1906), 67–70; Leonard, "Failure."

22. Leonard, "Failure."

23. Hawgood, "Collapse"; Leonard, "Failure."

24. Truscon display ad, *Los Angeles Times*, November 25, 1906, part 6, 18.

25. Bradley, Laura A., "Magnificent Hotel Virginia is Formally Opened," *Long Beach Press*, April 1, 1908, 1.

26. "The Virginia Closed," *Long Beach Telegram*, October 7, 1908, 7.

27. "Political Bluff," *Berkeley Gazette*, October 29, 1908, 4.

28. "Sidelights on Quake Damage in Southland," *Fresno Bee*, March 12, 1933, 7.

29. "Three Names on Death Roll of Accident at Kodak Park," *Rochester Democrat and Chronicle*, November 22, 1906, 15; "The Collapse During Construction of a Reinforced-Concrete Building of the Eastman Kodak Co., Rochester, N.Y.," *Engineering News* 57, no. 1 (1907): 1–5.

30. "Three Names on Death Roll of Accident at Kodak Park."

31. "Seeking to Place Blame," *Rochester Democrat and Chronicle*, December 5, 1906, 19. The testimony of John F. Ancona, chief draftsman for the Eastman Kodak Company, at the coroner's inquest as reported in the *Democrat and Chronicle*: "The plans for the building had been worked out at the Eastman office, and that the plans

together with a statement of the weights to go on each floor were forwarded to the construction company. Tracings were made by the Trussed Concrete Company and copies sent to Kodak park."

32. "Three Names on Death Roll of Accident at Kodak Park." The Eastman Kodak plant was located in the town of Greece, New York, a suburb of Rochester. Coroner Thomas Killip was employed by the town of Greece.

33. "Three Names on Death Roll of Accident at Kodak Park."

34. "May Be Hard to Get Money," *Rochester Democrat and Chronicle*, December 4, 1906, 15.

35. Engineer J. Y. McClintock's report to coroner Killip, reprinted in "The Collapse During Construction of a Reinforced-Concrete Building of the Eastman Kodak Co., Rochester, N.Y.," *Engineering News* 57, no. 1 (1907): 1–5.

36. "Coroner Causes Second Arrest," *Rochester Democrat and Chronicle*, December 21, 1906, 18; "Wilcox Held for Grand Jury," *Rochester Democrat and Chronicle*, December 28, 1906, 9.

37. "Coroner Causes Second Arrest."

38. "Coroner Causes Second Arrest."

39. "Letters to the Editor," *Engineering Record* 55, no. 5 (1907): 138–40. McClintock maintained the dead weight on the column was 84,645 lbs., while Thacher and Marx claimed 61,300 lbs. McClintock's value for the size of the column section was 142 square inches, while Thacher and Marx used 144. Most significantly, McClintock claimed the load on the column was eccentric, significantly increasing the computed load, whereas Marx and Thacher did not.

40. It was not clear in the report whether, as was the case with column 47, the column tested had only four reinforcement bars instead of eight, or whether it was constructed as intended.

41. "Letters to the Editor," *Engineering Record* 55, no. 5 (1907): 138–40.

42. "Collapse of the Eastman Kodak Company's Building at Rochester," *Fireproof* 10, no. 1 (1907): 22–23.

43. Henry Franklin Porter, "Failures of Reinforced Concrete," *Cornell Civil Engineer* 16, no. 3 (1907): 76–84.

44. "Victims Now Number Four," *Rochester Democrat and Chronicle*, November 24, 1906, 2.

45. "May Be Hard to Get Money."

46. Porter, "Failures." It is not clear from Porter whether the superintendent referred to was John Mullen.

47. Porter, "Failures."

48. "Frederich Given the Kodak Contract," *Rochester Democrat and Chronicle*, January 9, 1907, 20.

49. "Grand Jury Did Not Indict," *Rochester Democrat and Chronicle*, February 21, 1907, 12.

50. "Damage Action Against Kodak Company Settled," *Rochester Democrat and Chronicle*, November 27, 1907, 3.

51. Quoted in Porter, "Failures," and in D. T. Pierce, "The Lesson from Recent Failures of Reinforced Concrete Structures," *Engineering News*, 57, no. 1 (1907): 20. The quoted statement originally appeared in one of Truscon's promotional booklets.

52. See for example *Engineering Magazine*, March 1907, 113; and *Scientific American* 96, no. 8 (February 23, 1907): 179.

53. Maurice Goldenberg, "Accidents in Reinforced Concrete," *Engineering Record* 55, no. 11 (1907): 370.

54. Arthur B. Reeve, "Our Industrial Juggernaut," *Everybody's Magazine* 16, no. 2 (1907): 146–57.

55. P. Fountain, "The Remarkable Settlement of a Concrete Building in Tunis," *Engineering Record* 54, no. 18 (1906): 492–93; W. Noble Twelvetrees, *Concrete-Steel Buildings* (New York: Whittaker, 1907) 359–64.

56. "The Rochester Failure," *Concrete and Constructional Engineering* 2, no. 1 (1907): 3.

57. "Trade Publications," *Cement Age* 4, no. 6 (1907): 444.

58. "Short Talks and Encores," compiled by Oscar W. Loew, Remarks of Maurice Goldenberg at the Silver Anniversary Banquet in Honor of Mr. Julius Kahn, held in Youngstown, Ohio, December 12, 1928, (unpublished), in the collection of the Archives Research Center of the Mahoning Valley Historical Society.

59. For Mergenthaler Linotype and Grinnell Brothers buildings, see *Selected Illustrations Typical of Over 5000 Important Structures Built; Kahn System Reinforced Concrete* (Detroit: Trussed Concrete Steel Co., 1910), (pages unnumbered). For Hammond, Standish, see classified ads, "Carpenters wanted," September 6, 1908, 21; and "Building Permits," *Detroit Free Press*, November 15, 1908, 54. The Hammond, Standish building is located on the north side of Standish Street between Twentieth and Twenty-First Streets in Detroit.

CHAPTER 10

1. Carl W. Condit, "The First Reinforced-Concrete Skyscraper: The Ingalls Building in Cincinnati and Its Place in Structural History," *Technology and Culture* 9, no. 1 (1968): 1–33.

2. Parsons Brinckerhoff, *A Context for Common Historic Bridge Types*, NCHRP Project 25–25, Task 15 (National Cooperative Highway Research Program, 2005), 2–14.

3. Brinckerhoff, *Context for Common Historic Bridge Types*.

4. Henry Grattan Tyrrell, *History of Bridge Engineering* (Chicago: self published, 1911), 410.

5. The Alvord Lake Bridge is often stated to have been constructed in 1889, but

a well-researched article by Stephen Mikesell provides evidence that the bridge and its near twin were designed in 1890 and completed in 1891. See "Ernest Leslie Ransome; A Vital California Engineer and Builder" *California History* 96, no. 3 (2019): 77–96. Among the items cited by Mikesell is an announcement in the January 20, 1891, issue of *California Architect and Building News* (12, no. 1, p. 12) of the award by the Park Commissioners to architects Percy & Hamilton and contractors Ransome & Cushing for bridge cement work. The Alvord Lake Bridge is in the eastern end of the park, opposite the tiny Alvord Lake, and the second bridge is located beneath John F. Kennedy Drive in a direct line from the front of the Conservatory of Flowers.

6. Some sources state that the Melan bridge near Rock Rapids was constructed in 1893, but a letter from the Office of the City Recorder of Rock Rapids, Iowa, that appeared in the October 8, 1895, issue of *Engineering News* (p. 214) is accompanied by a caption that states, "The following is a testimonial bearing on the weatherproofness of the first Melan bridge built in this country in the summer of 1894." The bridge was originally located where Hickory Avenue (K52) crosses Dry Run Creek (43.389571, -96.136181), but was later moved to Emma Sater Park in Rock Rapids.

7. Brinckerhoff, *Context for Common Historic Bridge Types,* 2–17, 3–54.

8. The Melan Arch Bridge in Eden Park, Cincinnati, is located on Cliff Drive where it crosses Eden Park Drive. The ornate railing that once graced the bridge was replaced. "A Melan Concrete Arch in Eden Park, Cincinnati, O," *Engineering News* 34, no. 14 (1895): 214–25; "Contract Prices," *Engineering News* 32, no. 15 (1894): 307.

9. The ornate railing has been removed from the bridge and with it went the date stone that read "1885." "An Engineering Feat," *Detroit Free Press*, November 15, 1896, 18; "A Melan Concrete-Steel Railroad Bridge," *Railroad Gazette* 31, no. 9 (1899): 150–51; "A Melan-Arch Railway Bridge," *Engineering Record* 32, no. 18 (1895): 309–10; "West Grand Boulevard Railroad Overpass," HistoricBridges.org at https://historicbridges.org/bridges/browser/?bridgebrowser=michigan/westgrand/, accessed June 22, 2021.

10. "South Bridge," Historic American Engineering Record, IL-146, National Park Service (Susan Gordon, James Hanley, and Lisa Gardner delineators), 1999; biography of Peter J. Weber, *Explore Chicago Collections*, online at https://explore.chicagocollections.org/ead/artic/66/3x83q60, accessed June 23, 2021; "Jackson Park Animal Bridge," Contech Engineered Solutions, online at https://www.conteches.com/knowledge-center/case-studies/details/slug/jackson-park-animal-bridge, accessed June 23, 2021; "South Bridge (Stone Facing) Animal Bridge," HistoricBridges.org, online at https://historicbridges.org/bridges/browser/?bridgebrowser=illinois/jacksonsouthus41/, accessed June 23, 2021.

11. "Wabash, Ind., March 31," *Hamilton County (IN) Democrat*, April 10, 1880, 3.

12. "The Electric Light," Columbus, *Indiana Republic*, April 23, 1880, 2.

13. "Reinforced Concrete Bridges," *Cement Age*, 7, no. 2 (1908): 95–96.

14. "Bridge Contract Let," *Indianapolis News*, August 6, 1904, 3; "Question of City's Right," *Indianapolis Star*, August 8, 1904, 8; *Engineering News*—Supplement 52, "Bridges": no. 7 (August 18, 1904), 78; no. 15 (October 13, 1904), 180; no. 25 (December 22, 1904), 291; 53, no. 3 (January 19, 1905), 19; no. 7 (February 16, 1905), 55.

15. It is quite possible that yet another bridge deserves credit as the first concrete parabolic arch bridge. The Wealthy Avenue Bridge in Grand Rapids, Michigan, was a steel truss bridge across the Grand River and while it was under construction, the decision was made to extend the bridge across a channel that was to have been filled in. To span the channel a reinforced concrete arch was constructed that formed an approach to the steel bridge. The arch is described as having a 75 foot span and "consists of seven parallel parabolic arch ribs." Work is described as having begun in the spring of 1905, but it is not known when it was completed. Unfortunately, the bridge no longer exists and all information on it comes from a single *Engineering News* article. A subsequent article in *Municipal Engineering* from 1908 and the 1908 book *Concrete and Reinforced Concrete Construction* by Homer A. Reid mention the bridge but the information was likely drawn from the earlier *Engineering News* article. "Arch Rib Bridge of Reinforced Concrete at Grand Rapids, Mich.," *Engineering News* 55, no. 12 (1906): 321–23.

16. Official reference to the Sixteenth Street Bridge being the first parabolic concrete arch appears in the US Historic American Engineering Record, National Park Service Roads and Bridges Recording Project, 16th Street Bridge, DC-29, Doug Anderson delineator, 1995.

17. "Parabolic Concrete Arch Bridge over Piney Creek at 16th St., Washington, D.C.," *Engineering News* 54, no. 20 (1905): 510–12.

18. "A Concrete Arch Bridge," *Engineering Record* 52, no. 23 (1905): 637.

19. "A Modern Concrete Bridge," *Manufacturers' Record* 48, no. 21 (1905): 560.

20. "Parabolic Reinforced Concrete Arch Bridge at Wabash, Ind.," *Engineering News* 55, no. 11 (1906): 290; "Foundations of Reinforced Concrete Arch Bridges," April 5, 1906, 389–90; "Foundations of Reinforced Concrete Arch Bridges," April 19, 1906, 449; "Foundations of Concrete Arches and the Charley Creek Bridge," April 26, 1906, 473; Daniel B. Luten, "Empirical Formulas for Reinforced Arches," June 28, 1906, 718–20.

21. The Ferry Street Bridge is included in the National Bridge Inventory, number INNBI 8500635. Additional information on this and other bridges is available at BridgeReports.com and Bridgehunter.com. United Consulting, Indianapolis, Indiana, "Wabash County Bridge No. 505," online at https://ucindy.com/project/wabash-county-bridge-no-505/, accessed January 13, 2022.

22. According to "The Reinforced Concrete Bridge at Lake Park, Milwaukee," *Engineering Record* 52, no. 22 (1905): 609–10, "The design [of the bridge] was prepared by the contractor, and the contract let after some slight modifications had

been made with reference to the architecture." So while most of the recent documentation regarding the bridge credits A. C. Clas with its design (such as the "Ravine Concrete Arch Footbridge at Milwaukee Lake Park, A Cultural Heritage Assessment Study and Report," Historic Preservation Office, City of Milwaukee, 2016), it is more likely that Clas had little to do with the design of the bridge. "May Bar Mr. Clas," *Milwaukee Journal*, June 6, 1907, 9.

23. "Bridges," *Engineering Record* 51, no. 16 (1905): 48; "Make Plans for the Zoo," *Milwaukee Journal*, March 8, 1906, 4; "Holds Special Meeting," *Milwaukee Journal*, October 16, 1905, 4; *Annual Report of the Park Commissioners* 16, City of Milwaukee, 1907, 54.

24. Rich Rovito, "A Rehab of the Historic Footbridge in Lake Park is Finally Moving Forward," *Milwaukee Magazine*, September 9, 2020, online at https://www .milwaukeemag.com/a-rehab-of-the-historic-footbridge-in-lake-park-is-finally -moving-forward, accessed July 8, 2021; Alison Dirr, "Milwaukee County Board Allocates $1 Million," *Milwaukee Journal Sentinel*, May 20, 2021, online at https:// www.jsonline.com/story/news/local/milwaukee/2021/05/20/milwaukee-coun ty-board-allocates-1-million-lake-park-footbridge/5173316001/, accessed July 8, 2021.

25. Frederle J. Haskin, "Cement Users' Convention," *Dallas Morning News*, January 21, 1908, 6.

26. "A Novel Reinforced Concrete Viaduct," *Cement Age* 6, no. 2 (1908): 218–21.

27. Julius Kahn, "Reinforced Concrete in Bridge Work," *Cement World* 1, no. 9 (1897): 546–47.

28. "The Reinforced Concrete Viaduct of The Richmond & Chesapeake Bay Railway At Richmond," *Engineering Record* 55, no. 9 (1907): 226–28; "Reinforced Concrete Viaduct—Richmond & Chesapeake Bay Railway," *Railway Age* 44, no. 13 (1907): 427–31; "Great Viaduct Nearly Completed," *Richmond Times Dispatch*, January 13, 1907, 25; National Register of Historic Places Registration Form, "Richmond and Chesapeake Bay Railway Car Barn (127–6171)," United States Department of the Interior, National Park Service, 2006, continuation sheet, section 8, 3–5.

29. J. Kahn, "Reinforced Concrete in Bridge Work."

30. "Ashland Trolley Quits Operation," *Richmond Times Dispatch*, December 22, 1917, 1, 3.

31. "Richmond-Ashland Line Cars Resume Operation," *Richmond Times Dispatch*, June 1, 1919, 6; "Richmond and Chesapeake Bay Railway Car Barn (127–6171)," 3–5.

32. "Concrete Highway Bridge Over the French Broad River," *Engineering Record* 63, no. 18 (1911): 508–9; "Bridges," *Engineering Record* 60, no. 17 (1909): 39.

33. "New Concrete Bridge to West Asheville Now Almost Finished," *Asheville Citizen-Times*, January 20, 1911, 1; "Greystone Tract Sold," *Baltimore Sun*, March 12, 1911, 5.

34. Malverd A. Howe, *Symmetrical Masonry Arches* (New York: John Wiley &

Sons, 1914), Appendix A, Supplementary Table of Reinforced Concrete Arches, 182.

35. "Concrete Highway Bridge Over the French Broad River," *Engineering Record*.

36. "A Handsome County Bridge," *Scientific American Supplement* 71, no. 1839 (1911): 196; "Permanent Construction in the Growing South," *Concrete Age* 17, no. 3 (1912): 9–13.

37. "The French Broad River Bridge, Southern Railway," *Engineering Record* 63, no. 1 (1911): 12–13.

38. "Detour Established for Trucks, Buses Around Old Bridge," *Asheville Citizen-Times*, February 3, 1968, 9.

39. "SHC Approves Construction of New W. Asheville Bridge," *Asheville Citizen-Times*, August 7, 1970, 1.

40. Bob Terrell, "Old Fashioned Brush Arbor Meet Begins," *Asheville Citizen-Times*, June 20, 1972, 14.

41. Robert W. Hadlow, "Historic Columbia River Highway, Multnomah Falls Footbridge (Benson Footbridge)," Historic American Engineering Record, No. OR-36-I, 11.

42. Hadlow, "Historic Columbia River Highway," 11–12.

43. Hadlow, "Historic Columbia River Highway," 12; "Reinforced Concrete Arch Bridge over Lower Multnomah Falls, Office of Oregon Highway Commission, Nov. 14, 1913," drawing no. 306, bridge number 4534, Oregon Department of Transportation Bridge Program and Standards Unit, Salem; "Hy-Rib Steel Sheathing," *Cement World* 3, no. 11 (1909): 1034; *Hy-Rib Handbook* (Youngstown, OH: Trussed Concrete Steel Co., 1917), 5.

44. "Multnomah Falls crumbles," *Salem (OR) Statesman Journal*, September 5, 1995, 1; "Multnomah Falls to reopen Monday, Longview, Washington," *Longview (WA) Daily News*, September 6, 1995, 9.

45. Henry Grattan Tyrrell, *History of Bridge Engineering* (Chicago: published by the author, 1911), 409. That 100 bridges were constructed between 1894 and 1904 cannot be verified. However, a review of the bid requests for "concrete bridge" within *Engineering News* for the years 1900 to 1903 found only one in 1900, seven during 1901, about 12 during the last six months of 1902, and about 22 during the last six months of 1903, suggesting that the number of concrete bridges constructed prior to 1901 was quite small.

46. *Kahn System of Reinforced Concrete*, General Catalogue D (Detroit: Trussed Concrete Steel Co., 1904), 48–49.

47. J. Kahn, "Reinforced Concrete in Bridge Work."

CHAPTER 11

1. Concrete was considered fireproof based on the assumption that the reinforcing steel was embedded deeply enough within the concrete—typically about

two inches—that it was insulated from the heat of a building fire. The concept of fire resistance evolved over time into a more complex subject and the word "fireproof" is now rarely used, but for purposes of our understanding of history, the concepts of the period are used here.

2. Ira H. Woolson, "Report of Fire, Load and Water Test Made at the Fire-testing Station, Columbia University, N.Y., Upon a Kahn System, 15-foot Span," *Cement* 5, no. 6 (1905): 289–98.

3. "Baltimore's Conflagration," *Insurance Engineering* 7, no. 2 (1904): 123–45.

4. John Stephen Sewell, "Report to the Chief of Engineers, U.S.A., on the Baltimore Fire," *Engineering News* 50, no. 12 (1904): 276–79.

5. "Baltimore's Conflagration," *Insurance Engineering*.

6. Sewell, "Report to the Chief of Engineers."

7. *The Baltimore Conflagration*, 2nd ed. (Chicago: National Fire Protection Association, 1904), 118.

8. "Reinforced Concrete in the Baltimore Fire," *Engineering Record* 49, no. 12 (1904): 367.

9. *Baltimore Conflagration*, 72.

10. *Baltimore Conflagration*, 74.

11. This test is described in both "Report to the Chief of Engineers, U. S. A., on the Baltimore Fire" and "Reinforced Concrete in the Baltimore Fire." The descriptions agree in all particulars except the live loads for which the floors were designed. Sewell states 150 pounds, and the second article states 200.

12. "Report Upon the Condition of Concrete in the Fidelity & Guaranty Building of Baltimore," *Fireproof Magazine* 4, no. 6 (1904): 15–22.

13. *Baltimore Conflagration*, 72.

14. "Report Upon the Condition," *Fireproof Magazine*.

15. "Expert Tests at Baltimore," *Fireproof Magazine* 4, no. 6 (1904): 5–7.

16. *Baltimore Conflagration*, 72.

17. "Reinforced Concrete in the Baltimore Fire," *Engineering Record*.

18. *Baltimore Conflagration*, 72.

19. "More Claims Adjusted," *Baltimore Sun*, March 29, 1904, 7; "United States Fidelity and Guaranty Company's New Building," April 15, 1904, 16; and "To Build 100 Houses," December 4, 1904, 7.

20. The report by S. Albert Reed is quoted at length in "Report to the National Board of Fire Underwriters on the San Francisco Conflagration," *Engineering News* 56, no. 6 (1906): 136–40. *The San Francisco Earthquake and Fire of April 18, 1906*, Bulletin no. 324 (Washington, DC: US Government Printing Office, 1907) contains reports from four authors. However, Sewell's report was considered the most authoritative due to his experience. The preface by Joseph A. Holmes on page xi states, "Before going to San Francisco Captain Sewell had studied carefully the effects of fire on buildings and materials, especially as indicated by the results of the conflagration at Baltimore in 1904."

21. *San Francisco Earthquake and Fire of April 18, 1906*, 72.

22. *San Francisco Earthquake and Fire of April 18, 1906*, 119.

23. "Report to the National Board of Fire Underwriters," *Engineering News*.

24. *San Francisco Earthquake and Fire of April 18, 1906*, 147.

25. *San Francisco Earthquake and Fire of April 18, 1906*, 126.

26. "Reinforced Concrete Proved Best," *Cement World* 3, no. 3 (1909): 267.

27. *San Francisco Earthquake and Fire of April 18, 1906*, 109, 150.

28. Cinder concrete uses cinders as a lower cost aggregate than stone. This type of concrete was used for concrete floor slabs (sometimes in place of wood for the wearing surface) and as an alternative to terra cotta tile for fireproofing of structural steel. Though light in weight, it was less strong than stone concrete and so not generally used for reinforced concrete construction.

29. *San Francisco Earthquake and Fire of April 18, 1906*, 72; "Report to the National Board of Fire Underwriters on the San Francisco Conflagration," *Engineering News*. Sewell also praised the effectiveness of four inches of brickwork mortared with cement as being effective in protecting columns.

30. "Troubles of the Cement Workers," *Concrete* 7, no. 4 (1907): 48.

31. "Concrete Not Safe in Tall Buildings," *Daily Oklahoman*, July 20, 1906, 1 (and others).

32. "San Francisco's Wonderful Building Record," *Architect and Engineer of California* 10, no. 1 (1907): 76–77; "Reinforced Concrete Construction in San Francisco," *Concrete* 7, no. 2 (1907): 34c. There might have been even more reinforced concrete buildings, but the city limited concrete buildings to a maximum height of 102 feet.

33. *San Francisco Earthquake and Fire of April 18, 1906*, 113; "The Effect of the Earthquake at Stanford University, Cal.," *Engineering Record* 53, no. 19 (1906): 586–88.

34. "Building Conditions in San Francisco," *Concrete* 7, no. 4 (1907): 46–48.

35. The Bemis Bag Factory Building still stands at 1000 Sansome Street and the First National Bank Building at 1401 Broadway in Oakland. The Wellman, Peck and Co. building was located at the intersection of Embarcadero and Jackson Street (formerly 311 East Street) and the Scatena Building on the northwest corner of Sansome and Clay Streets. "Will Use the Kahn Bar," *Architect and Engineer of California* 7, no. 6 (1906): 100, and Truscon ad for the Kahn System, 105.

36. "Opens Coast Office," *Architect and Engineer of California* 10, no. 3 (1907): 80.

37. "Four Stories Too High," *Detroit Free Press*, November 3, 1907, 10.

38. "Reinforced Concrete Construction Popular," *Brooklyn Daily Eagle*, February 22, 1906, 13; "The First Concrete Strictly High-Class Elevator Apartments" (advertisement), *New York Times*, September 28, 1916, 15; "Apartments of Concrete," *New York Times*, October 7, 1906, 45; "First Concrete Apartment House," *Cement and Engineering News* 16, no. 12 (1906): 293.

39. J. W. Buzzell, "Concrete Coming Into More Favor," *New York Times*, April 14, 1907, R5. Buzzell was an 1893 graduate of the Worcester Polytechnic Institute and employed at the time of the article by Frank B. Gilbreth, General Contractor.

40. "Concrete Now Bricklaying," *New York Times*, September 15, 1906, 5; "Bricklayers Threaten War," *New York Sun*, September 15, 1906, 4; "Prevailing Rate of Wages in Building Trades," *Brooklyn Daily Eagle*, November 4, 1907, 18. Bricklayers were the highest paid among all construction trades at $5.60 per day. Plasterers, stone setters, and marble carvers earned $5.50, Carpenters, masons, framers, gas fitters, plumbers, stone cutters, steam fitters: $5.00. Concrete laborers: $3.00.

41. "May do Without Bricklayers," *New York Sun*, September 16, 1906, 4.

42. "Concrete Builders Oppose New Code," *New York Times*, December 22, 1907, 11 (quoting John C. Wait, C.E. of the Concrete Association of America). *Briefs on Portland Cement and Concrete*, Arguments Presented Before the Commission for the Revision of the Building Code of New York (New York, 1908), 8–9. The maximum of five-foot beams in industrial buildings would also have applied to steel frame structures. The reasoning behind this provision was that steel beams supporting floors in steel frame buildings, when softened by the heat of fire (due to partial failure of terra cotta fireproofing), often sagged or became deformed. Its structural support compromised, the floor often collapsed beneath the weight of heavy machinery, which plunged through, often stopping only upon reaching the basement. Limiting the length of beams and, thereby, increasing the number of supporting columns would reduce the likelihood of such floor collapses. There was, however, no reason for this restriction to be applied to concrete beams.

43. Henry C. Turner, "Vast Sums for Concrete Building," *New York Times*, April 26, 1908, 72: "Exclusive of all fireproofing, floors, subways, tunnels, bridge piers, and abutments, concrete was used in New York City during the year 1907 for $4,000,000 worth of building construction."

44. *Briefs on Portland Cement and Concrete*. The testimony came from: Association of American Portland Cement Manufacturers, National Advisory Board on Fuels and Structural Materials, Concrete Association of America, and Masters' League of Cement Workers.

45. "Concrete Building Fire a Problem for Fighters," *Brooklyn Daily Eagle*, March 7, 1907, 5; "Reinforced Concrete Building Stands Severe Test," *Detroit Free Press*, January 19, 1908, 8; *Briefs on Portland Cement and Concrete*, 15–16.

46. "Three Firemen Dead in $5,000,000 Blaze," *New York Times*, January 11, 1908, 1; W. C. Robinson, *Report on Fire, January 10th, 1908, in Parker Building* (New York: New York Board of Fire Underwriters, April 22, 1908), 8–9, 11–12.

47. "Three Firemen Dead in $5,000,000 Blaze;" "Fallon's Body Found; Met Death by Fire," *New York Times*, January 17, 1908, 4; Robinson, *Report on Fire*, 9.

48. "May Open Subway Section Today," *New York Times*, January 13, 1908, 1.

49. Robinson, *Report on Fire*, 7.

50. Robinson, *Report on Fire*, 11–12. The cast iron columns supporting the

building's interior were round and covered with one-inch terra cotta tiles. The building's wall columns (along the exterior wall line) were square cast iron columns fireproofed with four inches of brick in the lower stories and two inches in upper stories. The brick fireproofing was generally undamaged by the fire.

51. Robinson, *Report on Fire*, 18, 24.

52. "Skyscrapers for Fourth Avenue Block," *New York Times*, September 12, 1909, 10; "Down Town Firms Moving Northward," *New York Times*, October 30, 1910, 65.

53. "Concrete Construction is Booming in the City of Dayton, O.," *Concrete* 8, no. 2 (1908): 30–32; *Briefs on Portland Cement and Concrete*, 132–33; "Concrete Again Withstands Fire," *Cement Age* 6, no. 5 (1908): 493–95.

54. "Dayton Motor Plant Destroyed by Fire," *Buffalo Times*, February 21, 1908, 3; "Report of Fire Exaggerated," advertisement for American Automobile Co., *Minneapolis Star Tribune*, February 23, 1908, 25; "Reports Exaggerate Auto Factory Fire," *Fort Worth Telegram*, February 24, 1908, 2; "Telegraphic Briefs," *Baltimore Sun*, February 25, 1908, 5.

55. "Three Views of Stoddard Dayton Factory," *Dayton Herald*, February 29, 1908, 2; *Insurance Engineering* 15, no. 5 (May 1908): 373 (pictorial review section).

56. J. B. Gilbert, "The Fire at the Dayton Motor Car Works," *Engineering Record*, March 28, 1908, reprinted in *Briefs On Portland Cement And Concrete*, 132–141; "Reinforced Concrete," *Insurance Engineering* 15, no. 5 (1908): 476; "Fireproof Building Construction and Concrete Building Construction," *Engineering News* 59, no 24 (1908): 627–28; "Fire-Proof Buildings Fire Record," *Quarterly of the National Fire Protection Association* 1, no. 14 (April 1908): 139–41; Frank B. Ramby letter reprinted in *Briefs on Portland Cement and Concrete*, 141, 144.

57. "Limitations of 'Mill' or 'Slow Burning' Construction," *Insurance Engineering* 9, no. 4 (1905): 323–29.

58. "Commission Defends New Building Code," *New York Times*, May 20, 1909, 18.

59. "Concrete Men Fight," *New York Tribune*, May 18, 1909, 1. Buildings made of reinforced concrete in New York City as of 1909 included: the 12-story McGraw Building on Thirty-Ninth Street, the 12-story Monolith Building on Thirty-Fourth Street, and the 10-story McNulty Building on Fifty-Second Street.

60. "The Mayor Vetoes the Building Code," *New York Times*, July 24, 1909, 1.

61. "Report on the Asch Building Fire, New York," *Engineering Record* 63, no. 15 (1911): 417–18.

62. *Elmira (NY) Star-Gazette*, March 28, 1911, 6.

63. "Penned in Factories and no Fire Escapes," *New York Times*, October 12, 1911, 18; "Shorter Factory Hours," *New York Times*, October 1, 1912, 12; "Broke Fire Prevention Law," *New York Sun*, November 11, 1913, 12; "State Labor Department Had Ordered Owners," *New York Times*, November 7, 1915, 1.

64. "Rudolph P. Miller Resigns," *Brooklyn Daily Eagle*, April 15, 1914, 2; "The

Man Who Made City's New Building Code," *New York Times*, January 16, 1916, 53; William D. Brush, *Building Code of the City of New York as Amended to May 1, 1922* (New York: M. B. Brown Printing & Binding, 1922).

CHAPTER 12

1. "$1,000,000 Truscon Steel Company," *Detroit Free Press*, March 24, 1920, 20.

2. The Trussed Concrete Building, or Owen Building as it was later called, was located on the northeast corner of Lafayette Street and Wayne Street (now Washington Blvd.). It was completed September 1907 and demolished in 1957 to accommodate the widening of Wayne Street. "Old Landmark to Go," *Detroit Free Press*, August 31, 1906, 5; "Concrete Replaces Steel in Construction of Owen Building," *Detroit Free Press*, January 27, 1907, 7.

3. "Fall Nine Stories; One Will Live," *Detroit Free Press*, May 15, 1907, 8; "Building Inspector Claxton," *Detroit Free Press*, May 21, 1907, 5.

4. Joseph G. Butler, *History of Youngstown and the Mahoning Valley, Ohio*, vol. 1 (Chicago: American Historical Society, 1921), 726–27; *First Annual Report of the Youngstown Chamber of Commerce*, Youngstown, 1906, 9–10; "Trussed Concrete Steel Co.'s Plant, Youngstown, Ohio," *Western Architect* 20, no. 9 (1913): 86, XII, XV; "Trussed Concrete Steel," *Wall Street Journal*, May 28, 1914, 3; *Truscon: The First Fifty Years, 1907–1957* (London: Bay Tree Press, 1957).

5. "The Michigan Technical Laboratory," *Concrete* 7, no. 6 (1907): 61.

6. "New Plant Is Being Erected for Company, Moving to Detroit from Chicago," *Detroit Free Press*, December 11, 1912, 42; "See New Plant Opened," *Detroit Free Press*, May 4, 1913, 9; "R. A. Plumb, Executive, Dies at 71," *Detroit Free Press*, April 30, 1954, 11.

7. The Carpenter Paper Company Building was located at 815 Harney Street in Omaha and was demolished in 1989. "Building News and Notes," *Omaha Daily Bee*, April 14, 1907, 6; "Rigid Test of Floors," *Omaha Daily Bee*, May 8, 1907, 7.

8. The telephone exchange was on Harney Street west of Nineteenth Street (demolished). "Contract for 'Phone House," *Omaha Daily Bee*, June 11, 1907, 7.

9. The Brandeis store is a steel frame building with concrete floors located at 210 South Sixteenth Street in Omaha. It was converted to condominiums and is known as "The Brandeis." "Warehouse," *Omaha Daily News*, October 15, 1907, 1; "Contracts," *Engineering News*—Supplement 57, no. 13 (1907): 117; Louis Banny, "Concrete Construction," *Omaha Daily Bee*, July 19, 1908, 4.

10. "Montagues Build Big New Factory," *La Crosse Tribune*, August 10, 1907, 20; "3,000,000 Pounds of Candy a Year," *La Crosse Tribune*, July 29, 1910, 63.

11. Wallace Montague died in 1919, and La Crosse Cracker and Candy merged in 1927 with another firm. Beset by competition from national manufacturers, the company closed during the Depression, and the building was demolished in 1935.

12. "Julius Kahn Gets Patent on Invention," *Youngstown Vindicator*, February 23, 1934, 1, 8.

13. Sanford E. Thompson, "Forms for Concrete Construction," *Rock Products* 6, no. 6 (1907): 43: "Correspondence with a number of prominent contractors in various parts of the country, including the Aberthaw Construction Co. (Boston), the Expanded Metal and Corrugated Bar Co. (St. Louis), the Ferro Concrete Construction Co. (Cincinnati), the Trussed Concrete Steel Co. (Detroit), and the Turner Construction Co. (New York), indicate substantial agreement in the minimum time to leave forms."

14. "Trussed Concrete Steel Co., Monthly Statements, 1908" ledger book, December 31, 1908 (unpublished), in the collection of the Archives Resource Center of the Mahoning Valley Historical Society, 648 Wick Avenue, Youngstown, Ohio.

15. Dario A. Gasparini, "Contributions of C. A. P. Turner to Development of Reinforced Concrete Flat Slabs 1905–1909," *Journal of Structural Engineering* 128, no. 10 (2002): 1243–52.

16. Quoted in Gasparini, "Contributions," 1245; George A. Hool and William S. Kinne, *Reinforced Concrete and Masonry Structures* (New York: McGraw-Hill, 1924), 342.

17. William Sydney Wolfe and Harry Anthony Wiersema, "Comparison of Various Floor Systems in Reinforced Concrete," BS thesis in architectural engineering, College of Engineering, University of Illinois, 1913. Harry Wiersema (1892–1985) spent most of his career with the Tennessee Valley Authority, eventually serving as assistant to the chief TVA engineer.

18. C. A. P. Turner, *Concrete Steel Construction, Part I—Buildings* (Minneapolis: Farnham Printing & Stationery Company, 1909); Maurice Goldenberg, "Letters to the Editor," *Engineering Record* 52, no. 26 (1905): 725.

19. "The Rochester Failure," *Concrete and Constructional Engineering* 2, no. 1 (1907): 3.

20. "Gabriel Concrete Steel Co.," *Detroit Free Press*, April 5, 1906, 5.

21. Julius Kahn, "Some of the Causes of Recent Failures of Reinforced Concrete," *Engineering News* 51, no. 3 (1904): 66–68.

22. *Designing Tables for The Gabriel Concrete Reinforcement*, technical manual edited by the Gabriel Concrete Reinforcement Co., Detroit, 1908.

23. "The Gabriel System," *American Architect and Building News* 94, no. 1699 (1908): 14.

24. *Bayne v. Everham*, 197 Mich. 181, 1917.

25. *Bayne v. Everham*.

26. "Structural Member," US patent number 1,085,429, January 27, 1914; "Building Construction," US patent number 1,192,209, July 25, 1916; W. H. Faraday, "Some Impressions of Pressed Steel and its Uses," *Modern Building* 3, no. 8 (1916).

27. Julius Kahn, "Using Simplification to Increase Our Sales," *System* 48, no. 2 (1925): 151–56, 220–24.

28. H. W. Faraday, "The 'Sectional' Factory," *Modern Building* 3, no. 6 (1916): 10–16.

29. J. Kahn, "Using Simplification."

30. "A Fire-Resisting Construction for Apartments, Stores, Etc." *Modern Building* 4, no. 2 (1927): 20–21; "Kahn Pressed Steel Joists and Studs" advertisement, *Modern Building* 3, no. 9 (1916): 23; "Truscon Pressed Steel" advertisement, *Modern Building* 6, no. 4 (1919): 21; Truscon Steel Company ads, *Literary Digest* 8, nos. 4 and 8, October 23 and November 20, 1919; 1; Truscon Foundry Flasks advertisement, *Canadian Foundryman* 12, no. 2 (1921): 59.

31. "New Ford Factory Building is One Sixth of Mile Long," *Detroit Free Press*, July 4, 1909, 7; "Extensive Construction Work in Progress," *Detroit Free Press*, October 24, 1909, 47; *Insurance Maps of Detroit Michigan*, vol. 8, no. 2 (New York: Sanborn Map Co., 1910).

32. *Insurance Maps of Detroit Michigan*, vol. 10, nos. 75 and 76 (New York: Sanborn Map Co., 1915).

33. Moritz Kahn, *The Design and Construction of Industrial Buildings* (London: Technical Journals Ltd., 1917), plate XLVIII, "Interior of the Glass-covered Court between Two Units of the Works of the Ford Motor Co."

34. T. V. Buckwalter, "Motor Trucks for Railroad Service," *Transactions (Society of Automobile Engineers)* no. 5 (1910): 306–20.

35. Landon L. Goodman, "Materials Handling and Processing—Past and Present," *Journal of the Royal Society of Arts* 101, no. 4905 (1953): 672–94; "A Century of Lift Trucks; The Story of Elwell-Parker and its Contribution to Materials Handling is Woven into the Very Fabric of Modern Commerce," Elwell-Parker, online at https://elwellparker.com/our-history/a-century-of-lift-trucks/, accessed November 18, 2021.

36. Albert Kahn, "The Architects Problems in Designing Office Buildings," *Proceedings of the Twentieth Annual Convention of the National Association of Building Owners and Managers* (National Association of Building Owners and Managers, 1927), 264–79.

37. Albert Kahn, "Industrial Architecture," *Weekly Bulletin of the Michigan Society of Architects*, December 27, 1939, 5–10.

38. "Ford's Latest Invention," *New York Times*, June 19, 1915, 1; "Ford to Make Steel; Scores Sale for War," *Detroit Free Press*, June 19, 1915, 3.

39. The former Industrial Works (or Industrial Brownhoist), located at Columbus Avenue and North Water Street in Bay City, Michigan, was demolished. Maurice Goldenberg, "Modern Industrial Buildings," *Modern Building* 1, no. 1 (1914): 13–18; E. E. Harris, "Unusual Heating Conditions in the New Shops of the Industrial Works," *Modern Building* 2, no. 2 (February 1915): 12–15.

40. The former Curtiss plant, located at 2020 Elmwood Avenue, Buffalo, NY, has been demolished. W. R. Richardson, "The Largest Aeroplane Factory in the World Built in 90 Days," *Modern Building* 6, no. 2 (1919): 7–8; Norman Krickbaum, "A Trip Through the Curtiss Aeroplane Plant," *Modern Building* 6, no. 2 (1919): 9–14.

41. "Remarkable Speed in the Large Building Operation of the Ford Shipbuilding Plant," *Modern Building* 6, no. 2 (1919): 10–18; "From Daylight to Daylight" advertisement, *Literary Digest*, March 15, 1919, 1.

42. The Eagle boat factory, sometimes referred to as "building B," has been mostly demolished. Frank A. Cianflone, "The Eagle Boats of World War I," U.S. Naval Institute Proceedings, June 1973, online at https://www.usni.org/magazin es/proceedings/1973/june/eagle-boats-world-war-i, accessed November 22, 2021.

43. The plant remains in use, though the building has been modified. "Plant of New Hinkley Motors, Inc.," *Motor West* 36, no. 7 (1922): 45.

44. Packard remained in its location on Grand Blvd. until the company shut down its Detroit operations in 1956. Murray Corporation was located in what was originally the Anderson Electric Car Company complex, now known as the Russell Industrial Center at 1600 Clay Street in Detroit. Fisher Body operated a cluster of plants in the Milwaukee Junction area of Detroit (mostly extant) as well as Plant 18 on Fort Street at West End, later known as the Cadillac Fleetwood plant (demolished).

45. "Healthy Growth Shown," *Windsor Star*, November 19, 1928, 14; "Truscon Steel at Capacity," *Wall Street Journal*, July 3, 1928, 5; "Republic Iron & Steel," *Wall Street Journal*, December 4, 1928, 19; "Truscon Steel," *Wall Street Journal*, March 13, 1929, 15.

46. "Personal," *Iron Age* 105, no. 10 (1920): 686; *Transactions of the American Society of Mechanical Engineers*, 1927, 1433; "Steel Expert Dies Suddenly," *Canton Evening Repository*, October 12, 1926, 1.

47. "Kahn Given 75th Patent," *Youngstown Vindicator*, February 23, 1934, 1, 8.

48. Michael G. Smith, *Designing Detroit; Wirt Rowland and the Rise of Modern American Architecture* (Detroit: Wayne State University Press, 2017), 89.

49. United States patent number 2,069,966, David H. Morgan; Truscon Buildings Catalogue No. 220, edition 1930, Truscon Steel Company, Youngstown, Ohio; Truscon Manufacturers of a Complete Line of Steel Building Products, 1933, Truscon Steel Company, Youngstown, Ohio; Kanopy Steel Doors advertisement, *American Architect* 141, no. 2604 (1932): 89.

50. O. W. Irwin, "Memoir of Julius Kahn," *Transactions of the American Society of Civil Engineers*, vol. 110 (New York, 1945), 1742–47; "Steel Workers Are Offered Double Aid," *Pottsville (PA) Republican and Herald*, December 31, 1926, 4.

51. O. W. Irwin, "Memoir of Julius Kahn."

52. Letter from Maurice Goldenberg to Mrs. Julius Kahn, undated, O. W. Irwin letters, call number SC-5420, in the collection of the Jacob Rader Marcus Center of the American Jewish Archives, Cincinnati, Ohio.

53. *Iron and Steel*, report No. 128, second series, United States Tariff Commission (Washington, DC: US Government Printing Office,1938), 96; "Truscon Employees Turn Down Union," *Wall Street Journal*, July 13, 1933, 9.

1. *Historical Statistics of the United States, 1789–1945*, A Supplement to the Statistical Abstract of the United States, "Series H 1-26 Construction Expenditures-Estimates: 1915 to 1945," June 1949, Bureau of the Census, 168.

2. Albert Kahn Inc. job list (unpublished), maintained by Albert Kahn Associates Inc., Detroit, Michigan.

3. Letter from O. W. Irwin to Mrs. Julius Kahn, August 19, 1943, O. W. Irwin letters, call number SC-5420, in the collection of the Jacob Rader Marcus Center of the American Jewish Archives, Cincinnati, Ohio.

4. "New Steel Shop to Employ 250," *Newark (OH) Advocate*, September 30, 1939, 3; "Public Auction," *Cincinnati Enquirer*, July 7, 1991, 121; "Julius Kahn Dies at Home," *Youngstown Vindicator*, November 5, 1942, 1, 12; "Julius Kahn, 68, Steel Ex-official," *New York Times*, November 6, 1942, 23.

5. There were earlier underground parking facilities than the Union Square Garage, but none have come to light that are multi-story and open to the public, as opposed to garages located beneath or adjacent to a building and intended for the sole use of building occupants and visitors.

6. Confirming the exact number of patents is difficult due to variations in the manner in which the patents were recorded and the inexact nature of the search process.

7. "Make Vital War Goods," *Windsor (ON) Star*, December 31, 1942, 42; "Truscon Makes Airfield Reinforcing," *Windsor (ON) Star*, December 31, 1942, 56; "Strike at Truscon Plant Ends Today," *Salem (OH) News*, October 13, 1944, 1; "Laying Off Many Workers," *Delphos (OH) Daily Herald*, July 6, 1945, 1; *Truscon: The First Fifty Years, 1907–1957* (London: Bay Tree Press, 1957).

8. "Truscon Steel Co. Plant," *Wall Street Journal*, May 13, 1949, 14; "What Others are Saying," *Bucyrus (OH) Telegraph-Forum*, July 14, 1982, 4.

9. "Republic Steel to Start Four-Day Work Week at Truscon Division," *Wall Street Journal*, December 6, 1957, 15; "Ohio Mill Closing, Layoffs Hit USW," *Pittsburgh Press*, April 2, 1982, 1.

10. "Brick Gaining in Popularity," *Detroit Free Press*, October 26, 1924, 82.

11. "Concrete Cap Urged for Wooden Columns," *Detroit Free Press*, September 13, 1925, 70.

12. The reinforced concrete replacement plant eventually became Chrysler Corporation's Kercheval Plant, located at 12265–12275 E. Jefferson Ave., and was subsequently demolished. "Bricklayers—Immediate work," *Detroit Free Press*, July 2, 1916, 32; "$1,000,000 Fire Sweeps Plant of Wadsworth Co.," *Detroit Free Press*, August 2, 1919, 1; Rotogravure Supplement, photos and captions, *Detroit Free Press*, August 17, 1919, 100; "Lack of Fire Doors Blamed for Big Loss," *Eastern Underwriter*, October 3, 1919, 14; "Wadsworth Fire Holds City Record," *Detroit Free Press*, December 28, 1919, 54; "Wadsworth Manufacturing Co.'s New Plant" advertisement, *Michigan Architect and Engineer* 2, no. 1 (1920): 16 (advertising section).

13. "An Important Departure in Building Codes," *American Architect* 114, no. 2219 (1918): 25–30; "Work on Building Code is Finished," *Detroit Free Press*, April 27, 1919, 67.

14. "2 Are Dead; Blast Loss is $3,000,000," *Detroit Free Press*, April 24, 1927, 1, 3; "Toll in Briggs Fire 11," *Detroit Free Press*, April 25, 1927, 1–2; "Twentieth Victim of Briggs Fire Dies," *Detroit Free Press*, May 5, 1927, 1.

15. In 2019 Tim Trainor described it: "At $50 million (almost $500 million in today's dollars) it was—and still is—the most destructive industrial fire in American history." Tim Trainor, "American's Most Destructive Industrial Fire," *Assembly*, May 8, 2019, online at https://www.assemblymag.com/articles/95000-americas-most-destructive-industrial-fire, accessed January 10, 2022. This description is accurate if one disregards non-structure fires, wildfires, terrorist attacks, and explosions.

16. *General Motors Fire* (Boston: National Fire Protection Association International, 1953); "Michigan's Costliest Fire Destroys Auto Parts Plant," *Fire Engineering*, September 1953, 790–91, 855; Trainor, "American's Most Destructive Industrial Fire."

17. General Motors never released official loss figures; the numbers quoted were estimates from knowledgeable sources. Mac L. Hutchens, "Under the Surface," *St. Louis Globe-Democrat*, January 20, 1954, 20; Richard C. Allgood, *Lincoln (NE) Shopping News*, March 10, 1954, 2.

18. "A Fresh Look at Fire Prevention," *Business Week*, November 28, 1953, 56–57, 60, 62.

19. "GM to Continue to Use Big Plants," *Bedford (IN) Times-Mail*, August 17, 1954, 8.

20. "Packard Plant Hit By 2 Fires," *Detroit Free Press*, February 10, 1959, 1, 3; "Packard Fire Wasn't Set, Officials Say," *Detroit Free Press*, February 11, 1959, 2.

21. "Costly 7-Alarm Fire Sweeps Businesses in Packard Plant," *Detroit Free Press*, April 13, 1966, 1–2.

22. Captain John Sewell, "Reinforced Concrete in the United States," *Concrete and Constructional Engineering* 1, no. 2 (May 1906): 80; Sewell wrote, "So that—as my British colleague, Lieut.-Colonel Winn, so ably argued in the preceding issue of this journal—this century is truly likely to be known as the Concrete Age." In the article referred to by Sewell, Winn wrote, "There is little doubt that when our descendants review the past and speak of the dawn of the twentieth century, especially in its relation to structural engineering, the term 'Concrete Age' will not be inappropriate." Lieut.-Colonel J. Winn, "The Advent of the Concrete Age," *Concrete and Constructional Engineering* 1, no. 1 (March 1906): 7.

Index

cement, manufacturing of, 33–34
Century Association Club, 16, 216n5
Charles B. Clark and Company, 151
Charley Creek Bridge, 146–47, 247n21
Chess Hall of Fame (US), 107
Chicago Pneumatic Tool Company, 20–23, 41, 46, 60, 96, 218n35
Christie, Charles, 56
Chrysler Corporation, 194, 258n12
Church, Alfred B., 105–6, 235n54
Cincinnati College of Music, 64–65, 226n21
Cincinnati Ferro-Concrete Construction Company, 55, 65–66, 68, 71, 224n26, 226n23, 234n33
Cincinnati, Ohio: Anderson family, 54; early concrete buildings, 59, 64–72, 227nn27–28; history, 53; industries, 53; Palace of the Fans, 41, 55; railways, 53, 68
Cinder concrete, 24, 162–63, 171, 219n39, 251n28
Clark, Milton, 122
Clas, Alfred C., 147–48, 247n22
Cleveland Silex Stone Company, 27
coal handling equipment, 11–12, 22
code, building. See building codes
collapses, building. See building collapses
Collingwood Prize, 12
Committee on Safety of the City of New York, 172
Common Brick Manufacturers' Association, 204–5
concrete age, 210
concrete ship, 92, 201–2
Concrete Steel and Tile Construction Company: Anderson Carriage Company, 123–24; Automobile Club of America 112; Brown-Lipe Gear Company, 120; Burroughs, 113; Cadillac Motor Car Company, 113–15; closing of, 140; E. R. Thomas Company, *118*, 119; Eastman Kodak Company Emulsion Building, 133–40; founding, 98–99, Garford Company, 117; George N. Pierce Automobile Company, 116, 123; Grinnell Brothers Building, 140; Hammond, Standish & Company, 140;

Hanan & Son, New York, 104; Mergenthaler Linotype Company, 120; Michigan, 104, 113, 115, 117, 123–24, 140; negligence, 134; New York, 104; Olds Motor Works/Oldsmobile 112; Packard Motor Car Company 115, 117; speed of construction, 123; Stambaugh Building, 176; Star Watch Case Company, 106; Trussed Concrete Building, 175–76
concrete: advantages of, 126, 180; bridges, advantages of, 142, 154; automobile plant, first, 113–15, *114*; beam theory, 43–51, *44*, *47*; column cap, 205; construction standards, 180, 255n13; crushing test, 58; exterior treatment, 101, 104; first factory in Michigan of, 106; floor collapses, 27–28, 56, 59, 84–86; food safety, 178; growth of use, 180; manufacturing of, 34; mixture, 34, 86, 128; ship, 92, 201–2; single-story factories, 192; whiskey tanks, 67
Concrete Steel Construction (Claude Turner), 183
Condit, Carl W., 141, 149
Considère system, 139
Consolidated Pneumatic Tool Company (Scotland), 23. *See also* Chicago Pneumatic Tool Company
construction accidents. *See* building collapses
Costello, William, 132–34, 136–37
Couchot, Maurice, 164
COVID pandemic, 148
Cramp and Company, 95
Curtiss Aeroplane and Motor Corporation, 192–93, 256n40

daylight factory, 66–67, 99, 193, 207, 209, 226n23
Dayton Motor Car Company, 168–70, *170*
Detroit City Gas Company, 22, 46
Detroit Steel Products. *See* Fenestra windows
Detroit United Railway, 151
Dickhaut, Charles A., 111–12
Dittoe and Wisenall, 66

Johnson-Bovey Building, 182
Joy, Henry P., 60–61, 115
Judaism, Reform, 9

Kahn and Kahn, 15, 17, *17*, 20, 22–24, 46, 51–52, 60–64, 78, 96, 210
Kahn Bar: advertisement, 95; Army War College, 79–80; bridges, use in, 147, 153; Cadillac Motor Car Co. factory, 114; Columbia River Highway project, 154; columns, use in, 134, 139, 184; cost, 81; Detroit buildings, use in, 96; development of, 46–51, *47*, 77; Eastman Kodak collapse, 133–34; factory, 176–77; Frankford Arsenal, 95–96; Great Northern Portland Cement Warehouse, 79, *79*; journal articles by Julius Kahn, 82; Johnson, Albert L. criticism, 88–89, 183–84; licensing, 73, 91; Marlborough-Blenheim Hotel, 101; manufacturing, 179; Packard Motor Car Co., 62, *63*; patent, 46, 50, 52–53, 59, 74–78, 81–82, 91; praise for, 73–75; pre-production version, 62, *63*; press coverage, 94–95, 147; sales, 180, 189, 210; Sewell, Captain John use of, 78–80; shearing stresses, 89; similarity to truss, *47*; single-story buildings, 192; testing, *51*; typical use, 83; safety of, 87, 105, 184; testing, 78, 105; West Asheville Bridge, 153; Worlds' Fair of 1904 display, 97–98
Kahn floor, 77–78, *77*, 98, 129, 181–82, 184
Kahn Realty, 200
Kahn System of Reinforced Concrete catalog, 82–83, *83*
Kahn, Albert: aiding family members, 52; anticipation of future trends, 16–18; automobile factories, 116–17, 119–20, 128, 239n32; birth, 7; Boyer, Joseph, 21–22, 61, 142; brothers in architectural practice, 201; Brown, David, 22; Burroughs Adding Machine Co., 96; Concrete Steel and Tile Construction Co., 99; death, 201; Detroit City Gas Co., 22; business risks, 18, 20, 27, 29, 87; civil engineering in firm, 18, *63*, 64;

early concrete work, 107, 115, 116–20, 236n60; early work experience, 9–10, 215n19; education, 10; Eagle sub chaser, 193; Engineering Building, University of Michigan, 219n46; earliest factory design, 23; Ferry, Dexter, 22; Ford, Henry, 191; Ford Motor Co., 120, 193–94; glass plant, Ford Rouge, 194; Great Depression, 199; Great Northern Portland Cement Co., 78; hangar, US Army, 196; iconic designs, 194; Industrial Works factory, 192; inefficiency, 31; Kahn Realty, 200; letters from Julius, 11–13, 16, 74–76; Mergenthaler Linotype Co., 120; Multi-Color Co., 51; Packard Motor Co., 61–62, *63*, 64, 73, 115, 119, 210; Palms Building, 24, 27, 29, 87, 219n41, 219n43; partnerships, 15, 20, 80, 104, 128, 218n36; passport, 213n9; patents, 202; photo of, *10*, *17*, *93*, *202*; residential design work, 20–22, 81; reuse of building designs, 175; SS Albert Kahn, 201; steel sash windows, 121; Trussed Concrete Steel Company, 80–81, 175, 239n32, 240n41; Vinton Co., 128; Wadsworth Mfg. Co., 206; waste of materials, 31
Kahn, Felix, 9, *10*, 52, 81, 92, *93*, 164, 201–2
Kahn, Gisela. *See* Gresser, Gisela (Kahn)
Kahn, Gustave (Gus), 7–10, *10*, 49, 52, *93*, 201–2, 215n19
Kahn, Joseph, 7–10, *10*, 51–52, *93*, 201
Kahn Julius, *10*, *17*, *93*, *179*, *202*; birth, 7, 213n9; bridges, success with, 141, 149, 155; business philosophy, 62, 74, 187, 195–97; childhood, 10; children, 107; civil engineering degree, 12; collapses, causes of, 86–88, 133, 136; Collingwood Prize, 12; concrete theory, 29, 43–51, *44*, *47*, 59–60, 180, 210; Condit, Carl W. on, 141, 149; death, 201; education, 10, 215n23; employee relations, 195–97; engineering services, 98; inventions, 179; Japan, 12–13, 74; leadership, 197; naturalization, 213n9; Newton, Alfred and Ralph, 148; Packard Motor drawings, *63*, 64; Palms

Apartment Building floors, 29, 87; patents, 46, 50, 52–53, 59, 74–75, 77, 78, 81–82, 91, 179, 194; Republic Steel, 200; safety, 105; Sewell, John, recognition by, 80; simplification, standardization 187; terra cotta floor, 75–78, 77; trial testimony, 185–86; trip to east (1903), 73–76; University of Michigan, 10, 12; Washington, DC buildings, 80, 94; wedding, 83; work experience, early career, 10–13. *See also* Kahn and Kahn

Kahn, Louis, 9, *10*, 52, *93*, 201
Kahn, Margaret (Kohut), 83, 107
Kahn, Mollie, 7, *10*, 49–50, 52, *93*, 201
Kahn, Moritz, 7, *10*, 52, 76, 81, 91–92, *93*, 158, 201–2
Kahn, Paula, 7, *10*, 22, *93*, 201
Kahn, Rosalie, 7–9, *10*, 52, 201
Kane, Thomas, 121, 186, 195–96
Kelly and Jones factory, 39–40, 64, 66, 99, 226n23, 234n30
Keppele Hall Company, 168
Knapp Brothers, 93–94
Kodak Company. *See* Eastman Kodak Company Emulsion Building
Kohut, Margaret. *See* Kahn, Margaret (Kohut)
Krolik, Day, 80
Krolik, Herman, 80
Kubo Moyoro Sulphur and Iron Mining Company, 12

La Crosse Cracker and Candy Company, 178, 254n11
labor unions, 70, 162–65, 197, 252n40
La Flamboy, Henry C., 60
Lake Park Friends, 148–49
Lake Park Ravine Road Footbridge, 147–49, 247n22
Lawrence Savings and Trust Company, 84
Leland Stanford Jr. Museum (Cantor Arts Center), 36–37, 143, 163
Leland, Henry M., 21, 113–14, 217n22
Lockwood, Louis, 102
Lockwood, Greene and Company, 18, 116

Longworth, Nicholas, 54
Lots Road Power Station (England), 121

MacDonald and Kahn, 92, 201–2, 258n5
Macdonald and Kiley Company, 65–66
MacDonald, Alan, 92
Mark Hopkins Hotel, 92
Marlborough-Blenheim Hotel, 100–102, *102*, 103, 122, 234nn34–35, 235n40, 235n43
martini glass shaped column, 181
Marx, Christian W., 54, 57–58, 135–36, 244n39
Mason and Kahn, 15–17, 20, 23–24, 27, 128, 216n5, 218n36, 219n41
Mason and Rice, 15
Mason, George D., 15, 20, 99, 104, 107, 113–14, 123, 128, 215n19, 229n20, 236n60
mass transit, 192
Massachusetts Automobile Club, 112
material handling, 189–91
Maybury, William C., 97
McClintock, John Y., 133–36, 244n39
McKim, Mead, and White, 79
Melan arch bridges, 54, 144–45, 147, 153–54, 246n8
Melan Arch Construction Company, 144
Melan, Josef, 144
Mensch, Leopold J., 65–66, 71–72, 226n21, 227n24
Mergenthaler Linotype Company, 120, 140
Miami and Erie Canal, 53
Michigan Central Railroad, 60, 144
Michigan Bolt and Nut Works, 50, 223n9
Michigan Stove Company, *4–5*
Michigan Supreme Court case, 185–86
Michigan Technical Laboratory, 177
Michigan, first concrete factory in, 106
mild steel, 184
mill construction: automobile manufacturing, 110–11, *110*, 125–26; described, 4–5, 213n6; concrete column caps, 205; cost, 103; Elzner, Alfred, 67; fires, 4–5, 158, 169, *170*, 171, 205–7; George N. Pierce Automobile Co., 116; hybrid construction, 84; improvements to, 109; insurance

mill construction (*continued*)
companies and, 4–6; insurance costs, 38–39; interior, *110*; Kahn and Kahn, 61, 64; Lockwood, Greene and Co., 116; Michigan Stove Co., *4–5*; obsolescence, 6–7, Packard Motor Car Co., 63–64, *65*; problems with in cities, 171; promotion in 1920s, 204–5
Miller, Rudolph P., 173
modular buildings, 187
Montague, Wallace R., 178, 254n11
Morgan, David H., 196
Morgan, Octavius, 129
Mullen, John, 136–37
Mullgardt, Louis, 21–22
Multi-Color Copying Company, 52, 201
Multnomah Falls. *See* Benson Bridge
Murray Corporation (Detroit), 194, 257n44
mutual insurance companies, 4–6
Mushroom system, 181

Nash automobile, 207
National Board of Fire Underwriters, 162, 167–68, 250n20
National Fire Protection Association, 159–61, 170
National Fireproofing Company, 171
National Lumber Manufacturer's Association, 205
Nettleton and Kahn, 15, 216n5
Nettleton, Kahn and Trowbridge, 15
Nettleton, George W., 15
New York Expanded Metal Company, 74
Newton Engineering Company, 148
Newton, Alfred, 148
Newton, Ralph, 148
Norcross, Orlando, 182
Norden bombsight, 106
Norman Street School, 86, 231n36

O'Connor, George, 167
office building construction, fireproof, 3, 24. *See also* Baltimore fire; Ingalls Building; San Francisco earthquake and fire
Olds Motor Works/Oldsmobile, 1–2, 109–12, 237n10
Otsego Hotel, 28, 220n48

Owen Building. *See* Trussed Concrete Building

Pacific Building, 163
Pacific Coast Borax, 36, 38–40
Packard No. 10, 115, 238n26
Packard Motor Car Company: architecture and engineering, 64; Building No. 10, 115; concrete buildings, 115, 117; Concrete Steel and Tile Construction Co., 115; fires, 209–10; insurance costs, 62, 225n12; journal articles about, 123; Kahn, Albert and Julius, 61, 73, 116–17, 119–20; Kahn Bar use, 62, *63*; cost, 64; mill construction, 61, 64, *65*; move to Detroit, 61; multistory plant, 194; production efficiency in design of plant, 61–62; shut down of factory, 257n44; size of early buildings, 240n42; speed of construction, 64
Painter, Walter S., 104
Paddington Apartments, 28–29
Palace of the Fans (Cincinnati Reds), 41, 55
Palms Apartment Building, 16, 20, 23–27, *25–26*, 29, 87, 128, 216n5, 219n41, 219n43
Parker Building, 167–68, 252n50
Patterson, George W. Sr, 81
Penobscot Building (Detroit), 182
Pennsylvania Railroad, 190–91
Pierce Arrow automobile. *See* George N. Pierce Automobile Company
Pierce, J. Elliott, 56
Plumb, Alfred, 177
Pocono Building, 168
Ponce de Leon Hotel, 34
Porter, Henry F., 137
Portland cement, 33, 168
pressed steel products, 181, 186–87, 189, 195
Price, William L., 101
Procter and Gamble, 53
Pugh Printing Company, 66, 227n24

Queen and Crescent Railway, 68

Rambler automobile. *See* Thomas B. Jeffery Company

Thomas B. Jeffery Company, 111–12
Thompson and Norris Company, 166–67
Triangle Shirtwaist factory, 171–73, 204, 206
Tooker, Charles A., 55–58
Trowbridge, Alexander B., 15
Truscon. *See* Trussed Concrete Steel Company
Truscon Laboratories, 177, 200
Truscon Steel Building, 187, *188*, 196, 203
Truscon Steel Company. *See* Trussed Concrete Steel Company
Trussed Concrete Building, 175–76, 254n2
Trussed Concrete Steel Company: advertising, *95*, 106, *118*, *122*, 137–38; automobile factories (*see chapter 8*); best practices, 139; best year of sales, 199; bridge design, 149, 151; catalog, 82–83, *83*; company name, 189; construction accident risk, 127; construction services (*see* Concrete Steel and Tile Construction Company); decline, 203; Detroit buildings, 97; dominant supplier, 180–82; employee benefits, 196; employee motivation, 195–97; engineering services, 98; factory, *195*; first office, 81; floors, safety of, 131–32; food processing, 178; founding 80–81, founders, 80–81, 230n20; hangar doors, 196; invention, 196; marketing, 81–83, 91, 94–95, 102–3, 106–7, 115–16, *118*, 122–25, 182; name change, 189; new products, 180–81; offices (*see under* Trussed Concrete Steel Co., offices); patent, 82; pressed steel manufacturing, 186, 189, 195; Republic Steel, 200; roundhouse, 104–5; sales, 175, 180, 194–95; sales department, 196; second year of operation, 106; steel buildings, 187; steel fabricating, largest company, 195; steel I-beam, joist, 186; steel trusses, 187; steel type, 184; safety, steel type, 184; stockholders, 80–81, Truscon Laboratories, 177; Washington, DC buildings, 80, 94; World War II, 202–3; World's Fair gold medal, 98; Youngstown, Ohio, factory

and office, 175–76, 189, 195–97, *195*, 199–200, 202
Trussed Concrete Steel Company, offices: Chicago, 93–94; Cleveland, 92–93, 195; earliest, 81, 91; in operation during 1904, 94, international, 175, Japan, 195; London, 92, 176, 195; Los Angeles, 130, 195; New York, 91, 231n1; number of, 194–95; Omaha, 177–78; satellite factories, 95; San Francisco, 92; Seattle, 94; Toronto, 95; Walkerville, Ontario, Canada office and factory, 92, 176
Tunis (Tunisia) grain warehouse, 138–39
Turner Construction Company, 42, 99–100, 255n13
Turner, Claude A. P., 181–84
Turner, Henry C., 42, 100
Tuteur, Julius, 92
twisted reinforcement bars. *See* Ransome, Ernest L.

Unions. *See* labor unions
United Shoe Machinery factory, 39–40, 64, 66, 99, 121, 234n30
United States Fidelity and Guaranty Building annex, 160–61
United Steel Fabricators, 200–201
United Steel Sash, 121–22, *122*, 176, 189, 192–94
US Army Corps of Engineers, 59, 75, 80. *See also* Sewell, Captain John Stephen
University of Cincinnati, 54, 58
University of Michigan: Kahn, Felix, 52, 92: Kahn, Julius, education, 10, 12, 215n23; Kahn, Moritz, 52, 91; Engineering Building, 16, 23–24, 27, 216n5; Field, Hinchman and Smith, 226n19; Newton, Alfred, 148; Newton, Ralph, 148; Patterson, George W., 81; Plumb, Roy A., 177; Psychopathic Hospital, 16, 23; Schuett, Albert, 134; Smith, Hinchman and Grylls, 226n19; West Engineering Building, 16, 23–24, 27, 216n5

Van Leyen, Edward, 106
vibration, in buildings, 7, 126
vibration, in bridges, 142

Villa Zorayda, 34
Vinton Construction Company, 117, 128
vitrified tile, 61
von Treitschke, Heinrich, 8

W. H. Ellis and Company, 68
Wabash, Indiana, 145–46
Wadsworth Manufacturing plant, 205–6
Wadsworth, Frederick E., 205
Wagner, Richard (composer), 8
Walkerville, Ontario, Canada factory,
    92, 176
Ward, William E., 32–33, 43
Wason, Leonard C., 40–41, 57
waterproofing, 177
Weld, Fred F., 105
Wentworth, C. A., 74
Werner Brothers Storage building, 94,
    232n8
West 137th Street apartments (New York
    City), 164–65
West Asheville Bridge, 151–53, 155
West Engineering Building, University
    of Michigan, 16, 23–24, 27, 216n5,
    219n46
Westcott Paper Products Company, 115
White, Josiah, 100
Whittemore, James and Margaret, 52
Wilby, Ernest, 121, 240n47
Wilcox, Perley S., 134–37
Willys-Overland, 129
windows, in factories: daylight factory,
    39–40, 66, 193–94, 207; Dayton Motor
    Car Co. fire, 170, *170*; double hung,

66, 121; Ford Motor Highland Park,
120–21, 193; Ford Motor River Rouge
Glass Plant, 194; Fenestra, 121; flat,
light reflecting ceiling, 76; General
Motors Hydra-Matic fire, 207; Industrial Works, 192–93; Macdonald and
Kiley Company, 65–66; mill construction, 6–7, *6*, *110*; Mullgardt, Louis,
21; multi-story buildings, 191; Pacific
Coast Borax, 38–39; Ransome, Ernest,
38–39, 121; sawtooth roof, 21; single-
story buildings, 191, 193; steel sash,
120–21, 192; Superior Match factory,
61; Triangle Shirtwaist fire, 172; Trus-
con Steel Buildings, 187; United Steel
Sash, 121–22, *122*, 193–94; Wilby,
Ernest, 240n47
Wing and Bostwick Company, 86–87,
231n35
Wolfe, William S., 182
Wonderland Theater collapse, 18–20
Woodruff, Sydney H., 113, 119, 237n14
World War I. *See* First World War
World War II, 106, 193, 201, 207, 209
World's Columbian Exposition, 145
World's Fair, St. Louis (1904), 97–98
Worthington, Judge William, 56
wristwatches, 106

Yerba Buena Island torpedo shed, 36,
143
Youngstown, Ohio, factory and office,
121, 176–77, 189, 195–96, *195*, 199–
200, 202–3